Recent Research in Psychology

This book is to be returned on
or before the date stamped below

Hans-J. Hippler    Norbert Schwarz    Seymour Sudman
Editors

# Social Information Processing and Survey Methodology

With 20 Illustrations

Springer-Verlag
New York Berlin Heidelberg
London Paris Tokyo

Hans-J. Hippler
Project Director, Zentrum für Umfragen, Methoden und Analysen, Mannheim, FRG

Norbert Schwarz
Director, Zentrum für Umfragen, Methoden und Analysen, Mannheim, FRG

Seymour Sudman
Departments of Business Administration and Sociology, Survey Research Laboratory,
University of Illinois at Urbana-Champaign, Urbana, Illinois 61801 USA

Library of Congress Cataloging in Publication Data
Social information processing and survey methodology.
  (Recent research in psychology)
  Bibliography: p.
  1. Social surveys—Psychological aspects—Congresses.
2. Interviewing—Congresses.  I. Hippler, Hans-J.
II. Schwarz, Norbert.  III. Sudman, Seymour.  IV. Series.
HN29.S635  1987    301'.0723    87-16559

Text prepared by the editors in camera-ready form.
Printed and bound by Edwards Brothers, Ann Arbor, Michigan.
Printed in the United States of America.

9 8 7 6 5 4 3 2    (Second Printing, 1988)

ISBN 0-387-96570-X Springer-Verlag New York Berlin Heidelberg
ISBN 3-540-96570-X Springer-Verlag Berlin Heidelberg New York

## ACKNOWLEDGMENTS

The preparation of the present volume was supported by funds from the Center for Surveys,
Methods, and Analysis, ZUMA e.V., Mannheim. We
gratefully acknowledge the support and encouragement of ZUMA's former executive director Manfred
Kuechler at an early stage of this project. The
editorial assistance of Pamela Hormuth and the
technical support provided by Gabi Naderer greatly
facilitated our task.

# CONTENTS

# 1

EDITORS' INTRODUCTION

The main objective of this volume is to further the recently initiated dialog between survey researchers and cognitive psychologists. To date this dialog has involved only a few people. With this book we want to let others know what has been happening so that they can benefit from and contribute to what we believe is an exciting and valuable cross-fertilization of two deeply interrelated disciplines.

We see the audience for this book as consisting of both researchers who use and develop survey methods as well as cognitive psychologists who are interested in understanding how humans process social information. It is obvious that survey research can benefit greatly from theories that have been and are being developed by cognitive psychologists. The most optimistic expectation is that new methods will be developed based on cognitive theories that will substantially improve the quality of responses that are currently being collected. A less optimistic, but perhaps more plausible scenario is that we shall gain a more fully developed understanding of what is possible to ask of respondents and why? That is, we shall continue to have response effects, but they will be smaller than at present and we shall know that we are doing the best we can, given the task and the limitations of the human brain.

The contributions, however, are not only from cognitive psychology to survey research, but also in the other direction. As Bodenhausen and Wyer point out in their chapter, some critics have questioned whether processes of everyday cognition can be meaningfully studied in the laboratory. Bodenhausen and Wyer counter that laboratory experiments make major contributions if the theoretical principles supported by laboratory research also make important predictions about phenomena of the real world. Thus, the survey experiments presented in this volume help to support and to modify and improve the theories developed in the laboratory.

Most of the chapters in this book are revised versions of papers presented at an International Conference on Social Information Processing and Survey Methodology held in July, 1984, at the Center for Surveys, Methods, and Analysis (ZUMA e.V.) in Mannheim, West

Germany. This conference followed an earlier conference that was organized by the Committee on National Statistics of the National Research Council (Jabine, Straf, Tanur and Tourangeau, 1984). The earlier conference was primarily concerned with developing a research agenda. The ZUMA conference was organized so that researchers from both cognitive psychology and survey research, who were already convinced of the value of interaction, could present theoretical and experimental findings to each other and ultimately to the reader of this book.

At an ideal conference, the entire field is covered and there is no duplication. It will soon be clear to you that this was not an ideal conference, if such a conference ever existed. There is some duplication, but the duplication is not extensive and indeed is somewhat comforting. It is encouraging in a new area to see people using the same words and ideas. In the language of multiple regression, there is some multicollinearity of ideas, but it is not sufficient enough to be troublesome and, in fact, without it a joint research agenda could hardly be developed.

Far more troubling is what is omitted from this book. We would like to be able to present much more richly developed specific theories as well as empirical tests of these theories. Unfortunately, the state of the art does not yet permit that. But hopefully a review of our current knowledge, as it is presented in the present book, will contribute to the development of this new and exciting field.

The papers in this volume have been substantially modified since the conference. At a minimum they now take account of each other, although the crossdialog is still less than we would have liked. Almost all of the papers now include specific discussions of the implications of the theories to survey research. Some of these implications are still fuzzy and will require imaginative researchers to convert them to specific research projects.

Since there are 11 chapters in the book, there are 11 permutations of how these chapters could be arranged and no arrangement will meet all the criteria we established. We decided to put the more theoretical chapters together in the first part of the book and the more applied chapters in the second part. You will note, however, that the theoretical chapters have descriptions of experiments in them and the research studies usually start with a discussion of the theory that motivated the study. While we believe that the order we finally chose has some logic, the courageous reader has our encouragement to read in any order that fits his or her needs. If you prefer to read the research studies before reading the theory, go to it.

The first three chapters of the book are all tightly related to information acquisition, processing and use. The chapter by Bodenhausen and Wyer is organized so as to make it especially easy for a reader who is new to the field. Bodenhausen and Wyer present a dozen major postulates in the field of social cognition. For each postulate they present the evidence for and against it and the applicability of that postulate to real-world behavior. While these postulates have major significance for survey researchers, the paper does not always make them explicit, but leaves it to the reader. In some cases, the applications are obvious.

The chapter by Hastie is an overview of information processing theory at a fairly general level. Hastie is one of several authors who present discussions of schemata. His discussion is especially extensive describing the alternative formulations that have been used. Hastie uses his theory to explain the belief and knowledge structures underlying political behavior.

Ostrom in the third chapter also discusses information processing, but in a much narrower perspective – how respondents react to bipolar survey items. From this discussion comes the interesting speculation that respondents, in choosing a scale value, do so by a series of choices from two or three categories at a time, that is, a successive narrowing of the decision. He also speculates on how this is done but leaves the task of designing experiments to test these theories to the reader.

Whereas Ostrom concentrated on a task of measuring attitudes, Strube's chapter discusses the role of memory in responding to behavior questions. After presenting a general theory of memory, Strube presents some interesting examples of how these theories might impact on two major tasks asked of survey respondents, frequency judgments and time dating of events. A discussion of the survey literature on this issue, that complements Strube's chapter, is provided by Sudman and Bradburn (1974).

Those readers who are unfamiliar with survey research literature on response effects will find a summary of this work in the chapter by Hippler and Schwarz. It will be evident from this chapter that survey researchers have been looking at the same issues as cognitive psychologists, but not from the same theoretical perspective. Indeed, what is most obvious in the survey research literature is that there has been no general theoretical perspective. Instead, there has been some limited theorizing and many ad-hoc experiments. Given the insights generated by cognitive theories, it is possible to better understand why these survey response effects occurred in some cases and not in others.

The second part of the book begins with the chapter by Strack and Martin describing how context effects influence responses in attitude surveys. There is a detailed discussion based on theoretical and experimental insights from cognitive research on how respondents interpret questions, generate an opinion and format and edit their responses for reasons of social desirability.

Tourangeau also looks at attitude measurement and describes the four major steps necessary to answer a question - comprehension, retrieval, judgment, and response selection. The discussion parallels that of Strack and Martin, but there is a much more detailed discussion of scripts that parallels the Hastie chapter. Tourangeau concludes with a discussion of how these theoretical insights impact on questions dealing with the Korean War and confidence in instruction. He describes some experiments in progress to test the magnitude of response effects on vague and abstract as compared to concrete issues.

Schwarz and Hippler in their second chapter describe experimental results that demonstrate that not only do the values of a response scale provide information to respondents on how to answer the question being asked, but that these values also provide information that influences responses to later questions.

Bishop also describes the results of experiments on context effects in his chapter. He has studied the impact of first asking knowledge questions on subsequent respondent perceptions of their own interest in government and public affairs. A surprising finding is that the effects are not diminished or eliminated by substantial numbers of buffer questions between the knowledge and perception questions. At least during the time of the interview, and perhaps longer, responding to knowledge questions has changed people's perceptions about themselves.

In their chapter, Dijkstra and van der Zouwen make an important point that is not made very explicit in the earlier chapters--respondent motivation plays a significant role in how well the respondent accomplishes the task that the researcher determines. What respondents are told and the style of the interview, whether it is primarily task-oriented or empathetic, influence how they respond. To complicate the problem, respondent motivation interacts with the topic of the interview, as their own research demonstrates.

The final chapter by Sudman attempts to place the ZUMA conference and this book into the context of what will be the continuing work in this area. As with all attempts to predict the future, it will almost certainly be wrong. The book and this final chapter will succeed if we persuade its readers to think about and to participate in the development of the dialog between survey research and the cognitive sciences.

## REFERENCES

Jabine, B., Straf, L., Tanur, M., & Tourangeau, R. (Eds.). (1984). Cognitive aspects of survey methodology. Washington, DC.: National Academy Press.
Sudman, S., & Bradburn, N. (1974). Response effects in surveys: A review and synthesis. Chicago: Aldine.

# 2 SOCIAL COGNITION AND SOCIAL REALITY: INFORMATION ACQUISITION AND USE IN THE LABORATORY AND THE REAL WORLD

Galen V. Bodenhausen
University of Illinois at
Urbana-Champaign


Robert S. Wyer, Jr.
University of Illinois at
Urbana-Champaign

Social cognition research has generated widespread interest in recent years. Although researchers may differ in the specific concepts and methods they have in mind when they speak of "social cognition," they generally agree that the ultimate goal of their research is to identify the cognitive processes that presumably mediate people's responses to the information they encounter in social contexts. The "input" variables of concern include the content, source, and context of information available in the social environment. Prominently studied "output" variables include attitudes, beliefs, judgments, and occasionally, overt physical behavior. The objective of social cognition research is to specify the cognitive processes linking these variables.

This approach has not gone without criticism. For example, Wyer (1980) presented a summary of several of the basic concepts that appeared to guide social cognition theory and research in the late 1970s. The twelve postulates he discussed have in one form or another been incorporated into several theoretical accounts of the phenomena studied in social cognition laboratories. Underlying these postulates is a clear commitment to the information-processing paradigm that currently dominates cognitive psychology. However, Neisser (1980) has criticized the basic approach embodied in Wyer's postulates on a number of grounds. Perhaps the concern he voices most emphatically is a fear that social cognition researchers (and cognition researchers more generally -- see Neisser, 1976, 1982) have lost sight of the real-world phenomena that presumably motivate their research programs. In their exclusive concern over seemingly esoteric theoretical issues, Neisser argues, social cognition researchers take no time to consider the "social reality" that constitutes the true phenomena of interest. Neisser is by no means alone in his concerns about the ecological validity of much social cognition research (see, e.g., Forgas, 1983; Graumann & Sommer, 1984).

Despite the concerns of Neisser and others, research on social information processing has continued to flourish in the years since Wyer's postulates appeared. Moreover, many of the assumptions under- lying these early postulates have persisted. In this chapter, we will examine whether this persistence is justified, or alternatively, whether a theoretical inertia exists that leads conceptualizations to lag behind the empirical evidence that bears on their validity. We also wish to consider the extent to which the assumptions that un- derlie these postulates, which have been primarily applied in some- what restricted laboratory research, are in fact relevant to knowledge acquisition and use in real-life situations. To the extent that some of the processes embodied in these assumptions do in fact operate outside of the laboratory, these principles may be very important to consider in more naturalistic research strategies such as surveys and interviews.

It should be noted that some have questioned whether the processes of everyday cognition can in principle be meaningfully studied in experimental paradigms. These critics assert that whatever social reality may be, it is not amenable to the usual forms of experimental investigation (see Harr , 1980). Such a sweeping dis- missal of the laboratory seems to us to be both unwarranted and unwise. The arguments against such a pessimistic view of the value of the experimental approach in social psychology have been many and varied (see, for example, Berkowitz & Donnerstein, 1982; Henshel, 1980; Kruglanski, 1976; Turner, 1981), and we will not attempt to reproduce them all here. It is sufficient merely to assert that our most fundamental concern is not the extent to which the empirical phenomena observed in the laboratory "generalize" to the real world. Rather, it is with the extent to which _theoretical principles_ sup- ported by laboratory research also make important predictions about the phenomena of the "real world." (Turner, 1981, provides a par- ticularly thorough exposition of this point of view.) This is not a matter that can best be decided by the categorical rejection of any research method. A more useful strategy is to consider the warrant given to any theoretical principle by the available evidence from any

and all research methods and simultaneously to consider the potential
value of the principle in understanding or predicting behavior outside the laboratory. This strategy will be adopted in the remainder
of this chapter.

## Assessing the Current Status of Some Common Assumptions

Many different theoretical formulations of social cognition have
been developed in recent years (e.g., Hastie, 1980; E.R. Smith, 1984;
Wyer & Srull, 1985a,b). Rather than attempt a detailed assessment of
each individual conceptualization, it will be most useful to examine
assumptions about social information processing that are prominent
elements of several different formulations. In the interest of con-
tinuity, our discussion will focus on the postulates examined by Wyer
(1980). In each case we will state the postulate, briefly discuss its
theoretical importance and implications, and examine its plausibility
on conceptual and empirical grounds. After considering how well each
assumption stands up in the laboratory, we will turn to a consideration of its applicability and relevance (or irrelevance) outside of
the laboratory.

Postulate 1. Social knowledge is organized in memory into configural
representations of persons, objects, and events.

Mental representations of social entities are assumed to be
constructed to facilitate the individual's subsequent interactions
with these entities. Because interpersonal and cultural forces undoubtedly place important constraints on the nature of mental representations (D'Andrade, 1981; Freyd, 1983), certain regularities
presumably exist in the nature of the mental representations that are
formed. This basic assumption of organized representations that are
stored and retrieved from memory is so fundamental to most thinking
in social cognition that the issue of its validity is very rarely
raised. It is not, however, completely uncontroversial. Kolers and
Roediger (1984, p. 426), for instance, complained that "with little
if any supporting evidence ... cognitive psychologists stuff the
human mind with metaphorical structures."

Along related lines, Anderson (1978) pointed out that assumptions about the content and structure of mental representations of
stimulus information are evaluated on the basis of memory performance
(e.g., recall, recognition, etc.). However, the use of memory data
requires assumptions about the processes that underlie the retrieval
of the information contained in the representations as well as the
content and structure of the representations themselves. Anderson

asserts that in a large number of instances, it is virtually impossible to distinguish between (a) theoretical approaches that postulate differences in the structure of mental representations but assume a single set of retrieval processes and (b) those that postulate a single mental representation but different sets of retrieval processes. Models have indeed been developed that account very successfully for a wide variety of memory phenomena without making a commitment to any specific type of mental representation (Gillund & Shiffrin, 1984; Raaijmakers & Shiffrin, 1981).

Perhaps the most serious challenge to the assumption that specific mental representations are formed of persons, objects, and events has come from the development of distributed memory models (e.g., Kohonen, Oja, & Lehtiö, 1981; McClelland & Rumelhart, 1985). These models assume that memories are not localized in a particular structure that pertains to specific entities. Rather, a common set of "memory nodes" is postulated, each of which may become activated with varying intensities in response to different stimulus features. New stimuli that elicit a pattern of responses that is similar (although not necessarily identical) to the pattern elicited by other stimuli encountered in the past are "remembered" as similar to these past stimuli. This sort of model can account for many memory phenomena without assuming the existence of localized configural representation of stimuli. Unfortunately, distributed memory models are not yet developed at a level that permits them to be easily applied to the complex stimulus configurations that must be considered in research on social information processing. They nevertheless are a serious challenge to the ultimate validity of formulations that require the postulation of separate mental representations of information.

Research. We have just contended that specific claims regarding the structure of memorial representations are exceptionally difficult to substantiate. Nevertheless, the existence of some kind of organization in memory (whatever its specific internal structure) is strongly implied by a study conducted by Srull (1983b). Srull's subjects were either asked to try to memorize a set of behavioral information or to use the information to form an impression of the persons who performed the behaviors. He found that subjects with an impression set organized the behavioral information in terms of the persons who performed the acts, whereas those with a memory set did not. Given this, it seems reasonable to conclude that social information is in fact organized into knowledge domains that can be accessed by relatively few cues (in this case, a person's name). Beyond

providing general evidence for organization of some kind, this research reveals different organizational strategies resulting from
different processing objectives. It remains for future research to
determine whether greater precision is possible in the specification
of the structure of organized representations or whether the nature
of cognitive architecture is ultimately indeterminate.

Applicability. It seems obvious that much social knowledge is
organized in terms of persons. However, because of the radical differences in the way in which knowledge is acquired, both in and out
of the laboratory, it is unwarranted to assume that the organizational strategies suggested in laboratory research resemble those
employed in real-life situations. The information we accumulate about
others in the course of daily life is usually acquired on several
different occasions and in several different ways (e.g., direct
observation, reports from third parties, etc.). Perhaps even more
important, the goals that drive the processing of information are
often different and more varied in everyday life than in the
laboratory.

One specific difference in organization that might be expected
as a result of these differences is that in the real world, information about others may often be spontaneously thought about in terms
of its implications for the self. If I am told that someone I meet
has won a state-wide chess tournament, I may speculate about whether
she could help me with my calculus homework, or whether I would stand
a chance playing chess with her, and so forth. If I read about this
woman in a laboratory setting, none of this would occur to me. Thus,
the self-other relational quality that is prominent in everyday life
is largely absent in the laboratory when subjects are asked to form
impressions of hypothetical persons.

Postulate 2. New information about a person, object, or event is
interpreted by comparing its features to features of mental structures stored in memory.

These comparisons may be based on configurations of features as
well as on an analysis of individual features. Like Postulate 1, this
assumption has generally been regarded as a truism. Moreover, it
presupposes the validity of Postulate 1. As we have just pointed out,
whether it is accurate, meaningful, or useful to speak of mental
structures in memory is a matter of debate. Nevertheless it would
seem to be a logical necessity that prior knowledge, whatever its
nature, be used in the interpretation of new information, and the

most likely mechanism to accomplish this interpretation is some sort of feature-based comparison process.

The interpretation process implied by Postulate 2 either could be carried out automatically or, in some cases, require conscious effort. At the level of concrete perception, referencing prior knowledge to "recognize" a familiar stimulus clearly requires minimal if any effort. When the stimulus is complex or ambiguous, conscious effort may be necessitated. Interpretation may also involve either a holistic response to a stimulus as a configural unit (Laßerge, 1981; see also Zajonc, 1980), or an analysis of component features (E.E. Smith, Shoben, & Rips, 1974; Tversky, 1977). The postulate's unconstrained phrasing allows for all of these possibilities. To be theoretically useful, therefore, something more explicit must be said about the circumstances in which interpretation is holistic vs. piecemeal and unconscious vs. effortful.

Research. This postulate represents such a fundamental presumption that it is rarely if ever tested directly in social cognition research. However, one set of studies that bears on the validity of the postulate is the work of Snyder and colleagues on confirmatory hypothesis testing (Snyder & Cantor, 1979; Snyder & Swann, 1978). According to Snyder, when we want to determine whether Person $X$ has trait $Y$, we use features associated with $Y$ to interpret $X$'s behavior. The process is called confirmatory because attention seems to focus on behaviors that are good exemplars of the trait in question (even though disconfirming behaviors are presented in equal numbers). This research at least implies processing of the sort specified in Postulate 2 when the social perceiver has a specific hypothesis to test. Evidence concerning other cases is sparse.

Applicability. In the broadest sense, prior knowledge is probably involved in the interpretation of information in most social situations. However, in many cases the interpretation is at such a low level that it occurs without conscious effort. This process is unlikely to be strongly affected by differences in social situations or personal characteristics of individual perceivers. On the other hand, effortful feature-based interpretation, which is more likely in the face of complex and/or ambiguous stimuli, may indeed be affected by both individual and situational factors. These factors may affect either the motivation of the individual to make a thoughtful comparison or the difficulty of doing so. For example, an analytic interpretation of information is unlikely when such an analysis is difficult and the consequences of an incorrect interpretation are trivial. On the other hand, a person who is very emotional or anxious may be distracted and therefore may be less sensitive to important stimulus features, thus aborting the systematic feature comparison process implied by Postulate 2. Situational distractions that in-crease processing load may also interfere with a systematic com-parison process. Thus, for example, a telephone survey respondent who feels rushed may fail to carefully interpret questions in terms of an elaborate memory-based feature comparison process but may instead respond in a heuristic, or knee-jerk fashion based on a superficial construing of the question. The extent to which prior knowledge is carefully brought to bear in new situations, it would seem, is likely to be strongly affected by situational and personal factors during effortful interpretation processes.

Postulate 3. When several alternative concepts stored in memory are potentially applicable for interpreting new information, the one used is that which is most accessible in memory.

This postulate makes two basic claims. First, it asserts that, in general, not all relevant knowledge is brought to bear in the interpretation of incoming information. Then, it goes on to specify that the concept(s) used will be one(s) most accessible in memory. However, exactly what is meant by "most accessible" is not clearly specified. Without an independent conceptualization of the factors that determine accessibility, Postulate 3 cannot be meaningfully applied. Indeed, it becomes tautological. If the criterion for infer-ring the accessibility of a concept in memory is whether or not it is used to interpret information, the proposition that accessibility is a determinant of the use of the concept is impossible to invalidate.

Accessibility is often assumed to depend on recency of use (see Postulate 10). That is, the probability of a relevant concept being used in the interpretation of incoming information is a negative function of the amount of time since its last use. Some theories discuss other determinants of a concept's accessibility. Higgins, Bargh, and Lombardi (1985), for example, postulate that frequency of concept use is an important determinant of accessibility. Although frequently used concepts are more likely also to have been used recently, the two factors can lead to different predictions in some situations. Another factor that theoretically could influence acces-sibility is salience. We now turn to a discussion of research evidence bearing on these possibilities.

Research. Postulate 3 is particularly important in considera-tions of priming phenomena, in which the interpretation of ambiguous

information is affected by previously acquired but objectively irrelevant information that has made certain concepts more accessible.
Laboratory demonstrations of priming phenomena are reviewed by
Higgins and King (1981) and by Wyer and Srull (1981). In a recent
study, Higgins et al. (1985) constructed situations in which the
recency with which a concept had been activated and the frequency of
its activation theoretically have opposing effects on its use. They
found that if an ambiguous stimulus was presented very soon after
concepts were primed, the more recently activated concept  was used
to interpret it. When presentation of the ambiguous stimulus was
delayed, however, the more  frequently activated concept was used.

   The possibility that salience affects a concept's accessibility
is suggested in experiments by Taylor and Fiske (1978) and by Strack,
Erber, and Wicklund (1982). These studies show that attribution of a
person's responsibility for a social event depend on objectively
irrelevant factors that make the person distinctive in the situation
being judged (e.g., the person's sex or ethnicity, type of clothing,
spatial location, etc.). Research has also shown that the point of
view taken by subjects in experimental tasks can affect the accessibility of concepts by making different aspects of a situation
salient as a function of point of view (see Fiske, Taylor, Etcoff, &
Laufer, 1979; Taylor & Fiske, 1975, 1978).

   In evaluating the implications of these studies it is important
to bear in mind the concern previously expressed about the tautological nature of the accessibility construct. The research described
above can be interpreted as an indication that the salience of a
concept increases its accessibility and therefore increases the
likelihood that it is used to interpret information and social
experiences. But what if the results had not occurred. Would the
appropriate conclusion be that the salience does not affect a concept's accessibility, or that salience affects a concept's accessibility but that the most accessible concepts are not always used as
bases for interpreting information?

   In fact, some research by Martin (1985) suggests that accessibility per se is not a sufficient basis for predicting a concept's
use in interpreting information. In this research, subjects first
were asked to sort behaviors in terms of the trait concepts they
exemplified. The number of behaviors that subjects actually sorted
was the same in all conditions. However, some subjects were led to
believe that they had completed the sorting task whereas others were
ostensibly interrupted before the task was finished. Later, all

subjects read a paragraph describing behaviors of a target person
that were ambiguous with respect to the traits they implied. Subjects
under the "incompleted" priming task condition were more likely to
interpret these ambiguous behaviors in terms of the concepts primed
by the sorting task than in terms of other applicable concepts.
Subjects in the "completed" priming task, however, were _less_ likely
to use the primed concept. Because the recency and frequency of
priming relevant trait concepts was the same in both task conditions,
these results cannot be interpreted in terms of differences in the
accessibility of the concepts. Martin argues that subjects in the
completed task conditions were more aware that a concept applicable
for interpreting the information had been activated by the earlier
sorting task, so they intentionally suppressed the use of this concept in order to avoid being biased. Be that as it may, his results
obviously indicate that the accessibility of concepts alone is not
sufficient to account for their effects on the interpretation of
ambiguous information and that other factors may be equally or more
important. These factors are not dealt with by Postulate 3.

   _Applicability_. Postulate 3 implies that people make one interpretation of a stimulus and base this interpretation on whatever
concept is momentarily most accessible. This seems most likely to be
true only in those everyday situations in which persons have relatively little vested interest. In fact, indirect evidence for this
claim has been obtained in several field studies, which show that
people who have fortuitously been put into a good or bad mood (e.g.,
by receiving a small gift at a supermarket, by the weather, or by the
outcome of a soccer game) judged the quality of both specific aspects
of their lives (e.g., the service record of their automobiles) and
their general life satisfaction in a way that was affectively consistent with their mood state (see Isen, 1984; Schwarz & Clore, 1983;
Schwarz, Strack, Kommer, & Wagner, 1984). This suggests that concepts
activated by transitory mood states are applied in interpreting both
specific and general information that underlies  the judgment people
make. Alternatively, the affect-associated concepts may themselves be
used as a basis for judgments (see Schwarz & Clore, 1983).

   In the area of survey research, Postulate 3 has important implications for the effects of the order of questions in a questionnaire or interview. Specifically, early items may evoke concepts that
are used to interpret the meaning of later questions, thereby possibly biasing the responses. To the extent that the meaning of a

15

question is ambiguous, accessibility effects on interpretation are of considerable importance to the survey researcher.

An important issue arising from these considerations is exactly what determines the final interpretation given to an ambiguous stimulus event? Under what conditions will people consider several alternative interpretations before they accept some particular one? In many cases, this may often be determined in part by self-serving biases. People may continue to interpret and reconstrue information until they reach an interpretation that has pleasant implications for themselves (assuming this is possible). This analysis suggests that the processes described in Postulate 3 will exert their rather for- tuitous influence on social perception in everyday life only when the individual is indifferent to the implications of the information or when the initial interpretation has acceptably positive implications.

Although this possibility, to our knowledge, has not been directly investigated, a laboratory study by Arkin, Gleason, and Johnston (1976) is relevant. They found that subjects interpreted their failure on an experimental task as being their own fault only if no obvious situational factor could have accounted for the outcome. However, they took responsibility for success despite the availability of situation-based explanations. These data suggest that people prefer to interpret their own behavior in ways that reflect positively on themselves and that they actively seek alternative interpretations only when the more immediately obvious interpretation has negative implications for their self-image. Similar contingencies may exist in the effects of concept activation on the interpretation of information in daily life as well as in the laboratory.

Postulate 4. The selection of a concept for use in encoding and organizing new information can be affected by the purpose for which the information is to be used.

This postulate states that a person's goals can significantly influence the way he or she interprets information relevant to these goals. This implies, for example, that if one's current purpose is to screen applicants for a librarian position, concepts such as intro- verted, quiet, intelligent, and so forth, are likely to be used whereas concepts such as artistic, agile, or ostentatious would likely not, since they have little if any relevance to the goals at hand. Goals determine a range of relevant concepts. The actual selec- tion of specific concepts from this range presumably begins with the most accessible (see Postulate 3).

Most theoretical applications of this postulate assume that the goals or purposes of the recipient of information are conscious. However, it is conceivable that certain goals are so central to a person that they influence interpretational processes, regardless of whether or not the person is currently conscious of them. It is also possible that other unconscious factors can influence concept selection during interpretation. This has been suggested in the priming paradigm by Bargh and Pietromonaco (1982). They found that trait information presented to subjects so briefly that it presumably never reached consciousness influenced their subsequent interpretation of ambiguous stimuli. There must therefore be factors irrelevant to current goals that can affect concept selection in encoding and organizing operations.

Research. A great deal of research (summarized in Srull & Wyer, in press) has demonstrated that experimentally supplied goals do indeed result in differential organization and use of information. While this may be interpreted as general evidence for the importance of goals in social information processing, more specific evidence for Postulate 4 is generally lacking. With few exceptions (e.g., Carlston, 1980), the activation and use of specific goal-relevant concepts in the interpretation and use of social information has not been demonstrated. Consequently, despite its intuitive appeal, Postulate 4 remains largely unsubstantiated by social cognition research.

Applicability. Two bodies of evidence do provide rather convincing indications of the role of goals in the perception and organization of information. They are important because they deal with goals that are not supplied by an experimenter but rather are simply important aims of individuals in their everyday lives. One set of evidence is the work of Klinger (1975) on "current concerns." Current concerns are basically a person's salient transitory or enduring goals (e.g., to find a job, or to make a favorable impression). There is considerable evidence that these concerns play a major role in determining the aspects of the stimulus field to which people attend and respond. As just one example, Klinger cites the case of mothers who, even though asleep, are particularly sensitive to the cries of their neonates but not to other similar noise disturbances. Klinger concludes that goals induce a sensitization to goal-related stimuli.

The other set of evidence supporting the applicability of this postulate outside the social cognition lab is the work of Bruner (e.g., 1951). He tachistoscopically presented subjects with ambiguous visual stimuli and found that their interpretations of them could be predicted by assessment of their values. Values can be thought of as enduring, generalized goals. In this case, the visual image was interpreted in terms of these ongoing goals. The research of Bruner and Klinger provides better support for Postulate 4 than does research performed to date in the typical social cognition paradigm. Specifically, it demonstrates the power of important personal goals in guiding information processing, whereas most social cognition research has studied rather mundane and uninvolving goals imposed on the subject by the experimenter.

Postulate 5. (Selective Encoding) If a set of abstract concepts applicable for encoding information has already been activated at the time the information is received, only those features of the information that exemplify these concepts will tend to be encoded in more abstract terms.

This postulate states that if a (presumably limited) set of concepts is activated during information acquisition, the only higher-order encodings of the information that occur will generally be in terms of these concepts. The use of the qualifier "generally" is important. Some behaviors are such clear and striking examples of a specific trait that they will be encoded in terms of this trait regardless of whether it was among those concepts that have been activated recently. To return to the case of the person screening applicants for a librarian position, this person would likely have concepts such as "intelligent" and "well-read" in mind. Postulate 5 states that only these concepts will tend to be used for higher-order encodings. However, if one candidate's resume contains the fact that he or she won three Olympic medals in track and field, it is almost inevitable that this will be encoded in terms of the trait "athletic" even though this concept was not previously activated.

Research. The primary empirical implication of Postulate 5 is that subjects who are asked to recall previously presented information will tend to recall only those aspects that exemplify concepts that they had in mind at the time the information was received. One particularly robust laboratory finding that is consistent with this postulate is the better recall of a person's behaviors when they are relevant to trait-based expectancies than when they are irrelevant to them (Hastie, 1980; Srull, 1981; Srull, Lichtenstein, & Rothbart, 1985; Wyer, Bodenhausen, & Srull, 1984). A related example is the case of stereotypic beliefs. Stereotypes can influence judgments of the stereotyped target because stereotypic concepts (evoked by the

target's ethnicity, gender, occupation, etc.) facilitate the encoding
of any behaviors that are consistent with stereotypic expectancies
(Rothbart, 1981).

In much of this research, however, alternative theoretical
mechanisms could also account for the observed effects of
expectancies. An example may be subjects who are told that a person
is intelligent and subsequently show better recall of behaviors that
have implications for intelligence than behaviors that are irrelevant
to this attribute. This could indicate that subjects selectively
encoded and organized the person's behaviors in terms of expectancy-
related concepts (e.g., "intelligent") at the time the behaviors were
first read, and this led them to be relatively better recalled.
However, it is equally plausible that subjects encoded all of the
behaviors in terms of traits they appeared to exemplify regardless of
their relevance to intelligence. However, at the time they were asked
to recall the behaviors, they remembered that the person was
described as "intelligent" (during the expectancy-generation phase of
the experiment) and this concept cued the recall of the particular
behaviors that had some implications for this trait. In other words,
the recall bias could result from the selective retrieval of
expectancy-related behaviors and not from selective encoding of them
at the time they were first presented.

These possibilities can be distinguished by varying the point at
which expectancy-related concepts are activated. That is, suppose
some subjects are given trait descriptions of a target person before
receiving behavioral information about him or her, whereas others are
not given these characterizations until after the target's behaviors
have been read. If both groups of subjects show the same bias in
recall and judgments, it would suggest that selective retrieval
processes are operating. However, if biases in recall are obtained
only when the trait description of the target preceded the presentation of the target's behaviors, the selective encoding postulate
would be supported. In fact, quite different patterns of recall seem
to occur in the two cases (Wyer et al., 1984). Although Snyder and
Uranowitz (1978) report evidence that they interpreted as support for
selective retrieval, their memory test involved a forced-choice
recognition procedure that failed to correct for guessing bias.
Therefore, their results are equivocal regarding the merits of the
selective retrieval hypothesis (see Bellezza & Bower, 1981).

Applicability. It is quite reasonable to wonder whether the
selective encoding and organization phenomena assumed in social

cognition theorizing are as prominent in daily life as in the laboratory. One reason for questioning their generalizability is the fact that it is rare in real life to learn about 60 different behaviors of a person, most of which have clear trait implications, in a matter of minutes. Outside the laboratory, as we noted before, we typically acquire knowledge of a person's behaviors in several different situations over a fairly extended period of time. Consequently, we are quite capable of encoding these individual behavioral episodes as they are observed or learned about, at least at the level of generality with which they are usually described in an experiment (e.g., "helped a woman with her groceries"). Moreover, in contrast to the laboratory, we often learn about a person's behaviors without any particular objective in mind, and therefore we are unlikely to interpret them in terms of any specific goal-related concepts. Thus, the selective encoding and organization that often appear to occur in laboratory research seems likely to play a minor role in most everyday life situations.

In everyday life situations, selective retrieval may be a more critical factor. Which of the many behaviors that we have learned about a person over the course of our past interactions with him or her are we likely to retrieve and use to make a particular judgment (which we probably were not expecting to make at the time the behaviors were learned)? A related question was raised by Snyder and Uranowitz (1978). That is, motivational factors that come into play after information is presented may lead this information to be recalled and reinterpreted in a way that facilitates one's present need. Following a divorce, for example, one may reconstrue the behaviors of a spouse as exploitive even though they were originally viewed as loving.

Although the specific sort of selective encoding identified in laboratory research on person memory and judgment may have relatively little influence on information processing in daily life, this does not mean that selective encoding in general is unimportant. The processing demands placed on the human organism in daily life are often considerable. Moreover, these demands are often heightened by the need to pursue more than one cognitive objective simultaneously, necessitating attention to several different sources and types of information. Under these conditions, it seems inevitable that selective encoding does play an important role in information processing. However, whether the processes that underlie this sort of selectivity are in any way similar to the sort of selective encoding implied by current laboratory research in social cognition (i.e., selective encoding of particular types of information about a particular individual when we have a particular goal in mind to which the information is relevant) is not at all clear. Consideration of these everyday life phenomena again reveals a problem that could in principle be investigated in the laboratory, namely the influence of competing objectives, or processing demands, which are not directly related to one's primary goals, on selective encoding and use of goal-relevant information.

Postulate 6. If an object described by new information can be identified as an exemplar of a general concept (such as schema or script), a representation of the object may be formed on the basis of this concept. This representation is then stored in memory as a unit.

This postulation has several important theoretical implications. First, it asserts that the representational form of information is often determined primarily by the existing organization of relevant prior knowledge rather than by its presentational format. Second, it implies that information not contained in the original material may be added to the representation on the basis of prior knowledge. Third, it allows for the possibility that presented information will not be contained in a representation if it is not relevant to the knowledge structure guiding the construction of this representation (see Postulate 5). The generality of the postulate leaves open the specific mechanism involved in the construction of representations on the basis of prior knowledge. However, it should be noted that, inasmuch as it does posit the formation and storage of an organizational unit, it is subject to the various theoretical controversies discussed in the context of Postulate 1.

Two models proposed by Graesser and his colleagues offer more specific accounts of the way existing bodies of knowledge are used in creating new representations. The "script pointer + tag" model (Graesser, Gordon, & Sawyer, 1979) proposes that once the relevance of an existing memory structure is recognized, a mental "pointer" is created that indicates its applicability. The script or schema is conceived as a generic structure containing variables. Specific values of these variables, which can be extracted from the new information being presented, are stored along with the pointer. Script or schema variables, whose values are not contained in the information, may be assigned "default" values, or most likely guesses. This provides for later intrusions or spontaneous inferences. Any information in the presented material that deviates from the script (by being irrelevant or atypical) is "tagged" onto the pointer representation. The links between the tags and the main representation are sufficiently weak that the irrelevant or atypical material can become dissociated from the representation and therefore be lost. This provides for omissions in recall of atypical items.

A second, closely related conceptualization is the "schema copy + tag model" (Graesser & Nakamura, 1982). This model makes identical assumptions except that instead of a pointer referencing the generic memory structure, a copy of a relevant subset of the nodes in the schema is created and variable values are inserted into this copy. This model is equally capable of accounting for intrusions and omissions. Both approaches are compatible with Postulate 6, and others are also possible. However, Graesser's models are among the best specified in this area.

Research. In addition to the research conducted by Graesser in support of his own models, other evidence exists for the basic claims of Postulate 6. One of the most interesting demonstrations of the use of generic knowledge structures in the formation and organization of new mental representations is the research reported by E. Lichtenstein and Brewer (1980). They presented subjects with both videotaped event sequences and prose descriptions of events. The particular events they examined involved goal-directed behavior, and they found evidence in five experiments for the use of a general "plan schema" in organizing the informational content of behavior. They also found relatively poor recall for presented behavior that was not goal-directed, providing evidence of a tendency to omit information that is irrelevant to the generic knowledge structure guiding representation formation.

Applicability. In what situations outside the laboratory would someone be expected, on the basis of generic mental structures, to form a new "unit of knowledge?" One likely prerequisite is a higher-order processing objective such as "forming an impression." This goal is usually pursued when someone or something is encountered for the first time. Thus, a new neighbor may be construed as a "typical accountant type" or a new restaurant may be seen as a "run-of-the-mill fast-food joint." In such situations, it seems quite plausible that we would rely on general knowledge to "pidgeon-hole" new entities. However, once we begin to acquire more particular, episodic information about these specific entities, generic knowledge structures probably become obsolete. There is also no need to form a new knowledge unit; new information can be incorporated into the existing one(s).

As knowledge of some entity or class of entities becomes more complex and generic schemas become largely obsolete, domain-specific knowledge structures may be used to facilitate further learning. For example, Srull (1983a) found that individuals who had more familiarity with automobiles were better able to learn information about the attributes of several brands of cars (such as statements that might appear in an advertisement). Moreover, the recall performance of low-familiarity subjects was clearly inferior when the information was presented in a random order compared to when it was blocked by brand name. This was not the case with the high-familiarity subjects, who apparently used their better articulated knowledge structures to organize more efficiently the incoming information.

The role of generic knowledge structures in survey application is suggested by research conducted by Bishop, Tuchfarber, and Oldendick (in press), who asked survey respondents questions about fictitious (but to the respondent, ostensibly real) entities and events. Many people responded as if they had specific knowledge relevant to these entities. Having identified the fictitious entity as a member of some domain, their general knowledge apparently permitted them to make a response. This suggests that responses to survey items about which the respondent has relevant general knowledge may be determined by guess-work based on schemata or scripts rather than a retrieval of specific information that may also be available (see also Postulate 9).

Postulate 7. When a large amount of information about a target is presented, the only aspects of it that are stored in memory are those sufficient to permit the original material to be reconstructed, based on more general relevant knowledge structures.

A primary implication of this postulate is one of cognitive parsimony and efficiency. The claims for this assumption are mostly made on theoretical grounds. The commitment to cognitive parsimony is a legacy of network theories of semantic memory (cf. Johnson-Laird, Herrmann, & Chaffin, 1984). Some evidence for the notion of cognitive efficiency was provided by Collins and Quillian (1969) who measured the time required for subjects to verify various semantic relations (e.g., a robin is a bird). Based on the pattern of data they collected, they concluded that information was not redundantly distributed throughout memory but could be described in terms of a hierarchical structure in which attributes possessed by all members of a class were stored only at the superordinate level of the class and not repeated in representation of each class member. Johnson-Laird et al., however, suggest that semantic memory may involve more redundancy than has previously been believed. Their specific argument is that many semantic relations (links between objects and their attributes) are so well-learned that they must be included in representations of some individual members of a class as well as at the superordinate level.

Claims for parsimony in mental representation have also been made in the case of memory for episodic information. Wyer (1980) asserted that this postulate is especially important in conceptualizing memory for ongoing behavior sequencies, which often involve a great deal of information that could easily be recaptured simply by storing "highlights." On intuitive grounds, this claim is quite plausible. A specific theoretical implementation of Postulate 7 in terms of event memory is the work of Graesser et al. (1979), discussed in the previous section. In the script pointer + tag model, an action sequence that is an instance of some more general type of activity (e.g., eating lunch at Nature's Table with Rhonda and Peter is a specific instance of "eating at a restaurant") is remembered by the use of a cognitive "pointer" to the restaurant script and an indication of the specific information that is not in the script but is necessary to reconstruct the event. This additional information takes the form of "tags" and instantiation values of script variables. Graesser's model demonstrates one theoretical use of this postulate.

Research. Obtaining supporting or disconfirming evidence regarding this postulate is difficult. One set of findings that supports the basic idea is the research on the atypicality effect (Graesser & Nakamura, 1982). Stated in the broadest terms, the atypicality effect refers to the fact that people can discriminate presented and unpresented atypical aspects of a stimulus passage fairly well. In contrast, people are quite poor at discriminating between presented and unpresented typical aspects. This is presumably because they only store the distinctive and informative aspects of the material at the time it is presented and do not bother to retain other material that would be redundant with general knowledge. A recent study by Nakamura, Graesser, Zimmerman, and Riha (1985) replicated the atypicality effect in a nonlaboratory setting. Students were given a recognition memory test for the behaviors performed by a lecturer 20 min after the lecture ended. Aspects of the lecturers behavior that were not inherent in a generic "lecture" script were better discriminated from distractors than were more typical behaviors.

More evidence that only "highlights" of action sequences are stored in memory is suggested in the work of Newston (1976). In his research, he presents subjects with videotaped action sequences and "unitizes" them into meaningful segments. He finds that breakpoints occur at significant events. Recall of these breakpoint events themselves is theoretically all that is required to reconstruct the general sequence. Mundane interpolated actions can be inferred from information contained at the breakpoints. However, some evidence argues against such strong claims of representational parsimony. Cohen and Ebbesen (1979), in a paradigm similar to Newtson's, found that subjects forming an impression of an event sequence divided it into fewer action units than those who were trying to memorize the sequence. Nevertheless, recognition memory for details of the sequence a short time later was not appreciably different for these two groups of subjects. Cohen and Ebbesen conclude that a dual-coding system must be involved, in which more than one representation is formed with information overlap in the two representations. If this is the case, it argues against Postulate 7. Thus, the evidence regarding Postulate 7's status in the laboratory is mixed.

Applicability. In real life, we encounter so much information in the course of any given day that it seems very unlikely that we would store anything other than the highlights or the gist of the events. However, there is some evidence that we can remember much of the specific detail of real-life events. In a study by Keenan, MacWhinney, and Mahew (1977), colleagues were unexpectedly asked to recall the content of a prior conversation. Subjects not only demonstrated a clear ability to remember the gist of comments that had been made, but in many cases they also remembered the surface structure as well. Contrary to Postulate 7, this suggests that very detailed information may be available in memory representations of ongoing events.

It is true that after substantial time delays, details of information are often hard to remember. For example, if someone is asked to recall the specific details of a movie they saw a month ago, she or he may be unable to generate many of the events that occurred. However, if a specific event is mentioned by someone else, the person may often not only immediately remember it, but the event may trigger memories of related specific incidents in the film that she or he was previously unable to call to mind. This example intuitively seems to support a dual-coding notion over a single, parsimonious representation. One representation of the film may consist of the general gist of the plot and the main characters, and perhaps one's own affective reactions to the film. The details of the film may be contained in another representation, one that is typically not assessed. It would not be necessary to access it, for example, in making a recommendation to someone else about whether to see the film. Nevertheless it can be accessed if specific retrieval cues are provided.

In terms of implications for survey research, this means that appropriate retrieval cues contained in a question may lead respondents to access a more richly detailed memory representation and respond on the basis of this representation, whereas a global or vague question may result in a failure to consult these specific details. Instead, a more abbreviated, highlights-only representation may be used. The question, once again, is what sorts of cues are required to elicit effective retrieval of fine details -- a question not adequately considered in social cognition research to date.

Postulate 8. Information is more likely to be retained in long-term memory if it has been processed more extensively.

The general idea of "amount of processing" has been used in many different ways. Originally, when first discussed by Craik and Lockhart (1972), there was a notion of "depth" or differing levels at which processing can occur. Although this point of view has been largely abandoned, there are still several other senses in which "amount of processing" is or could be used. One general sense is the amount of time devoted to the consideration of specific information. If more time is spent thinking about something, it should be more likely to be remembered (cf. Raaijmakers & Shiffrin, 1981).

One type of information that is likely to receive more processing time and thus to be more memorable is salient or distinctive information. This postulate also applies to the amount of repetition or rehearsal an informational item receives. Obviously this also involves more time, but it specifies that the time is spent in the rote process of repeating the item. A third sense of amount of processing also deals with more processing time, but rather than spending the additional time on rehearsal, it is spent on elaboration. This is the usage adopted in the Hastie (1980)-Srull (1981) model of impression formation. The basic idea is that the presence of an item that contradicts an expectancy leads to attempts to explain or reconcile the item in terms of other available knowledge. It is the elaboration, and the concomitant formation of interitem associative linkages that theoretically leads to greater ease of recalling contradictory items in this paradigm, rather than the amount of processing time per se.

Research. The expectation that salient or distinctive information will receive more processing and thus be better remembered has received mixed support. Evidence for this proposition includes the finding that perspective or point of view affects the content of recall protocols in a systematic manner. Material that is salient from one point of view is better remembered relative to conditions in which another point of view is taken from which the same material is not salient (Fiske et al., 1979).

However, two reviews of research on salience effects recently concluded that evidence for superior recall of salient information is not consistent (McArthur, 1981; Taylor & Fiske, 1978).

The hypothesis that inconsistent information will be better remembered due to elaborative processing has received much more substantial empirical support (Hastie, 1980; Srull, 1981; Srull et al., 1985; Wyer et al., 1984). Moreover, researchers have begun to examine the specific conditions in which elaborative processing will or will not result from encountering inconsistent information. Crocker, Hannah, and Weber (1983), for example, found that behavior that is inconsistent with a trait-based expectancy is better recalled only when it cannot be easily attributed to a situational factor. If it can be attributed to a situational cause, the inconsistency poses no cognitive dilemma and therefore does not stimulate further processing (see also Hastie, 1984). Srull (1981) and Wyer et al. (1984) found that inconsistencies in information about members of a group are better remembered only when the group is a cohesive unit for which one has strong expectations of uniformity along certain trait dimensions. Otherwise, the usual diversity found in most loosely-knit collectives is sufficient to account for the inconsistent behavior of individual members, thereby precluding the need for more extensive processing.

The available evidence clearly supports Postulate 8 when "extensive processing" is interpreted as elaborative processing. However, there is some evidence that merely repeating or rehearsing an item may not be sufficient to produce greater recall performance. Srull (1981) found that having subjects repeat inconsistent behaviors four times after hearing them actually decreased recall. Thus, the repetition interpretation of "extensive processing" has not received the extensive support that the elaboration interpretation has.

Applicability. There is no compelling reason to believe that the effect of amount of cognitive elaboration found in the laboratory will not also be obtained in real-world situations. In these situations, as in the laboratory, the likelihood of long-term storage should increase with more extensive processing. However, in relation to other factors, amount of processing may play a less important role in determining which of several items will be recalled in the situation. In the laboratory, effects of amount of processing on recall may be substantial primarily because of the unique nature of the recall task. That is, amount of processing may have a major influence on the probability that an item will be recalled only when subjects are instructed to recall information in general, without regard to type. In everyday life situations, however, we are rarely called upon to make vague or general recollections. Instead, memory searches are conducted for specific reasons or in response to specific cues. The range of relevant information is likely to be much more restricted than in the "recall everything you can" task. Conceivably the amount of processing/elaboration is an important determinant of recall in these more restricted search situations only within the range of information that is considered on other bases to be goal relevant.

Postulate 8, in combination with the impression formation literature, implies that we should often be much more likely to store information about people in long-term memory if it contradicts our expectations about them. Hence, our minds should be full of disconforming evidence. This is inconsistent with phenomena such as the perseverance of beliefs and stereotypes in the face of contradictory evidence (Jelalian & Miller, 1984). Postulate 8 can be reconciled with belief perseverance through the introduction of motivational factors. In some situations, people are unwilling to accept contradictory evidence so they dismiss it out of hand and are not motivated to reconcile it with other knowledge. They may simply make a situational, transitory attribution for the occurrence of a belief-inconsistent event, regardless of whether evidence exists to support such attributions. Through motivational mechanisms, we may indeed be able to "overlook the incongruent."

<u>Postulate 9. When making judgments, people do not generally search memory for all previously acquired information that is relevant to the judgment; rather, they retrieve and use only a small subset of this information that is most easily accessible at the time.</u>

This postulate states that judgments are usually the result of a <u>heuristic</u> search process rather than an exhaustive, systematic search. Moreover, heuristic processes may bypass information search entirely. Many theorists have claimed that what is actually retrieved and used in many judgment-making situations are not instances of evidence contained in memory but is rather a personal theory relevant to the judgment domain. This is the claim for theory-based rather than data-based judgments (Jennings, Amabile, & Ross, 1982; Shweder, 1982; Wright & Murphy, 1984).

Postulate 9 has important implications for data-based judgments. One possible form of heuristic data-based decisions could involve the serial retrieval of pieces of decision-relevant information, beginning with the most accessible, until the preponderance of the evidence overall exceeds some judgmental threshold. Whatever the specific theoretical mechanism, the claims for heuristic processes in judgment and decision making are among the most well-substantiated in social and cognitive psychology.

The tone of many discussions of this heuristic quality of human information processing is decidedly pejorative. This is undoubtedly because in order to distinguish heuristic-based processing from more systematic (algorithmic) processing, one must construct conditions in which the use of a heuristic and the use of an algorithm lead to different judgments. In fact, this is often difficult to do. The lamentations over the supposed inferiority of heuristic-based judgments often ignore the fact that in the vast majority of situations encountered in everyday life, the use of a heuristic generates judgments that quite closely approximate those that would result from more extensive cognitive activity. It seems more appropriate to regard heuristic processing as a useful means of coping with complex judgment situations rather than as a "shortcoming" of the human information processor (cf. Nisbett & Ross, 1980).

<u>Research.</u> One of the most famous demonstrations of heuristic processing is the research of Tversky and Kahneman (1973) on the use of availability as a heuristic for judging frequency and probability. Events that come easily to mind are judged to be both more frequent and more probable. Research supporting the availability heuristic, as

well as many of the others that have been identified (e.g., representativeness, simulation), is well documented by Sherman and Corty
(1984). The operation of this postulate as it pertains to survey
research is described by Bishop (this volume).

Bodenhausen and Wyer (1985) provide interesting evidence regarding the relationship between heuristic strategies and the information
search process. In that study, we found evidence that ethnic
stereotypes were used in making punitive decisions (a theory-based
judgmental strategy). Subsequent to making these decisions, however,
the available information was apparently reviewed in an attempt to
corroborate the implications of the theory-based judgment. This
indicates that information search may be greater than the postulate
would  assume, but the searching may occur after a judgment has
already been made, primarily in an effort to confirm the judgment and
thereby justify the use of the heuristic.

Applicability. One obvious objection to laboratory demonstrations of heuristic processing is the fact that subjects in experiments often do not have sufficient interest and motivation in the
judgment tasks presented to them to adopt more systematic strategies.
This claim has been substantiated in the laboratory by Gabrenya and
Arkin (1979), who documented greater reliance on heuristic under
conditions in which judgments had low hedonic relevance. Similarly,
Chaiken (1980) found that in a personally involving persuasion situation, subjects used more systematic processing styles, while those in
less involving situations adopted heuristic styles. As a final example, Harkness, Deßono, and Borgida (1985) found that personally
involved subjects used more complex judgment strategies in a contingency judgment task and were also more accurate than relatively less
involved subjects.

Another potential difference between laboratory judgments and
real-world judgments lies in the fact that people in their everyday
lives are often able to reflect upon a decision, make a tentative
judgment, and then later modify it. This may occur several times en
route to a final decision. Thus, even if a limited set of available
information is used in arriving at each intermediate judgment on the
road to an ultimate decision, different subsets of information are
likely to be involved in each case. Therefore, over the course of
time the implications of several different types of information may
be considered, and most of their implications may ultimately be taken
into account. This phenomenon contrasts sharply with laboratory
situations in which a single judgment is expected to be made quickly.

The bottom line is that judgmental processes in the real world are complex and varied, and are not always heuristically based. Although we seldom if ever stop to consider all information relevant to a judgment, in everyday life our judgments may be more systematic than they typically are in laboratory and survey settings.

Postulate 10. The concepts of mental structures that are most likely to be retrieved from long-term memory for use in interpreting new information or making judgments are those that have been most recently used in the past.

This postulate explicitly equates cognitive accessibility with recency of use (not recency of acquisition). Many of the theoretical issues raised in the discussion of accessibility effects at encoding (Postulate 3) also apply here. For example, alternative factors that may rival recency in determining accessibility (e.g., frequency, salience, etc.) are important to consider in both cases. In making judgments, still other factors may become important that were not considered in the previous discussion. Most obviously, the effect of more recently used information about a person or event may be over-ridden by the effects of other attributes when these attributes are particularly strongly associated with the entity being judged.

Research. Postulate 10 is of potential importance in understanding a great variety of laboratory phenomena. One example is the research on priming effects in judgment, discussed earlier in the context of Postulate 3. Another important example is the finding that if people make a judgment after receiving experimentally presented information, they will rely on this more recent judgment, rather than the original material, in making subsequent judgments (Carlston, 1980; Sherman, Ahlm, Berman, & Lynn, 1978 -- see also Postulate 11). Still another example is research indicating that concepts that have been used to explain feedback concerning one's own (or someone else's) failure or success may affect predictions of future success or failure even after the feedback has been discredited as bogus (Ross, Lepper, & Hubbard, 1975).

However, the effects of recency are often hard to separate from those of other factors. For example, Carretta and Moreland (1982) found that people who voted for Richard Nixon in 1972 continued to regard him positively during the subsequent Watergate hearings. This could mean that the initial concepts formed about Nixon, which became strongly associated with him, were used as bases for judgments rather than the more recently acquired information about his role in Watergate. On the other hand, it could also indicate that the favorable concepts about Nixon, although acquired before the Watergate hearings, were typically recalled and were continually used in the course of hearing about Watergate and attempting to rational-ize the events that took place. Thus, knowledge about Watergate, although more recently acquired, was not necessarily more recently used.

   Applicability. The applicability of recency effects in terms of encoding operations was discussed in the context of Postulate 3 and will not be repeated here. The effect of recency  in real-world judgment processes can be viewed as a by-product of heuristic processing strategies. To this extent, an evaluation of its role in making judgments is susceptible to considerations similar to those we raised in the context of discussing heuristic processes in general. That is, recency may be important in determining an initial "kneejerk" judgment. However, in real life, many judgments are not of this sort. Unfortunately, the short time span of experimental tasks, and the limited importance that these tasks have for subjects, usually mitigate against such deliberate decision making, and there-fore may make recency effects appear more common than they actually are in everyday life.

Postulate 11. Once a representation of a target has been formed and stored in memory, this representation will tend to be used in sub-sequent judgments of the target rather than the original information.

   Postulate 11 is really a combination of the implications of several of the other postulates. Postulate 4 stated that a person's goals strongly affect the way information is encoded and organized. This postulate asserts that it is this goal-determined representation that will be retained in memory. Under ordinary circumstances, the original information will not be stored in long-term memory, and after a certain period of time, it will be lost from short-term or working memory. Given the processes assumed by Postulates 3 and 5, the information that ends up being stored in memory may differ sub-stantially from the original information. The implications of the representation for subsequent judgments may be quite different from the implications of the original information. Further discussion of theory relevant to this postulate can be found in the discussions of Postulates 3,4,5,7, and 10.

   Research and Applicability. In addition to research cited in the previous sections, one other set of findings has implications for a specific implementation of this postulate. The concept of working memory is central to this assumption. One version of this concept is the "Work Space" discussed by Wyer and Srull (1985b). In their model, the construction of representations occurs in the Work Space, which contains the original information. Only the representations migrate to long-term memory; the original information remains in the Work Space until it is displaced by more immediate processing goals. At such time, it is irretrievably lost. Srull and Wyer (1983) report six experiments that support this conceptualization. Basically, these studies show that factors that theoretically lead information in the Work Space to be displaced both decrease the recall of this informa- tion and increase the influence of abstract concepts that were used to encode it at the time the information was first received. Postulate 11 receives some credibility from these studies.

Issues surrounding the applicability of this postulate have been discussed in the context of previous postulates. Particularly relevant is the discussion in the "applicability" section of Postulate 7, in which it is contended that the details of the original information may be more likely to be stored and recalled in certain real-life situations than Postulate 11 implies.

Postulate 12. If information has been encoded and organized in terms of certain concepts or prototypic structures, the subsequent activa- tion of these concepts or structures may serve as retrieval cues for the information, thereby facilitating recall.

The organizing concepts that are described in Postulate 12 could be any of several different types. However, trait concepts are the most commonly studied kind. In the domain of person perception, Postulate 12 could be translated as: Recall of behavioral informa- tion, which has been encoded in terms of personality traits, can be effectively cued by the trait terms themselves.

As we noted at the outset, the effects of retrieval processes are often difficult to isolate from effects that occur at earlier processing stages (cf. Anderson, 1978). Nonetheless, most of the theoretical "action" has occurred in conceptualizing these earlier stages, and retrieval processes have received far less attention in social cognition theory and research than they deserve. One reason for this may be that the theories are developed to account for laboratory research in which the information presented is recalled after a relatively short retention interval. A conceptualization of strategic retrieval processes may become much more important when greater intervals occur between information acquisition and usage.

Research. Evidence that personality traits serve as retrieval cues for behaviors that exemplify them has been obtained by Wyer and

Gordon (1982; see also Winter & Uleman, 1984). It is interesting to note that in the Wyer and Gordon study, trait concepts cued the recall of behaviors exemplifying them only when subjects learned about these behaviors with the objective of forming an impression of the person who performed them. When the subjects' goal was simply to memorize the behaviors, there was no evidence that traits were effective retrieval cues. This can be explained simply by assuming that the behaviors were encoded in trait terms only in the impression formation condition. It would seem, then, that at least in the laboratory situations frequently investigated by social cognition researchers, Postulate 12 is quite likely to hold, provided the retrieval cues correspond to features involved in the original encoding.

Applicability. As stated above, consideration of retrieval cues may be much more important in real life than in the laboratory because retention intervals tend to be longer. One common real-life situation in which retrieval cues are important is question answering. Cues provided in a question may frequently have an important impact on the response that is generated. This is because different information may be accessed in response to different cues. This has obvious ramifications for survey research. A concrete example may clarify the point. Suppose that someone has recently had the flu and all the accompanying discomforts, including a nagging headache. The person may encode the entire episode at a general level as about with the flu rather than as a headache, fever, nausea, and so forth. If the person is contacted by an analgesic manufacturer's marketing research division and is asked when she or he last had a headache, she or he may overlook the flu-induced headache because the specificity of the question leads to a search for instances in which an episode was encoded as "a headache" specifically. The respondent may report that the last time she or he had a headache was months ago.

A final consideration in conceptualizing the role of retrieval processes in daily life is the fact that the retrieval cues we use to access prior knowledge may be selected strategically and intentionally. A common example occurs in trying to recall the names of the 50 United States. In performing this task, a person may first use geographical location as a basis for recall. If this strategy does not result in recall of all of the states, the person may run through the alphabet, attempting to recall the names of states beginning with each letter. Finally, the person may recall the states represented by various football conferences, or perhaps the states she or he passed through on a recent automobile trip to California. Each strategy may elicit a different subset of knowledge. One way of conceptualizing this phenomenon is to assume that different sets of cues access different subsets of information. Similar processes may be used in attempting to recall the names of persons in one's high school class, or the movies that one saw last year. These processes have in fact been discussed more formally by Norman and Bobrow (1979). A specification of both the determinants and effects of retrieval cues in accessing social knowledge may be of considerable importance in understanding the bases of judgments and decisions we make in daily life.

## Naturalistic Approaches to the Study of Social Cognition

It seems reasonable to conclude from the discussion above that existing research on social-cognitive processes has potentially more to say about real-world cognition that Neisser (1980) wishes to believe. At the same time, it is important to realize that there are constraints on the applicability of the conclusions drawn from experimental research that are in some cases substantial. These must be carefully considered. Moreover, there can be no doubt that important questions about real-world cognition still remain unanswered, some (but not all) of which are susceptible to laboratory investigation. In the final section of this chapter, we will briefly discuss the mutual benefits that could emerge from the use of naturalistic research strategies to complement and augment experimentation in the study of social cognition.

Ongoing Interaction. Ostrom (1984) recently pointed out that social knowledge is not passively acquired. As active participants in society, we gather knowledge in the course of complex interactions with the elements of the social environment. For this reason, it is important to study the cognitive processes of persons who are assuming a more active role than those often imposed by laboratory tasks. What is called for are more naturalistic strategies that involve the observation of ongoing interaction (e.g., Harr , 1980). We are quick to add that we do not advocate this _instead_ of the usual laboratory strategies but rather in addition to them. McGrath (1982) has noted that only through methodological pluralism can the social sciences hope to advance.

The extensive work of Newston (1976; for a concise summary, see Knowles & D. Smith, 1981) represents a research program that has begun to tackle the job of discovering those aspects of ongoing behavior (in videotaped form) that significantly affect an individual's cognitive responses to behavioral sequences. Despite these important contributions, the subject in Newtson's studies retains a predominantly passive orientation. We have recently undertaken a line of research that places the subject in a much more active and socially rich role. In this research, cohabiting couples are asked to engage in discussions of various issues of personal concern. These conversations are videotaped and the participants subsequently make numerous judgments and interpretations of their own and their partner's behavior. It is our ultimate goal to use discourse analytic strategies to identify the regularities that may exist in the nature of the conversation that evoke different patterns of perceptions and responses. (For preliminary findings and an elaboration of the methodology, see Gaelick, Bodenhausen, & Wyer, 1985.) This approach clearly involves the investigation of a real-world-type situation using a methodology quite different from much social cognition research, and hopefully the findings it generates will complement those coming from more traditional experimental techniques.

Real-World Memory. Another important approach to social cognition that involves a more naturalistic strategy is work concerned with memory for real-world persons and events that occur outside the laboratory. Examples of this include the extensive work of Bahrick (1984; Bahrick, Bahrick, & Wittlinger, 1975). Bahrick et al., for example, used a cross-sectional design to study people's memory for the names and faces of acquaintances over a fifty-year span. Memory for real-world events has been studied by Keenan and her colleagues (Keenan & Baillet, 1980; Keenan et al. 1977), by Linton (1975, 1982), and by Loftus (e.g., Loftus & Marburger, 1983). Memory for personally and socially significant events represents an area that is ripe for future exploration and is an important complement to experimental investigations of cognition.

Survey Research. Before concluding this chapter, we want to point out the possible role of survey research in bridging the gap between laboratory findings and what we have called real-world cognition. That is, not only may information-processing principles help to elucidate the determinants of response in interviews and questionnaires, but surveys and interviews may, as Loftus, Fienberg, and Tanur (1985) recently put it, "provide new sources of data for learning about human cognition" (p. 176). Loftus et al. document this

possibility in some detail. Interestingly, they conclude their ar-
ticle by noting that survey research may be an important mechanism
for addressing the complaints of Neisser (1982).

By now we hope it is clear that, although we dispute the strong
form of Neisser's claims about the irrelevance of much laboratory
work to an understanding of social cognition in the real world, we
agree that social cognition researchers must take his advocacy of
naturalistic research settings and strategies quite seriously. We
have argued that the postulates we described in this chapter have
implications outside the laboratory, but more work is needed to begin
to document their role in nonlaboratory situations.

### ACKNOWLEDGMENT

Preparation of this chapter was supported by grants from the National
Science Foundation (BNS83-02105) and the National Institute of Mental
Health (RO1 MH38585). We wish to express our appreciation to Meryl
Lichtenstein and Norbert Schwarz for their helpful commentary on a
draft of the chapter.

# REFERENCES

Anderson, J.R. (1978). Arguments concerning represenations for mental imagery. Psychological Review, 85, 249-277.

Arkin, R.M., Gleason, J.M., & Johnston, S. (1976). Effect of perceived choice, expected outcome, and observed outcome of an action on the causal attributions of actors. Journal of Experimental Social Psychology, 12, 151-158.

Bahrick, H.P. (1984). Memory and people. In J. Harris (Ed.), Everyday memory, actions, and absentmindedness. New York: Academic Press.

Bahrick, H.P., Bahrick, P.O., & Wittlinger, R.P. (1975). Fifty years of memories for names and faces: A cross-sectional approach. Journal of Experimental Psychology: General, 104, 54-75.

Bargh, J.A., & Pietromonaco, P. (1982). Automatic information processing and social perception: The influence of trait information presented outside of conscious awareness on impression formation. Journal of Personality and Social Psychology, 43, 437-449.

Bellezza, F.S., & Bower, G.H. (1981). Person stereotypes and memory for people. Journal of Personality and Social Psychology, 41, 856-865.

Berkowitz, L., & Donnerstein, E. (1982). External validity is more than skin deep: Some answers to criticism of laboratory experiments. American Psychologist, 37, 245-257.

Bishop, G.F., Tuchfarber, A.J., & Oldendick, R.W. (in press). Opinions on fictional issues: The pressure to answer survey questions. Public Opinion Quarterly.

Bodenhausen, G.V., & Wyer, R.S. (1985). Effects of stereotypes on decision making and information-processing strategies. Journal of Personality and Social Psychology, 48, 267-282.

Bruner, J.S. (1951). Personality dynamics and the process of perceiving. In R.R. Blake & G.B. Ramsey (Eds.), Perception: An approach to personality. New York: Ronald Press.

Carlston, D.E. (1980). The recall and use of traits and events in social inference processes. Journal of Experimental Social Psychology, 16, 303-328.

Carretta, T.R., & Moreland, R.L. (1982). Nixon and Watergate: A field demonstration of belief perseverance. Personality and Social Psychology Bulletin, 8, 446-453.

Chaiken, S. (1980). Heuristic versus systematic information processing and the use of source versus message cues in persuasion. Journal of Personality and Social Psychology, 39, 752-766.

Cohen, C.E., & Ebbesen, E.B. (1979). Observational goals and schema actionation: A theoretical framework for behavior perception. Journal of Experimental Social Psychology, 15, 309-329.

Collins, A.M., & Quillian, M.R. (1969). Retrieval time from semantic memory. Journal of Verbal Learning and Verbal Behavior, 8, 323-343.

Craik, F.I.M., & Lockhart, R.S. (1972). Levels of processing: A framework for memory research. Journal of Verbal Learning and Verbal Behavior, 11, 671-684.

Crocker, J., Hannah, D.B., & Weber, R. (1983). Person memory and causal attributions. Journal of Personality and Social Psychology, 44, 55-66.

D'Andrade, R.G. (1981). The cultural part of cognition. Cognitive Science, 5, 179-195.

Fiske, S.T., Taylor, S.E., Etcoff, N.L., & Laufer, J.K. (1979). Imaging, empathy, and causal attribution. Journal of Experimental Social Psychology, 15, 356-377.

Forgas, J.P. (1983). What is social about social cognition? British Journal of Social Psychology, 22, 129-144.

Freyd, J.J. (1983). Shareability: The social psychology of epistemology. Cognitive Science, 7, 191-210.

Gabrenya, W.K., & Arkin, R.M. (1979). Motivation, heuristics, and the psychology of prediction. Motivation and Emotion, 3, 1-17.

Gaelick, L., Bodenhausen, G.V., & Wyer, R.S. (1985). Emotional communication in close relationships. Journal of Personality and Social Psychology, 49.

Gillund, G., & Shiffrin, R.M. (1984). A retrieval model for both recognition and recall. Psychological Review, 91, 1-67.

Graesser, A.C., Gordon, S.E., & Sawyer, J.D. (1979). Recognition memory for typical and atypical actions in scripted activities: Tests of a script pointer + tag hypothesis. Journal of Verbal Learning and Verbal Behavior, 18, 319-332.

Graesser, A.C., & Nakamura, G.V. (1982). The impact of a schema on comprehension and memory. In G.H. Bower (Ed.), The psychology of learning and motivation, Vol. 16. New York: Academic Press.

Graumann, C.F., & Sommer, M. (1984). Schema and inference: Models in cognitive social psychology. In J.R. Royce & L.P. Mos (Eds.), Annals of theoretical psychology. Vol. 1. New York: Plenum Press.

Harkness, A.R., Deßono, K.G., & Borgida, E. (1985). Personal involvement and strategies for making contingency judgments. Journal of Personality and Social Psychology, 49, 22-32.

Harr , R. (1980), Social Being. Totowa, NJ: Littlefield, Adams & Co.

Hastie, R. (1980). Memory for behavioral information that confirms or contradicts a personality impression. In R. Hastie, T. Ostrom, E. Ebbesen, R. Wyer, D. Hamilton, & D. Carlston (Eds.), Person memory: The cognitive basis of social perception. Hillsdale, NJ: Erlbaum.

Hastie, R. (1984). Causes and effects of causal attribution. Journal of Personality and Social Psychology, 46, 44-56.

Henschel, R.L. (1980). The purposes of laboratory experimentation and the virtues of deliberate artificiality. Journal of Experimental Social Psychology, 16, 466-478.

Higgins, E.T., Bargh, J.A., & Lombardi, W. (1985). Nature of priming effects on categorization. Journal of Experimental Psychology: Learning, Memory, and Cognition, 11, 59-69.

Higgins, E.T., & King, G.A. (1981). Accessibility of social constructs: Information-processing consequences of individual and contextual variability. In N. Cantor & J.F. Kihlstrom (Eds.), Personality, cognition, and social interaction. Hillsdale, NJ: Erlbaum.

Isen, A.M. (1984). Toward understanding the role of affect in cognition. In R.S. Wyer & T.K. Srull (Eds.), Handbook of social cognition, Vol. 3. Hillsdale, NJ: Erlbaum.

Jelalian, E., & Miller, A.G. (1984). The perseverance of beliefs: Conceptual perspectives and research developments. Journal of Social and Clinical Psychology, 2, 25-56.

Jennings, D.L., Amabile, T.M., & Ross, L. (1982). Informal covariation assessment: Data-based versus theory-based judgments. In D. Kahneman, P, Slovic, & A. Tversky (Eds.), Judgment under uncertainty: Heuristics and biases. New York: Cambridge University Press.

Johnson-Laird, P.N., Hermann, D.J., & Chaffin, R. (1984). Only connections: A critique of semantic networks. Psychological Bulletin, 96, 292-315.

Keenan, J.M., & Baillet, S.D. (1980). Memory for personally and socially significant events. In R.S. Nickerson (Ed.), Attention and Performance VIII. Hillsdale, NJ: Erlbaum.

Keenan, J.M., MacWhinney, B., & Mayhew, D. (1977). Pragmatics in memory: study of natural conversation. Journal of Verbal Learning and Verbal Behavior, 16, 549-560.

Klinger, E. (1975). Consequences of commitment to and disengagement from incentives. Psychological Review, 82, 1-25.
Knowles, P., & Smith, D. (1981). The ecological perspective applied to social perception. Journal for the Theory of Social Behavior, 11, 189-206.
Kohonen, T., Oja, E., & Lehtiö, P. (1981). Storage and processing of information in distributed associative memory systems. In G.E. Hinton & J.A. Anderson (Eds.), Parallel models of associative memory. Hillsdale, NJ: Erlbaum.
Kolers, P.A., & Roediger, H.L. (1984). Procedures of mind. Journal of Verbal Learning and Verbal Behavior, 23, 425-449.
Kruglanski, A.W. (1976). On the paradigmatic objections to experimental psychology. American Psychologist, 31, 655-663.
Laßerge, D. (1981). Unitization and automaticitiy in perception. Nebraska Symposium on Motivation, 28, 53-71.
Lichtenstein, E.H., & Brewer, W.F. (1980). Memory for goal-directed events. Cognitive Psychology, 12, 412-445.
Linton, M. (1975). Memory for real-world events. In D.A. Norman & D.E. Rumelhart (Eds.), Explorations in cognition. San Francisco, CA: W.H. Freeman.
Linton, M. (1982). Transformations of memory in everyday life. In U. Neisser (Ed.), Memory observed: Remembering in natural contexts. San Francisco, CA: W.H. Freeman.
Loftus, E.F., Fienberg, S.E., & Tanur, J.M. (1985). Cognitive psychology meets the national survey. American Psychologist, 40, 175-180.
Loftus, E.F., & Marburger, W. (1983). Since the eruption of Mt. Saint Helens, has anyone beaten you up? Improving the accuracy of retrospective reports with landmark events. Memory and Cognition, 11, 114-120.
Martin, L.L. (1985). Categorization and differentiation. New York: Springer Verlag.
McArthur, L.Z. (1981). What grabs you? The role of attention in impression formation and causal attribution. In E.T. Higgins, C.P. Herman, & M.P. Zanna (Eds.), Social cognition: The Ontario symposium, Vol. 1. Hillsdale, NJ: Erlbaum.
McClelland, J., & Rumelhart, D.E. (1985). Distributed memory and the representation of general and specific information. Journal of Experimental Psychology: General, 114, 159-188.
McGrath, J.E. (1982). Dilemmatics: The study of research choices and dilemmas. In J.E. McGrath, J. Martin, & R.A. Kulka (Eds)., Judgment calls in research. Beverly Hills, CA: Sage.
Miller, A.G. (Eds.) (1972). The social psychology of psychological research. New York: Free Press.
Nakamura, G.V., Graesser, A.C., Zimmerman, J.A., & Riha, J. (1985). Script processing in a natural situation. Memory and Cognition, 13, 140-144.
Neisser, U. (1976). Cognition and reality. San Francisco, CA: W.H. Freeman.
Neisser, U. (1980). On "Social Knowing". Personality and Social Psychology Bulletin, 6, 601-605.
Neisser, U. (1982). Memory: What are the important questions? In U. Neisser (Ed.), Memory observed: Remembering in natural contexts. San Francisco, CA: W.H. Freeman.
Newtson, D. (1976). Foundation of attribution: The perception of ongoing behavior. In J. Harvey, W. Ickes, & R. Kidd (Eds.), New directions in attribution research, Vol. 1. Hillsdale, NJ: Erlbaum.
Nisbett, R.E., & Ross, L. (1980). Human inference: Strategies and shortcomings of social judgment. Englewood Cliffs, NJ: Prentice-Hall.

40

Norman, D.A., & Bobrow, D.G. (1979). Descriptions: An intermediate stage in memory retrieval. Cognitive Psychology, 11, 107-123.

Ostrom, T.M (1984). The sovereignty of social cognition. In R.S. Wyer & T.K. Srull (Eds.), Handbook of social cognition, Vol.1. Hillsdale, NJ: Erlbaum.

Raaijmakers, J.G.W., & Shiffrin, R.M. (1981). Search of associative memory. Psychological Review, 88, 93-134.

Ross, L., Lepper, M., & Hubbard, M. (1975). Perseverance in self-perception and social perception: Biased attributional processes in the debriefing paradigm. Journal of Personality and Social Psychology, 32, 880-892.

Rothbart, M. (1981). Memory and social beliefs. In D.L. Hamilton (Ed.), Cognitive processes in stereotyping and intergroup behavior. Hillsdale, NJ: Erlbaum.

Schwarz, N., & Clore, G.L. (1983). Mood, misattribution, and judgments of well-being: Informative and directive functions of affective states. Journal of Personality and Social Psychology, 45, 513-523.

Schwarz, N., Strack, F., Kommer, D., & Wagner, D. (1984). Soccer, rooms and the quality of your life: Further evidence for informative functions of affective states. Paper presented at the meeting of the European Association of Experimental Social Psychology, Tilburg, Netherlands.

Sherman, S.J., Ahlm, K., Berman, L., & Lynn, S. (1978). Contrast effects and their relationship to subsequent behavior. Journal of Experimental Social Psychology, 14, 340-350.

Sherman, S.J., & Corty, E. (1984). Cognitive heuristics. In R.S. Wyer & T. K. Srull (Eds.), Handbook of social cognition, Vol.1. Hillsdale, NJ: Erlbaum.

Shweder, R.A. (1982). Fact and artifact in trait perception: The systematic distortion hypothesis. In B.A. Maher & & W.B. Maher (Eds.), Progress in experimental personality research, Vol. 11. New York: Academic Press.

Smith, E.E., Shoben, E.J., & Rips, L.J. (1974). Structure and process in semantic memory: A featural model for semantic decisions. Psychological Review, 81, 214-241.

Smith, E.R. (1984). Model of social inference processes. Psychological Review, 91, 392-413.

Snyder, M., & Cantor, N. (1979). Testing hypotheses about other people: The use of historical knowledge. Journal of Experimental Social Psychology, 15, 330-342.

Snyder, M., & Swann, W.B., Jr. (1978). Hypothesis testing processes in social interaction. Journal of Personality and Social Psychology, 36, 1202-1212.

Snyder, M., & Uranowitz, S.W. (1978). Reconstructing the past: Some cognitive consequences of person perception. Journal of Personality and Social Psychology, 36, 941-950.

Srull, T.K. (1981). Person memory: Some tests of associative storage and retrieval models. Journal of Experimental Psychology: Human Learning and Memory, 7, 440-463.

Srull, T.K. (1983a). The role of prior knowledge in the acquisition, retention, and use of new information. In R.P. Bagozzi & A.M. Tybout (Eds.), Advances in consumer research, Vol. 10. Ann Arbor, MI: Association for Consumer Research.

Srull, T.K. (1983b). Organizational and retrieval processes in person memory: An examination of processing objectives, presentation format, and the possible role of self-generated retrieval cues. Journal of Personality and Social Psychology, 44, 1157-1170.

Srull, T.K., Lichtenstein, M., & Rothbart, M. (1985). Associate storage and retrieval processes in person memory. Journal of Experimental Psychology: Learning, Memory, & Cognition, 11, 316-345.

Srull, T.K., & Wyer, R.S. (1983). The role of control processes and structural constraints in models of memory and social judgment. Journal of Experimental Social Psychology, 19, 497-521.

Srull, T.K., & Wyer, R.S. (in press). The role of chronic and temporary goals in social information processing. In R.M. Sorrentino & E.T. Higgins (Eds.), Handbook of motivation and cognition: Foundations of social behavior. New York: Guilford Press.

Strack, F., Erber, R., & Wicklund, R.A. (1982). Effects of salience and time pressure on ratings of social causality. Journal of Experimental Social Psychology, 18, 581-594.

Taylor, S.E., & Fiske, S.T. (1975). Point of view and perceptions of causality. Journal of Personality and Social Psychology, 32, 439-445.

Taylor, S.E., & Fiske, S.T. (1978). Salience, attention, and attribution: Top of the head phenomena. In L. Berkowitz (Ed.), Advances in experimental psychology, Vol. 11. New York: Academic Press.

Turner, J.C. (1981). Some considerations in generalizing experimental social psychology. In G.M. Stephenson & J.H. Davis (Eds.), Progress in applied social psychology, Vol. 1. New York: Wiley.

Tversky, A. (1977). Features of similarity. Psychological Review, 84, 327-352.

Tversky, A., & Kahneman, D. (1973). Availability: A heuristic for judging frequency and probability. Cognitive Psychology, 5, 207-232.

Winter, L., & Uleman, J.S. (1984). When are social judgments made? Evidence for the spontaneousness of trait inferences. Journal of Personality and Social Psychology, 47, 237-252.

Wright, J.C., & Murphy, G.L. (1984). The utility of theories in intuitive statistics: The robustness of theory-based judgments. Journal of Experimental Psychology: General, 113, 301-322.

Wyer, R.S. (1980). The acquisition and use of social knowledge: Basic postulates and representative research. Personality and Social Psychology Bulletin, 6, 558-573.

Wyer, R.S., Bodenhausen, G.V., & Srull, T.K. (1984). The cognitive representation of persons and groups and its effects on recall and recognition memory. Journal of Experimental Social Psychology, 20, 445-469.

Wyer, R.S., & Gordon, S.E. (1982). The recall of information about persons and groups. Journal of Experimental Social Psychology, 18, 128-164.

Wyer, R.S., & Srull, T.K. (1981). Category accessibility: Some theoretical and empirical issues concerning the processing of social stimulus information. In E.T. Higgins, C.P. Herman, & M.P. Zanna (Eds.), Social cognition: The Ontario symposium, Vol. 1., Hillsdale, NJ: Erlbaum.

Wyer, R.S., & Srull, T.K. (1985a). Cognitive bases of personality impression. Unpublished manuscript, University of Illinois, Urbana.

Wyer, R.S., & Srull, T.K. (1985b). Human cognition in its social context. Unpublished manuscript, University of Illinois, Urbana.

Zajonc, R.B. (1980). Feeling and thinking: Preferences need no inferences. American Psychologist, 35, 151-175.

# 3 INFORMATION PROCESSING THEORY FOR THE SURVEY RESEARCHER

Reid Hastie
Northwestern University,
Evanston

Psychology in the second half of the twentieth century is dominated by the cognitive point of view. Based on foundational work by Chomsky (1957) on syntactic structures in language, by Newell and Simon (1972) on computer simulation of thinking, and by a host of researchers interested in memory and perception (Miller, Galanter, & Pribram, 1960; Neisser, 1967), a new mentalism has emerged that serves as the central theoretical orientation in all subfields of psychology. Neighboring social sciences have started to use some of these theoretical concepts in their analyses of individual behavior.

Within the cognitive approach one set of concepts seems to be coalescing into a coherent core of principles, called "Information Processing Theory." The body of this paper is a summary of the essentials of Information Processing Theory stated as a list of general principles. This list is designed to be useful to survey researchers. There are several excellent texts (e.g., J.R. Anderson, 1980; Lachman, Lachman, & Butterfield, 1979) and survey articles (e.g., Bower, 1978; Estes, 1978; Simon, 1979) that provide alternative treatments of the same material.)

## KEY CONCEPTS IN INFORMATION PROCESSING

### Information

1. The fundamental material in an information processing analysis is information. Sometimes information is measured or represented in terms of quantitative metrics (Garner, 1962; N.H. Anderson, 1981). However, the most common practice is to represent information qualitatively as lists of features, natural language sentences and phrases, or geometric diagrams. Since the most common experimental stimuli are words, sentences, and pictures these formats for representation, closely matching the structures of the stimulus materials,

are convenient and have proven successful as theoretical symbols. The types of representation that will be most useful for survey researchers concerned with respondents' thoughts about their personal lives, medical practices, consumer goods, the political world, and other everyday events should be closest to the theoretical solutions developed by cognitive psychologists interested in text comprehension (Rumelhart & Norman, 1985).

Typical practice would be to represent a concept as a location in a graph that is described by a word or phrase and associated with a list of attributes. In the case of noun categories, these features are usually properties of the entity referenced by the concept that are to verify whether or not an object is an instance of the concept (Figure 1). Relations between idea nodes are symbolized theoretically as links in the network or pointers that connect the nodes. These links are given with labels selected from a short list of quasi-formal relationships that are allowed in the specific representational system. The attribute lists associated with the nodes correspond loosely to the concept's reference and the links in the network correspond loosely to the concept's sense.

Figure 1: Attribute list representations of concepts (based on Smith & Medin, 1981).

| PIGEON | CANARY | CHICKEN | COLLIE | DAISY |
|---|---|---|---|---|
| $A_1$: animate | $A_1$: animate | $A_1$: animate | $A_1$: animate | $A_1$: inanimate |
| $A_2$: feathered | $A_2$: feathered | $A_2$: feathered | $A_2$: furry | $A_2$: stem |
| $A_3$: flies | $A_3$: flies | $A_3$: pecks | $A_3$: tan | $A_3$: white |
| $A_4$: lives-in-cities | $A_4$: yellow | $A_4$: squawks | $A_4$: barks | |
| | | $A_5$: lays eggs | | |
| | | $A_6$: cannot fly | | |
| | | $A_7$: edible | | |

The emphasis on semantic attribute representations for stimuli is characteristic of Information Processing Theory and it highlights one of its major limits. How are <u>nonsemantic</u>, nonpropositional types of information (e.g., emotions, sensory experiences such as rare tastes or melodies, <u>dense</u> impressions such as images of works of art, etc.) represented mentally? Of the problematic information types, survey researchers will be most interested in theoretical analyses of the relationship between cognition and affect (Clark & Fiske, 1982). The clearest proposal of a representational format for affect is as a set of semantic tags (corresponding to alternate emotional states) that are linked to concept nodes as features or as alternate concept nodes in the same network (Bower & Cohen, 1982). Thus, affect information is treated like any other semantic information in the network. However, there is considerable controversy on this issue and some theorists (e.g., Zajonc, 1980) argue that the semantic representation solution is inadequate.

The influence of emotional reactions to a candidate or issue on voting behavior has been of interest to survey researchers for a long time (Campbell, Converse, Miller, & Stokes, 1960; Lippman, 1922). Recent research by cognitive psychologists has reaffirmed the significance of emotional factors in political choice (Abelson, Kinder, Peters, & Fiske, 1982) although specific models of the representation and processing of emotion-provoking political stimuli have not been applied to politically significant stimuli. Leventhal (1982) has contributed an original and integrative treatment of the roles of emotion and cognition in thinking about medical experiences. Johnson and Tversky (1983) have demonstrated effects of affect on judgments of personal risk. Other researchers are attempting to analyze the role of emotion in knowledge about consumer products and consumer choice (Tybout, Calder, & Sternthal, 1981).

## Memory Structures

2. Information is stored in memory in one of several alternate structures. One of the major contributions of the information processing reliance on the analogy between human and machine information processing has been an increased sophistication about structures for information (Winograd, 1975). These structures usually apply to the relationship between conceptual nodes (see above) and a small set of structures appear again and again in the cognitive psychology literature. The most common structure is a list of concepts, with each concept linked to one or two adjacent nodes. The list structure is popular because many of the stimulus materials in memory research

45

Figure 2: A simple semantic network chosen to illustrate inheritance
relations among concepts (based on Rumelhart & Norman,
1985).

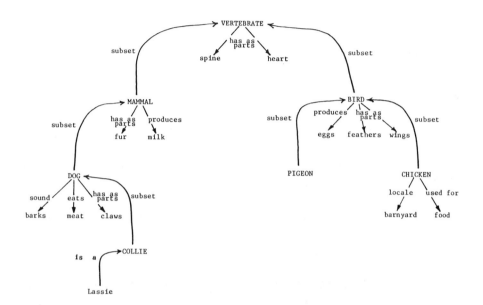

Figure 3: Examples of structural representations for narrative text
(based on Kintsch, 1978; and Trabasco, Secco, & Van Den
Broek, 1984).

(a)

Text          Text Base

This Landolfo, then,     1(PURCHASE,agent:L,object:SHIP)
having made the sort    2(LARGE,SHIP)
of preliminary calcu-    3(VERY,2)
lations merchants        4(AFTER,1,5)
normally make, pur-     5(CALCULATE,agent:L)
chased a very large     6(PRELIMINARY,5)
ship...                 7(LIKE,5,8)
                    8(CALCULATE,agent:MERCHANT)
                    9(NORMAL,8) ...

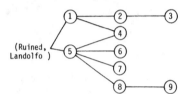

(Ruined,
Landolfo )

(b)

① Judy is going to have a birthday party.

2   She is ten years old.

③ She wants a hammer and saw for presents.

4   Then she could make a coat rack...

5   and fix her doll house.

⑥ She asked her father...

7   to get them for her.

⑧ Her father did not want to get them for her.

9   He did not think that girls should play with
     a hammer and saw.

⑩ But he wanted to get her something.

⑪ So he bought her a beautiful new dress.

12   Judy liked the dress...

⑬ but she still wanted the hammer and saw.

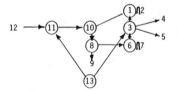

have been presented as lists (e.g., word lists, digit strings, etc.). We also noted that the features for concept nodes are typically represented as lists.

The hierarchy, a directed graph, in which some nodes are super-ordinate to other (subordinate) nodes with the hierarchical ordering extending over several tiers is also popular. These structures are common in theoretical descriptions of long-term conceptual memories (Smith & Medin, 1981; Smith, 1979) because of the manner in which many natural language nomenclature systems are structured. Linguistic concepts frequently have an "embedded" character where one concept can be used to reference many levels of abstraction. As I noted above, these interconcept networks correspond to the sense of the concepts and the links are usually labeled by a small set of relationships that are fundamental to the meanings of the concepts (see detail of Figure 2). Additionally, many other linguistic en-tities such as sentences, paragraphs, and narrative texts can be described in terms of hierarchical phrase structure diagrams or text outline hierarchies (J.R. Anderson & Bower, 1973; Kintsch, 1974) (Figure 3). In these cases comprehension is hypothesized to involve the application of rules that "parse" texts or events into meaningful units that are stored separately but linked together, often in a hierarchical structure. The hierarchical structure is also useful to represent plans for actions which can be described at many levels of specification (Miller et al., 1960; J.R. Anderson, 1980).

A third type of structure, the undifferentiated network, is frequently used to represent the organization of material where time or semantic constraints do not impose the orderly relations implied by the list or hierarchy. For example, Hastie (Hastie & Kumar, 1979) and Srull (1981) have proposed such structures to characterize the organization of facts in memory that refer to a single casual acquaintance. A speculation that I would like to advance as a hypothesis about the knowledge underlying attitudes is that the undifferentiated network is the structure for this information in memory. For example, Figure 4 depicts a plausible structure for some of the ideas elicited from a respondent using the cue Abortion. I have used the unlabeled links and undifferentiated nodes of the network to summarize the associations observed in the respondent's verbal protocol. It appears that there are three "clusters" of ideas: (a) a "pro-choice" cluster of abstractions (e.g., freedom); (b) a "pro-life" cluster of abstractions (e.g., Catholic Church); and (c) a

Figure 4: An associative network representation of one respondent's ideas about the topic Abortion.

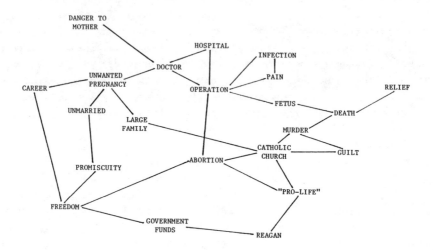

package of more concrete ideas relevant to the procedure of an abortion (e.g., antecedents, details, and consequences). In the example mental representation in Figure 4, a series of questions concerning attitudes towards the United States presidency (Reagan) or religion (Catholic Church) could serve to activate the "pro-Life" node, producing negative responses to subsequent questions concerning abortion. On the other hand, a context of questions concerning career goals, or teenage pregnancies might activate contrasting ideas and yield relatively positive responses on abortion. A further speculation would be that some response effects in surveys might be understood in terms of the activation of one portion of the network or another as determined by the context preceding or accompanying a question as it is put to an interview respondent. One context might elicit a positive response keyed by the "pro-choice" cluster of ideas, while another context would elicit a more negative response from the "pro-life" cluster or from the "procedure" sequence.

One popular type of structure is often referred to by the label "schema" in psychology. The term raises some problems in usage because its referents are not precisely limited and different writers seem to refer to different theoretical structures when they use the common label. For example, some theoreticians (e.g., Rumelhart, 1984) use the term schema to refer to almost any mental element, while others (e.g., Mandler, 1980) restrict the usage to one or two specific knowledge structures (e.g., that describe certain pictorial scenes and certain narrative stories). Recent reviews (Hastie, 1981; Taylor & Crocker, 1981) provide a sampling of the knowledge structures to which the label has been applied and emphasize the breadth and variety of referents. However, papers by Alba and Hasher (1983), Axelrod (1973), and Brewer and Nakamura (1984) give an impression that there is a precisely limited usage of the term "schema" and that there is a circumscribed theory associated with the concept. This impression is misleading and the Alba and Hasher paper, in particular, attributes a "prototypical schema theory of memory" to memory researchers that I do not believe applies to any current theorist.

Although there is no commonly accepted schema theory, there are a number of theoretical constructs associated with the label "schema" that are well-defined and in common usage by certain theorists. An enculturated member of any society will have a large stock of schemata stored in long-term memory. When a schema is activated by the occurrence of a relevant event (the schema's "entry conditions" are satisfied), the schema functions as a scaffold for the orderly encoding of incoming information. Relationships among disparate elements of the experienced event are provided by the schema. The perceiver is motivated to seek missing information that has not been experienced, but which is "anticipated" by the provision of "slots" in the schema. And, sometimes when information is missing, it is inferred as a "default" value to fill an empty slot in the schema.

Probably the best way to describe the notion of a schema is to give some examples from the theoretical literature in cognitive psychology. Figure 5 is a diagram of a schematic structure for the familiar "restaurant script" (Abelson, 1981; Schank & Abelson, 1977). This knowledge structure summarized the entry conditions, settings, roles, props, sequentially dependent stages, and exit conditions for the characters and events that occur in a visit to a typical restaurant in America. If the respondent learned about restaurants in another country, the restaurant script would doubtless differ slightly from this example. In Germany, for instance, certain customs such as asking other patrons to share a table would be part of the script, although they would not be familiar to a person who had experienced only American restaurants. Similar stereotyped action routine templates have been described for other social events (e.g., taking an airplane flight, visiting the dentist, etc.) and it is presumed that such knowledge structures are involved in the comprehension of many everyday activations.

A second example of an abstract knowledge structure is the "episode schema" that is found in many theories of text comprehension. Figure 6 provides a simple summary diagram of the elements of the highly abstract episode schema with the relations among them. A schema of this type is invoked in the comprehension of narrative discourse and it serves to summarize parts of the explicit text, to indicate the relations among them, and to direct the reader to "fill in the blanks" by inferring missing information that belongs in the schema structure. For example, we read the headline, "U.S. Jets Hit Libya," and immediately wonder about initiating events (What did Libya do to the U.S.?) and consequences (Now, what will Libya do to the U.S.?). If answers to these questions are not provided by the newspaper report or from another source, we are likely to infer an answer of our own to "fill the gap" (The U.S. is retaliating for recent terrorist activity by Libyan nationals, or, Reagan is reacting to recent put-downs by Russian leaders, and so forth).

Figure 5: Example script structure for comprehension of everyday events (based on J.R. Anderson, 1983 and Schank & Abelson, 1977).

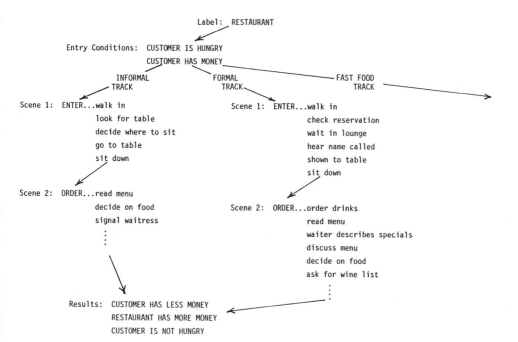

Label: RESTAURANT

Entry Conditions: CUSTOMER IS HUNGRY
CUSTOMER HAS MONEY

INFORMAL          FORMAL          FAST FOOD
TRACK             TRACK           TRACK

Scene 1: ENTER...walk in                    Scene 1: ENTER...walk in
         look for table                              check reservation
         decide where to sit                         wait in lounge
         go to table                                 hear name called
         sit down                                    shown to table
                                                     sit down

Scene 2: ORDER...read menu
         decide on food                     Scene 2: ORDER...order drinks
         signal waitress                             read menu
         ⋮                                           waiter describes specials
                                                     discuss menu
                                                     decide on food
                                                     ask for wine list
                                                     ⋮

Results: CUSTOMER HAS LESS MONEY
         RESTAURANT HAS MORE MONEY
         CUSTOMER IS NOT HUNGRY

Figure 6: Schema to represent the abstract structure of episodes (based on Pennington & Hastie, 1981).

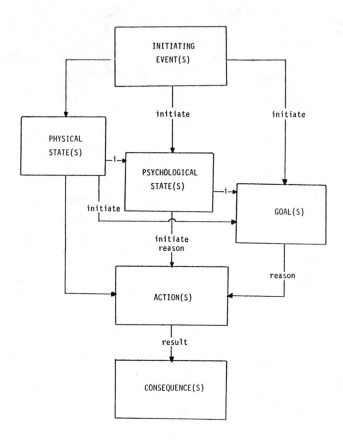

Spreading Activation

3. Information in memory is available according to simple "spreading activation" principles. The major role played by knowledge structures in the Information Processing Theory is to prescribe and constrain the patterns of activation of information in the mind. Although phenomenal experience provides an incomplete picture of information activation, the subjective impression that we are aware of only a few ideas at once is a fundamental assumption of all types of modern psychology. Information structures provide a metric that measures the number of ideas that are active, that is, available for use (i.e., to influence behavior), at any point in time. Furthermore, the structure predicts the direction and speed of changes in active mental content; experienced subjectively as movement from idea to idea.

The most common assumption of information processing theorists is that activation spreads from a currently active location in a knowledge structure to other nearby locations; that the spread is rapid; that the amount of activation of proximate locations is inversely related to the number of locations (number of efferent links); and that it diminishes sharply with increasing distance from the source of activation. We will emphasize the localization of ideas in geometric representational structures and the serial manner in which ideas become conscious in this paper. However, we would like to point out that there is considerable controversy and excitement over information processing models that relax one or both of these assumptions. Currently the "new look" in memory theories involves the use of distributed representations of information and parallel activation of excitatory and inhibitory connections (Hinton & J.A. Anderson, 1981; McClelland & Rumelhart, 1985). These models appear to be especially promising as descriptions of cognitive processes and structures that will map onto the physiological medium of the brain.

Additional factors affect the level of activation of ideas in memory. First, ideas that represent the immediate environment, being experienced through the sense organs, are activated (stimulus-driven activation). The "Encoding Specificity Principle" (Tulving, 1983) for retrieval of information from memory is an important closely-related conclusion: a stimulus event (cue) will effectively activate an idea in memory, if and only if information about the cue and its relation to the to-be-remembered idea was stored in memory at the same time as the original idea. Second, ideas that are closely linked to goals

that have priority in guiding current processing of the systems are
activated (goal-focussed activation). The implications of goal-
focussed activation depend on the system's rules for goal development
and ordering by priority. Goals will be determined by specific requirements of the task the subject performs, but some general rules
for the "executive" are emerging (see Sections 4 and 5 below).

## Transforming Symbolic Information

4. The basic processes of thinking involve the transformation of
symbolic information from one representation into another. An overview of the information processing system would show physical signals
in the environment converted to sensory feature information; sensory
information would be transformed into intermediate, semantic
information; later stages of processing would involve the elaboration
by inference and association of the semantic information (including
visual information); and then the transformation of semantic information into appropriate codes to generate responses. The analogy to
computer program functions and operators is strong and theoreticians
have attempted to reduce the complexity of information processing
theory models by agreeing on a limited set of elementary information
processes (Chase, 1978; Posner & McLeod, 1982). The elementary operations would include processes such as reading and writing into and
out of memories, recoding information from one format or structure
into a second format or structure, and comparing and testing two
pieces of information to determine the relationship between them
(e.g., to return a judgment of similarity of identity). Thus, the
economy of the information processing theory comes from increasing
consensus among theoreticians on an elementary set of formats for
information, structures for information, and elementary information
processes that transform one representation into another.
    Probably the most common organization of the elementary
processes is in terms of production systems. The analogy to computer
programming languages is dominant and the production system architecture used to describe many computer programs is a popular charac-
terization of the human organization of a system of elementary information processes. The basic unit of a production system is a  two-
part "condition-action" pair directly analogous to the S-R unit from
old learning theories. The condition part of the unit specifies a
state of the operating system (the presence of a certain pattern of
information) and the action part of the unit describes an operation

Figure 7: Elementary information processes (based on Newell & Simon, 1972).

1. <u>Discrimination</u>. It must be possible for the system to behave in alternative ways depending on what symbols are in its short-term memory.

2. <u>Tests and Comparisons</u>. It must be possible to determine that two symbol tokens do not belong to the same symbol type.

3. <u>Symbol Creation</u>. It must be possible to create new symbols and set them to designate specified symbol structures.

4. <u>Writing Symbol Structures</u>. It must be possible to create a new symbol structure, copy an existing symbol structure, and modify existing symbol structures, either by changing or deleting symbol tokens belonging to the structure or by appending new tokens with specified relations to the structure.

5. <u>Reading and Writing Externally</u>. It must be possible to designate stimuli received from the external environment by means of internal symbols or symbol structures, and to produce external responses as a function of internal symbol structures that designate these responses.

6. <u>Designating Symbol Structures</u>. It must be possible to designate various parts of any given symbol structure, and to obtain designations of other parts, as a function of given parts and relations.

7. <u>Storing Symbol Structures</u>. It must be possible to remember a symbol structure for later use, by storing it in the memory and retrieving it at any arbitrary time via a symbol structure that designates it.

or process to occur in the system. Actions are restricted to the basic operations provided by the set of elementary information processes (Figure 7). A set of these basic production units, when coupled together into a larger procedure, is called a production system. Production systems constitute a general, uniform descriptive language for many types of computer programs and, since information processing models are usually implemented in the programming medium, they provide a useful vocabulary to describe cognitive processes.

The Executive Monitor

5. At any point in time the information processing system is under the control of an executive monitor operating on a series of goals and plans are organized into a control structure hierarchy. It is the development of this executive that gives cognitive psychology the characteristics that most sharply distinguish it from traditional learning theory. A clear forerunner of current conceptions of the executive appeared in the Atkinson and Shiffrin (1968) distinction between structural features and control processes in a larger memory system. Newell and Simon (1972) introduced the notion of a hierarchy of goals along with an executive that executed plans according to goal priorities. These developments gave cognitive theories an active, planful character that was lacking in previous analyses of learning and problem-solving. Furthermore, with the aid of computer simulation methods, the theories of executive control were stated precisely in a respectable, scientific form, which was not susceptible to learning theorists' criticism of "mysterious homunculus" models.

The hierarchical organizational principle appears as a description of the relationships between superordinate goals, subordinate goals, and plans that are under consideration or under execution to achieve the superordinate goals (J.R. Anderson, 1983). For the most part simple goal-plan hierarchy structures have been the relationships between coordinate, independent, and competing goals, and single and multiple-function plans as characterizations of the logic of the executive (e.g., Schank & Abelson, 1977; Wilensky, 1983).

Figure 8: Example goal structures produced in the slution of a
planning problem (based on J.R. Anderson, 1983 and
Sacerdoti, 1977).

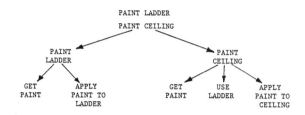

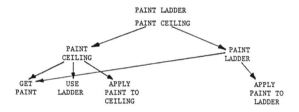

One application of these theoretical developments to survey
research phenomena is Carbonell's (1979) description of political
ideologies as goal-plan structures (see also Schank & Abelson, 1977).
Carbonell hypothesized that an ideological belief structure is organized as a goal-subgoal tree with higher-level goals such as
"Communist Containment" and lower-level goals such as "Strong U.S.
Military" and "Elect Reagan" ordered accordingly. The system was
implemented as a computer program that could enact the role of a
citizen with a conservative or a liberal ideology and evaluate
policies or events to assign desirabilities to them.

Independent Memories

    6. The larger information processing system is composed of a
series of component "locations" that are referred to as independent
memories. The typical system (see Figure 9) distinguishes between
sensory registers, short-term memory, long-term memory, and sometimes
a working memory. The memories are often hypothesized to be associated with separate physical structures of the brain. They are
characterized by distinctive formats for symbol representations and
capacity limits for representation and processing. Many of the important predictions of early information processing analyses came from
the assumption of a limited capacity short-term memory store. A
short-term memory limit on the amount of information that could be
represented or actively transformed at any point in time implied that
information processes would exhibit an orderly sequential character
(serial processing). Furthermore, many errors in subjects' performance on perception and memory tasks could be explained with
reference to the loss of information as it was passed from sensory
registers to the limited capacity  short-term memory.
    The long-term memory store is assumed to be extremely capacious
and to exhibit great representational flexibility in accepting a
variety of formats and structures for knowledge. Many  theoreticians
further subdivide the long-term store into two functionally distinct
components, one to represent temporally coded, episodic information
(e.g., information about a specific experience that occurred once in
the person's history) and a generic, semantic memory that is an
encyclopedia-like repository for general knowledge about the world,
including nonlinguistic information such as melodies and motor skill
routines (Tulving, 1972, 1983).
    The emphasis on the transformation of symbolic information
according to a production system hierarchy of elementary information
processes and the "geographic" organization of the mind into a series
of submemories, with the most active memories (i.e., short-term
memory) restricted in capacity, has given information processing
models the characteristic appearance of organizing complex cognitive
performances into a series of temporally ordered discrete stages.
This organization is most obvious in simple models for recognition
memory scanning (e.g., Sternberg, 1969) and certain perceptual tasks
(e.g., Broadbent, 1958). However, the same character can be discerned
in models for much more complicated accomplishments such as chess
playing, logical reasoning, and computer programming (Newell & Simon,

Figure 9: The principal components of the perception and memory
system (based on Wyer & Srull, 1985).

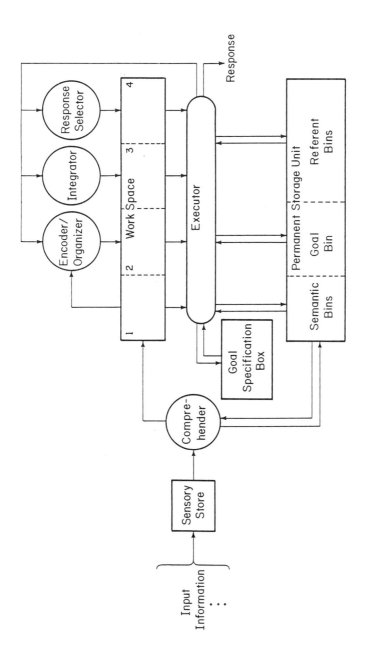

1972; J.R. Anderson, 1983). Tourangeau (1984) has proposed a conceptual breakdown of the survey respondent's task into four major stages: comprehend the question; activate relevant facts, beliefs, and emotions; generate a judgment; select or compose a response. He argues persuasively that the four-stage breakdown provides a useful framework for the analysis of many of the well-known survey response effects.

## Limited Resources

7. Principles of limited resources ("mental energy" and representational capacitiy) describe the performance of the information processing system. There is a general tendency for the information processing system to behave in an economical fashion to accomplish its goals by expending a minimum of time, processing resources, and strain on its memory system. For example, in choice and decision tasks, people will typically act to "satisfice" by terminating search when an acceptable, but possibly not optimal solution has been achieved. Similarly, in memory and judgment tasks, speed of performance and accuracy will be traded off so that when task demands restrict one aspect of the response (e.g., accuracy), the other aspect (execution time) will be used more liberally. Another example occurs in the typical model for long-term memory search where "self-terminating" search rules operate such that the system stops searching for information when any item that is sufficient to render an answer has been obtained.

## Processing Errors

There is a common misconception that the Information Processing Theory emphasis on computer simulation models implies that the human mind is as orderly, tireless, and error-free as a well-tested piece of computer software. This impression is completely false. Information processing theorists use the computer simulation medium to express their theories so that they (the theorists) can be precise and accurate about their theory's implications. However, the theory describes the behavior of humans and this behavior is frequently errorful, imprecise, and haphazard. The theory, if it is correct, must simulate these properties of human behavior, as well as other more orderly characteristics of human behavior. One of the major conditions that introduces the haphazard and errorful quality (to the extent it is present) to an information processing model's predictions of behavior comes from the implications of principles of limited resources. For example, a plan for behavior, generated by the model's executive, may be incomplete or may be executed in an inadequate manner, because of hypothesized limits on the model's (and the human's) memory capacity. Thus, a considerable portion of the human-like character of an information processing model will be produced by the limited resource principles.

## AN EXAMPLE: MEASURING POLITICAL BELIEFS AND KNOWLEDGE

It may clarify the relationship between information processing models and survey research phenomena if we outline the steps that would be necessary to apply a specific model to deduce testable predictions in a simple cognitive task. We will use a simple person memory task as an illustration because it is relevant to the belief and knowledge structures that underlie responses to questions concerning political behavior, namely voting. The task is important because the manner in which information about a political candidate is stored in memory and retrieved underlies important judgments and decisions, including evaluations of the candidate and his or her actions as well as the respondent's voting behavior.

For this example we will use the Information Processing Theory, ACT, that has been developed by John Anderson and his colleagues at Carnegie-Mellon University (1983). The ACT "system" is a language with which to write a specific model. The system provides three formats for declarative knowledge representation (temporal string, spatial images, and abstract propositions); a production system notation for the representation of processes; and system-wide rules limiting the capacitiy to activate declarative or procedural knowledge to "execute" procedures, and to alter declarative or procedural knowledge structures. Expositions of the ACT approach provide numerous examples of applications of the theoretical "language" in the form of specific models for task performance with an emphasis on learning, skill acquisition, and problem solving. Probably the easiest route to a new application is to find a close analogy between a task to which ACT has been applied (e.g., sentence memory) and a new task (e.g., candidate memory) that is important in survey research.

We will apply the ACT system to describe a respondent's long-term memory for information about Ronald Reagan. Declarative information ("facts") about Reagan can be represented in several formats in the ACT model. The likely representation will include propositional formatted information (most of the entries in Figure 10), image information (information depicted in little frames in Figure 10); goal information (in propositional format in Figure 10); and emotional responses (which would probably be represented as propositional information --see Bower & Cohen, 1982-- noted by broken-bordered surrounds in Figure 10). The structure of the information in Figure 10 is a sprawling network that J.R. Anderson would call a "tangled hierarchy" (1983, Chapter 2). Some instantiations of the ACT system do not specify labels on links in the network, and for simplicity we will use unlabeled links in this example. Another example of a survey response relevant knowledge structure was provided in Figure 4, where the ideas associated with the concept Abortion, for one respondent were diagrammed in an undifferentiated network.

Note, that in order for the model to be applied to a domain such as political candidate memory or opinions about abortion, an exact specification (perhaps still a hypothesis) of the memory structure must be provided in the vocabulary of the ACT representation system. This is no simple task and the ACT theory itself provides only very general guidelines for the structure of specific memory representations. The task of establishing the representation usually involves a back-and-forth bootstrapping process in which the theoretician starts with intuitions about the memory structure, evaluates those intuitions by making assumptions about processes, derives implications, and checks those implications against empirical data. Then the researcher typically has to modify the original assumptions about representation, evaluate again based on predictions assuming certain processes, and so forth until a working representation is in hand.

There has been considerable success in establishing memory representations for complex lexical (Smith, 1979), pictorial (Kosslyn, 1980), text (Kintsch, 1974), social (Hastie, Park, & Weber, 1984), and problem-solving (Chase & Simon, 1973) domains (see examples in J.R. Anderson, 1983). Nonetheless, establishing the memory representation is a big job and deductions concerning performance cannot be derived without the representation. Furthermore, the task of providing a representation to the information processing theorist falls most heavily on the shoulders of the collaborator who wishes to

Figure 10: Network structure for a fragment of one respondent's memories of Ronald Reagan.

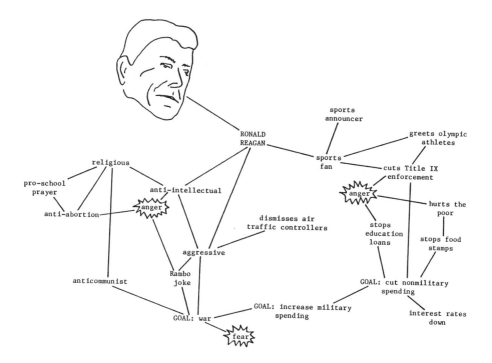

apply the model to a specific content domain. A laboratory
psychologist interested in the ACT model would not be able to provide
a hypothesized memory representation for political candidates or for
an attitude issue without help from an expert in the relevant content
domain. I predict that a subfield within cognitive psychology concerned with the description of knowledge structures for various
domains of experience will develop during the next decades. There are
already signs of such a development in the growth of "knowledge
engineering" methods in expert systems applications (e.g., Hayes-
Roth, Waterman, & Lenat, 1983) and in discussions of psycholexicog-
raphy by leading psycholinguists  (Miller & Johnson-Laird, 1976).
This subfield may eventually play a role in the cognitive sciences
that is analogous to the role of some classificatory specialities in
biology.

Anderson has spelled out explicit spreading activation rules
that yield predictions of probability of recall, order of recall,
speed of recall, and so on, once a memory representation has been
identified as a foundation on which to calculate predictions.
Anderson has developed explicit production system models that perform
the recall retrieval task. Thus, we would be able to derive exact
predictions concerning retrieval times and probabilities for a subject's behavior when asked to answer questions such as, "Recall what
you can about Ronald Reagan;" "Recall what you can about Reagan's
career before he became governor of California;" "Recall what you can
about Reagan's fiscal policies," or "Recall what you can about
Reagan's family." Similarly, the knowledge structure for the abortion
topic would be a basis for predictions of response times and probabilities for queries about abortion; for example, "Does Reagan favor
government funds for abortions?" "How do you feel about abortions?".
Earlier, I even suggested that the knowledge structure plus assumptions about memory activation could yield predictions of patterns of
context effects in survey responses.

## LIMITS TO INFORMATION PROCESSING THEORIES

There are several warnings to be derived from this quick sketch
of a specific application of ACT to candidate or issue memory. First,
the example foregrounds the large contribution that must  come from
the survey researcher. A theory of the mind based on laboratory
analyses of perception, memory, and reasoning processes demands many
domain-specific ingredients before a theoretical cake is ready for

the deductive oven. Even commitment to a specific model within the information processing approach does not purchase quick, cheap profits in the form of predictive power; the predictions will still be expensive. Second, we listed some of the many obstacles to successful applications; even with commitment and expensive ingredients the cake can fall. Third, the application is likely to require extensive developments before the theoretical questions of major interest to survey researchers are addressed. The political candidate memory model would require a large investment from the researcher; but an account of candidate memory is only a first step towards a major contribution to survey research such as a model of voting behavior. The abortion issue knowledge structure is only the first step towards predictions of responses or response effects in survey interviews.

A second limitation of Information Processing Theory is its impoverished treatment of motivational factors. Although many seminal formulations (Miller et al., 1960; Newell & Simon, 1972) dealt extensively with goals and plans, modern formulations have tended to downplay motivation (e.g., Nisbett & Ross, 1980). Typically, in the experimental laboratory research that provides the empirical grist for Information Processing Theory, motivation levels are assumed to be relatively constant and variations in factors that would affect motivation are excluded from the research. One of the most important consequences of efforts to extend the approach to phenomena such as those in survey research will be to force the theory to develop explicit principles to characterize the relationship between motivation, affect, and cognition. Signs of this development are already present in the psychological literature, many of them stimulated by social psychologists, clinical psychologists, and educational psychologists who have attempted to extend the theory (Clark & Fiske, 1982; Schank & Abelson, 1977; Zajonc, 1980). Hartmut Esser (personal communication) has suggested that economic utility theory can provide a firm foundation for an analysis of motivation in the survey interview. His conceptual analysis of the utility functions of the interviewer and respondent is a convincing demonstration of the power of the utility theory application. Perhaps an integration of the utility and information processing approaches offers hope for a practical theory of the interview (cf. Feldman & Yakimovsky, 1974; Feldman & Sproull, 1977).

Third, current Information Processing Theory does not include sophisticated measurement theories or scaling techniques. The major products of the field of survey research are methods used to assess opinions and to predict behavior. However, information processing theorists exhibit a very casual attitude towards measurement and scaling. Although it is probably healthy for the development of the field, the topic of measurement is rarely addressed and most Information Processing Theory research is sloppy when it comes to these matters. Granted, information processing psychology has developed and exploited in a clever fashion many dependent variables, some new and some old (e.g., reaction time measures, think-aloud measures, etc.). However, the scale properties of the most common Information Processing Theory dependent variables are unknown, even after decades of research (e.g., percent correct measures in memory tasks, confidence ratings in perception tasks, etc.).

This may be a major problem for the survey researcher who wishes to extend information processing theory to the phenomena he or she wants to study. For example, there is considerable discussion, uncertainty, and discomfort concerning the manner in which a mental schema should properly be measured. In fact, there are no uniform methods used by experimental psychologists to take "a snapshot" of a schema. There are numerous converging operations varying in precision and utility that, when taken together, make a convincing case for the existence of a schema and even for some of its structural properties. However, there are no generally accepted "index measurements" that are used to define, identify, and measure a schema. This means that a survey researcher who accepts the Information Processing Theory point of view has not purchased a set of well-developed and agreed upon measurement methods.

Although this section of our review has emphasized imperfection, incompleteness, and the cost of application of the information processing approach, we do not want to be unduly negative. Earlier sections emphasized the considerable merits of the approach, merits that seem even more important when comparisons are made to alternate theories of the mind.

This paper has attempted to explicate the basic concepts of Information Processing Theory so that a reader interested in applications to survey research phenomena will be able to use the theory. I believe that Information Processing Theory is the most successful and most promising theory of the mind available in the social sciences today. However, the presentation has made it clear that Information Processing Theory is not a universal solution for every theoretical or practical problem. The paper was written to make the reader self-conscious about the gains and losses associated with the use of

Information Processing Theory. Still, I hope the present chapter will encourage researchers to apply information processing concepts to survey phenomena.

## ACKNOWLEDGMENT

The author is grateful to Nancy Pennington, Norbert Schwarz, and Roger Tourangeau for helpful comments on this chapter.

# REFERENCES

Abelson, R.P. (1981). Psychological status of the script concept. American Psychologist, 36, 715-129.

Abelson, R.P., Kinder, D.R., Peters, M.D., & Fiske, S.T. (1982). Affective and semantic components in political person perception. Journal of Personlity and Social Psychology, 42, 619-630.

Alba, J.W., & Hasher, L. (1983). Is memory schematic? Psychological Bulletin, 93, 203-231.

Anderson, J.R. (1980). Cognitive psychology and its implications. San Francisco, CA: Freeman.

Anderson, J.R. (1983). The architecture of cognition. Cambridge, MA: Harvard University Press.

Anderson, J.R. & Bower, G.H. (1973). Human associative memory. Washington, DC: Winston.

Anderson, N.H. (1981). Foundations of Information Integration Theory. New York: Academic Press.

Atkinson, R.C., & Shiffrin, R.M. (1968). Human memory: A proposed system and its control structures. In K. Spence (Ed.), The psychology of learning and motivation. Vol. 2., New York: Academic Press.

Axelrod, R. (1973). Schema Theory: An information processing model of perception and cognition. American Political Science Review, 67, 1248-1266.

Bower, G.H. (1978). Cognitive psychology: An introduction. In W.K. Estes (Ed.), Handbook of learning and cognitive processes. Vol. 1, Hillsdale, NJ: Erlbaum.

Bower, G.H., & Cohen, P.R. (1982). Emotional influences in memory and thinking: Data and theory. In M.S. Clark & S.T. Fiske (Eds.), Affect and cognition. Hillsdale, NJ: Erlbaum.

Brewer, W.F., & Nakamura, G.V. (1984). The nature and functions of schemas. In R.S. Wyer, Jr. & T.K. Srull (Eds.), Handbook of social cognition. Vol. 1, Hillsdale, NJ: Erlbaum.

Broadbent, D.E. (1958). Perception and communication. London: Pergammon Press.

Campbell, A., Converse, P.E., Miller, W.E., & Stokes, D.E. (1960). The American Voter. New York: Wiley.

Carbonnel, J.G. (1979). Subjective understanding: Computer models of belief systems. (Research Report #150). New Haven, CT: Yale University, Department of Computer Science.

Chase, W.G. (1978). Elementary information processes. In W.K. Estes (Ed.), Handbook of learning and cognitive processes, Vol. 5, Hillsdale, NJ: Erlbaum.

Chase, W.G., & Simon, H.A. (1973). Perception in chess. Cognitive Psychology, 4, 55-81.

Chomsky, N. (1957) Syntactic structures. The Hague: Mouton and Co.

Clark, M.S. & Fiske, S.T. (Eds.) (1982). Affect and Cognition. Hillsdale, NJ: Erlbaum.

Estes, W.K. (1978). The information processing approach to cognition. In W.K. Estes (Ed.), Handbook of learning and cognitive processes, Vol. 5., Hillsdale, NJ: Erlbaum.

Feldman, J.A., & Yakimovsky, Y. (1974). Decision theory and artificial intelligence I: A semantics-based region analyzer. Artificial Intelligence, 4, 349-371.

Feldman, J.A., & Sproull, R.f. (1977). Decision theory and artificial intelligence II: The hungry monkey. Cognitive Science, 1, 158-192.

Garner, W.R. (1962). Uncertainty and structure as psychological concepts. New York: Wiley.

Hastie, R. (1981). Schematic principles in human memory. In E.T. Higgins, C.P. Herman, & M.P. Zanna (Eds.), Social cognition: The Ontario symposium, Vol. 1, Hillsdale, NJ: Erlbaum.

Hastie, R., & Kumar, P.A. (1979). Person memory: Personality traits as organizing principles in memory for behaviors. Journal of Personality and Social Psychology, 37, 25-38.

Hastie, R., Park, B, & Weber, R. (1984). Social memory. In R.S. Wyer, Jr. & T.K. Srull (Eds.), Handbook of social cognition, Vol. 2, Hillsdale, NJ: Erlbaum.

Hayes-Roth, F., Waterman, D.A., & Lenat, D.B. (Eds.) (1983). Building expert systems. Reading, MA: Addison-Wesley.

Hinton, G.E., & Anderson, J.A. (Eds.) (1981). Parallel models of associative memory. Hillsdale, NJ: Erlbaum.

Johnson, E.J., & Tversky, A. (1983). Affect, generalization, and the perception of risk. Journal of Personality and Social Psychology, 45, 20-31.

Kintsch, W. (1974). The representation of meaning in memory. Hillsdale, NJ: Erlbaum.

Kintsch, W. (1978). Comprehension and memory of text. In W.K. Estes (Ed.), Handbook of learning and cognitive processes, Vol. 6. Hillsdale, NJ: Erlbaum.

Kosslyn, S.M. (1980). Image and mind. Cambridge, MA: Harvard University Press.

Lachman, R., Lachman, J., & Butterfield, E.C. (1979). Cognitive psychology and information processing. Hillsdale, NJ: Erlbaum.

Leventhal, H. (1982). The integration of emotion and cognition: A view from the perceptual-motor theory of emotion. In M.S. Clark & S.T. Fiske (Eds.), Affect and cognition, Hillsdale, NJ: Erlbaum.

Lippman, W. (1922). Public Opinion. New York: Macmillan.

Mandler, J. (1980). Categorical and schematic organization in memory. In C.R. Puff (Ed.), Memory organization and structure. New York: Academic.

McClelland, J.L., & Rumelhart, D.E. (1985). Distributed memory and the representation of general and specific information. Journal of Experimental Psychology: General, 114, 159-188.

Miller, G.A., Galanter, E., & Pribram, K. (1960). Plans and the structure of behavior. New York: Holt, Rinehart, & Winston.

Miller, G.A., & Johnson-Laird, P.N. (1976). Language and perception. Cambridge, MA: Harvard University Press.

Neisser, U. (1967). Cognitive Psychology. New York: Appleton-Century-Crofts.

Newell, A. & Simon, H.A. (1972). Human problem solving. Englewood Cliffs, N.J.: Prentice-Hall.

Nisbett, R., & Ross, L. (1980). Human inference: Strategies and shortcomings of social judgments. Englewood Cliffs, NJ: Prentice Hall.

Pennington, N., & Hastie, R. (1981, August). Juror decision making: Story structure and verdict choice. Paper presented at the meeting of the American Psychological Association, Los Angeles, CA.

Posner, M.I., & McLeod, P. (1982). Information processing models -- In search of elementary operations. Annual Review of Psychology, 33, 477-514.

Rumelhart, D.E. (1984). Schemata and the cognitive systems. In R.S. Wyer, Jr. & T.K. Srull (Eds.), Handbook of social cognition, Vol. 1, Hillsdale, NJ: Erlbaum.

Rumelhart, D.E., & Norman, D.A. (1985). Representation in memory. In R.C. Atkinson, R.J. Herrnstein, G. Lindzey, & R.D. Luce (Eds.), Handbook of experimental psychology, New York: Wiley.

Sacerdoti, E.D. (1977). A structure for plans and behavior. New York: Elsevier North-Holland.

70

Schank, R.C., & Abelson, R.P. (1977). Scripts, plans, goals, and understanding. Hillsdale, NJ: Erlbaum.

Simon, H.A. (1979). Information processing models of cognition. Annual Review of Psychology, 30, 363-396.

Smith, E.E. (1979). Theories of semantic memory. In W.K. Estes (Ed.), Handbook of learning and cognitive processes, Vol. 6. Hillsdale, NJ: Erlbaum.

Smith, E.E., & Medin, D.L. (1981). Categories and concepts. Cambridge, MA: Harvard University Press.

Srull, T.K. (1981). Person memory: Some tests of associative storage and retrieval models. Journal of Experimental Psychology: Human Learning and Memory, 7, 440-463.

Sternberg, S. (1969). The discovery of processing stages: Extension of Donders' method. In W.G. Koster (Ed.), Attention and performance II. Amsterdam: North-Holland (reprinted from Acta Psychologica, 1969,30)

Taylor, S.E., & Crocker, J. (1981). Schematic bases of social information processing. In E.T. Higgins, C.P. Herman, & M.P. Zanna (Eds.), Social cognition: The Ontario symposium, Vol. 1, Hillsdale, NJ: Erlbaum.

Tourangeau, R. (1984). Cognitive sciences and survey methods. In T.B. Jabine, M.L. Straf, J.M. Tanur, & R. Tourangeau (Eds.), Cognitive aspects of survey methodology. Washington, DC: National Academy Press.

Trabasso, T., Secco, T., & Van Den Boek, P. (1984). Causal cohesion and story coherence. In H. Mandl, N.L. Stein, & T. Trabasso (Eds.), Learning and comprehension of text. Hillsdale, NJ: Erlbaum.

Tulving, E. (1972). Episodic and semantic memory. In E. Tulving & W. Donaldson (Eds.), Organization of memory. New York: Academic Press.

Tulving, E. (1983). Elements of episodic memory. New York: Oxford University Press.

Tybout, A.M., Calder, B.J., & Sternthal, B. (1981). Using information processing theory to design marketing strategies. Journal of Marketing Research, 18, 73-79.

Wilensky, R. (1983). Planning and understanding. Reading, MA: Addison-Wesley.

Winograd, T. (1975). Computer memories: A metaphor for memory organization. In C.N. Cofer (Ed.), The structure of human memory. San Francisco, CA: Freeman.

Wyer, R.S., Jr., & Srull, T.K. (1985). Human cognition in its social context. Unpublished manuscript, University of Illinois, Champaign, IL.

Zajonc, R.B. (1980). Feeling and thinking. References need no inferences. American Psychologist, 35, 151-175.

# 4 BIPOLAR SURVEY ITEMS: AN INFORMATION PROCESSING PERSPECTIVE

Thomas M. Ostrom
Ohio State University

Survey items range from the explicitly factual to the highly subjective. Factual questions ask respondents for information such as their name, address, age, marital status, salary, or occupation. For most people most of the time, the answer to these questions is well rehearsed and easily accessed from memory. The same cannot be said, however, for questions of a more subjective nature. People often do not have a ready answer to questions about product preferences, about their perceptions of political candidates, or about proposed civic improvements.

Subjective survey items probe a wide variety of affective, inferential, and judgmental concepts. Preferences and choices, likes/dislikes, beliefs/disbeliefs, levels of certainty or confidence, strength of agreement, judgments of similarity/dissimilarity, and perceptions of an object's attributes are all subjective responses that survey researchers attempt to uncover.

The present chapter focuses on one particular type of survey item, those designed to assess bipolar subjective responses. Typical examples are questions that ask whether the respondent feels positively or negatively toward a particular social issue (such as abortion), perceives a political candidate as being conservative or liberal, favors or opposes a given policy stand, or believes a particular breakfast cereal is healthy or unhealthy.

Bipolar questions are of particular interest to survey researchers for several reasons. Some theorists have argued that people naturally think in bipolar terms about their world. Measurement techniques such as Osgood's (Osgood, Suci, & Tannenbaum, 1957) semantic differential and Kelly's (1955) Repertory Grid derive from this assumption. Second, bipolar questions are clearly preferred in situa-

tions where overt actions (such as product purchases, voting decisions, and financial contributions) are guided by which side of the
midpoint a respondent endorses.

The primary aim of this chapter is to contrast two alternative
conceptual approaches toward understanding how people respond to
bipolar items. The main question is, "How do people go from their
head to their hand?" (Or "from mind to mouth" in the case of oral
responses.) That is, how do people draw upon their cognitive world
when they write down their answers in a survey? Historically, survey
researchers have employed a dimensional representation of the
response process. Limitations to this traditional approach are now
becoming evident with the advent of information processing models of
cognitive activity.

The chapter has two main sections. The first outlines the traditional, dimensional approach to modeling the response process, and
shows how it is applied to bipolar survey items and to different item
formats. The second section outlines several alternative response
models that are suggested by the information processing approach. It
provides an extension of earlier work that contrasted the dimensional
with the information processing approaches to understanding attitude
theory (Ostrom, 1981a) and attribution theory (Ostrom, 1981b), and to
understanding the role of inconsistency in impression formation
(Devine & Ostrom; 1985, in press).

## THE DIMENSIONAL APPROACH

Since the time of Wundt and Fechner, researchers have struggled
to understand how people answer questions that probe their subjective
reactions to significant objects, events, and concepts. The earliest
research addressed the psychophysical problem of how people make
judgments about sensory stimuli. For example, Weber and Fechner found
evidence supporting a logarithmic relation between stimulus magnitude
(e.g., weight or length) and subjective magnitude (e.g., ratings of
heaviness or length).

We see here the very beginnings of the dimensional approach. As
Guilford (1954) subsequently formalized, the psychophysical problem
was reduced to the analysis of three continua. The stimulus continuum
was used to represent the particular property of the stimulus being
judged. If objects were being judged for their length, the physical
length (say in centimeters) would be used to locate the object on the
stimulus continuum.

A second continuum was the <u>response continuum</u>. This is how the person's subjective (i.e., mental) response to the stimulus was conceptually represented. A stimulus item would evoke an implicit response, which took the form of a point on the response continuum. One category of theoretical effort in psychophysics is to explore the relation between the stimulus continuum and the response continuum. For example, Thurstone's (1927) law of comparative judgment offered one of the earliest models of this kind involving stochastic processes.

The third continuum was the <u>judgment continuum.</u> This continuum is used to represent the observable judgment made by the respondent to the stimulus. A second category of theory emerged in classical psychophysics that deals with the relations between the response and the judgment continua. Helson's (1964) Adaptation Level theory is in this category. Phrased another way, this category focuses on the problem of how people draw upon their mental representation of the stimulus when making overt responses to survey items. It is this category of theory that is of central concern to the present chapter.

This dimensional representation of subjective experience is very plausible in the context of understanding sensory experiences. The dimensional approach was developed to explain the obvious relation between objective and subjective stimulus magnitude. Physical stimulus properties do indeed vary on a continuum and our sensory receptors are capable of detecting small shifts of stimulus magnitude. So it is reasonable to assume that people (at least in some circumstances) may be capable of preserving the features of a continuum in their subjective representation of the stimulus features.

Judgments of Social Objects.

Although the continuum representation was developed for responses to physical stimuli, it was quickly adopted by researchers interested in responses to social objects. Questions such as "How conservative or liberal is the President?" were analyzed in the same way as questions such as "How bright is the light?" From the early work by Thurstone (1927, 1931; Thurstone & Chave, 1929) to more recent work in social psychophysics (Wegener, 1982), we can see explicit endorsement of this position.

It is accepted that the first continuum (the stimulus continuum) plays no role in the judgment of social objects. We have no way to physically measure the extent to which ice cream is likable or capital punishment is morally acceptable. Consequently, social applications of the dimensional approach focus attention on only the response continuum and the judgment continuum.

The dimensional approach carries with it some direct implications regarding how people subjectively respond to a survey item. Let us take the question mentioned above, "How conservative or liberal is the President?" as an example. The question identifies both the continuum (from Very Conservative to Very Liberal) and the stimulus object (the President). Presumably a subjective representation of both the continuum and the object are activated upon reading the question.

As in the case of sensory stimuli, a social object comes to be represented as a point on the response continuum. This point reflects where the respondent ultimately locates the object on the subjective continuum. The process of determining this point may occur through some form of information averaging (Anderson, 1981) or expectancy-value operation. However, this issue need not be resolved here; the explicit combinatorial process is of peripheral interest to the present arguments. It represents a separate issue for the dimensional approach, but one that is not germane to questions regarding the relation between the response continuum and the judgment continuum.

The dimensional approach views the process of going from the subjective to the overt (i.e., from the response continuum to the judgment continuum) as being a direct mapping. If several objects are rated on the same scale (as is typically the case in psychophysical research), the linear spacing of the objects on the judgment scale should correspond directly to their linear spacing on the subjective response continuum. Factors such as adaptation level (Helson, 1964) and end anchors (Ostrom & Upshaw, 1968; Parducci, 1965) can affect the origin and slope of this linear function. But except for some small perturbations (such as those due to a skewed distribution of stimuli; Parducci, 1965) most psychophysical research finds a linear relationship between the two continua. People attempt to accurately communicate all their subjective discriminations when making overt reports.

Bipolar Judgments.

In most cases, bipolar judgments are not regarded as fundamentally different from unipolar judgments. The dimensional approach would be applied in an identical fashion regardless of whether the question about the President were phrased "how conservative" (from high to low), "how liberal" (from high to low), or "how conservative or liberal" (from very conservative to very liberal). Support for this assumption derives from research showing that a very high negative correlation can exist between the ratings of social stimuli on scales phrased in these three different ways (e.g., Green & Goldfried, 1965).

Bipolar scales do have a midpoint (sometimes referred to as the zero point) that represents the transition from one polarity to the other. It is this feature that makes such items especially attractive for predicting behavior. Presumably the midpoint is used as a reference point for two purposes. One is in locating the stimulus on the response continuum. People may explicitly decide to place the object above or below that midpoint. The second purpose is in coordinating the response continuum with the judgment continuum. If a respondent subjectively places the President on the conservative side of the midpoint, the respondent will be sure to reflect that relative location when making an overt response.

Format of the Survey Item.

A final issue to consider before proceeding to the information processing perspective is the effect of item format on overt judgments. A variety of alternative formats could be given to a respondent who is asked to judge the President's level of conservatism. A continuous scale could be presented asking the respondent to place a check mark anywhere on a line (anchored with the labels "conservative/liberal"). A set of ordered categories ranging from highly conservative to highly liberal may be presented. The minimum number of categories would be two, forcing the respondent to choose between the two alternatives. Another possibility is to ask the respondent to rank order the President along with a number of other persons in terms of their conservative/liberal characteristics. And with any of these above possibilities, the respondent may or may not be allowed to give a "don't know" response.

The dimensional analysis strives for a direct mapping of the response continuum onto the judgment continuum for all possible formats. In the case of a continuous scale or a category scale with a very large number of categories, respondents can preserve their subjective discriminations in their overt judgments. It is possible for them to maintain a linear transformation when going between the two continua.

New problems arise when there are fewer categories than stimulus objects. As was argued by Thurstone in his method of Successive Intervals (Torgerson, 1958), respondents are viewed in this case as locating category boundaries from the judgment scale onto their response continuum and using them as a guide for making the overt response. In the two-category case, respondents presumably use the midpoint on the response continua as the sole guide for selecting a judgment scale category. In the case of pair comparisons and rank order, the respondent locates a pair of objects on the response continuum and places the higher above the lower when responding to the survey item.

## THE INFORMATION PROCESSING APPROACH

Several chapters in this volume (e.g., those by Hastie and by Bodenhausen & Wyer) have provided an overview of the information processing perspective and shown its relevance to survey research. Other chapters (e.g., those by Hippler & Schwarz, by Strack & Martin, by Bishop, and by Schwarz & Hippler) show how this perspective helps us better understand some of the methodological problems that arise in survey research. The present section of this chapter applies the information processing perspective to analyzing the problem of how respondents access their cognitive representation when responding to survey items, with special emphasis on bipolar items. It represents a radical departure from the solution offered by the dimensional approach.

Both the dimensional and information processing approaches recognize that people often draw upon a wide variety of beliefs when responding to survey items. But one of the key differences separating the two approaches is the conceptual analysis of those beliefs. As is argued by Ostrom (1981a, 1981b) and Devine and Ostrom (1985, in press), the dimensional approach is only concerned with locating each of those beliefs on the response continuum. Combinatorial theories like those of Fishbein and Ajzen (1975) and Anderson (1981) are primarily interested in determining the scale value and weight of each belief. Little interest is paid to the interrelation between the beliefs. In fact, theorists like Anderson (1981) explicitly argue that the scale value of each information item is independent of the other items in the system.

In contrast to this focus on the dimensional properties of beliefs, the information processing approach emphasizes the structural interrelation among the beliefs. A great deal of work has been done to identify what qualitatively different structures might be employed by people when cognitively organizing their beliefs about a stimulus object. For example, hierarchical structures, linear orders, schemas, and temporal scripts have all been explored. Knowing the nature of the structure should allow one to predict what beliefs will become salient (and therefore serve as the basis of item response) under what circumstances.

One implication of this analysis is that the "weight" assigned to any belief is a function of the structure in which it is imbedded and the manner in which that structure is activated. It is not an invariant property of the belief. In fact, the term "weight" is not even part of the information processing lexicon. The term implicitly suggests that the contribution of a particular belief to the overt response varies in a continuous manner. It implies that people may allow a belief to contribute slightly, moderately, or extensively to their responses. In contrast to this dimensional reasoning, most models of information processing view the contribution of a belief as being all-or-none. A cognition is either activated or it isn't, it either contributes or it doesn't.

From head to hand: Whereas the dimensional perspective has a well developed conception of how the person goes from the response continuum to the judgment continuum, the information processing perspective has not yet provided clear answers to this problem. This is particularly true for the question of how people answer survey items. However, there is an evolving area of research in cognitive science on the problem of question answering (e.g., Graesser & Clark, 1985; Lehnert, 1978). This chapter shares the perspective adopted by workers in this area.

The purpose of the present section is to outline a number of the relevent issues raised by the information processing approach toward understanding how people go from head to hand. It examines some of the information processing assumptions that underlie the empirical work reported in this volume by Hippler and Schwarz, by Strack and Martin, and by Schwarz and Hippler.

At the heart of the information processing approach to this problem is the need to identify what cognitive representations are activated by the survey question. The approach requires that we consider two kinds of representations. One corresponds to that evoked by the stimulus object (e.g., the President). The other is the set of representations evoked by the format of the response scale (e.g., the extent to which the President is viewed as conservative or liberal). This set will vary in number and quality depending on the exact nature of the response scale. The task of the respondent is to find the best match between the object representation and the alternative response representations.

As an example, consider the case where the respondents are presented in the questionnaire with only two response categories, conservative and liberal, for communicating their impression of the President. Each of the category labels will activate its own struc- ture, probably prototypes of the typical conservative President and the typical liberal President. The task of the respondent is to determine which of those two prototypes provides the best match to the structure they activated about the President.

Although this example is silent on the details of the activation process and the matching process, it does serve to illustrate the special importance placed on item format by the information process- ing perspective. Format is not viewed as being "merely" of methodological concern. It is not just a matter of finding the best way to linearly project the response continuum onto the judgment continuum. Instead, format is integral to determining what cognitive activity precedes the overt act of answering the survey question.

Two different item formats are considered in greater detail in the next two subsections. The two-category case is examined because it is one of the most common formats used in surveys. Also, it is simple enough to allow an examination of some of the complexities involved in the activation and matching processes. The case of a continuous rating scale is examined to show how responses on a con- tinuous scale can be generated by a cognitive system that operates on an "all-or-none" basis.

Two-category Format.

As described above, two response representations are activated with a two-category item format. A number of issues are relevant to understanding the details of the activation and matching process. The specifics of these processes have yet to be worked out in the context of survey items, so many of the ideas offered here should be regarded as speculative. The reader should consult sources like Lingle, Altom, and Medin (1984) and McCloskey and Glucksberg (1979) for analyses of the category assignment process. In a real sense, this chapter offers an agenda of conceptual issues that require formal solutions.

Staying with the "conservative vs. liberal" example, the first set of issues pertain to the nature of the representation that is activated upon presentation of the survey item. People can only activate prototypes that actually exist in their memory. If people have a good idea of what a conservative President is like, the prototype activated by the conservative category label will contain features of Presidents who are conservative. But if the respondent is unfamiliar with how conservatism manifests itself in presidential behavior, that person may need to generate the needed representation. The respondent might proceed by integrating knowledge from a general conservative trait-based schema with knowledge drawn from a general presidential behavior schema. The details of when and how such an integration occurs have not yet been well investigated by researchers in social cognition.

The above analysis assumes people have the time and motivation to generate and search the relevant knowledge structures. But there are alternative routes to producing an overt response. The simplest solution would be to take the response category labels (e.g., "conservative" and "liberal") and determine whether one or the other exists explicitly as an element in the cognitive representation evoked by the stimulus object (e.g., the President). If one of the labels is located in the representation (e.g., possessing the belief that "this President supports every conservative cause"), that category label could be directly endorsed when responding to the survey item. Lingle and Ostrom (1979) were one of the first to show that this process occurs. Such a strategy is probably most likely to occur under conditions where the respondents are not obligated to explain their choice.

A second set of issues pertains to the matching process. How does the respondent determine which of the two response alternatives is better? There are unresolved complexities even in the case of matching an item category label to a corresponding element in the cognitive representation (as was described in the paragraph above). What if the search of a President Reagan representation locates both a conservative and a liberal element? How is the inconsistency resolved? Presumably further search of the representation would ensue. If it were discovered that conservative was linked to President and liberal was linked to "movie actor," then the direct match would determine the response. But what if conservative was linked to "opposes abortions" instead of "President?" The nature of the search process and matching processes under such complications have yet to be worked out.

Let us now turn to the case where prototype structures are activated for the two response alternatives. How do respondents go about determining which of the alternatives best matches their representation of the object? Tversky (1977; Tversky & Gati, 1982) has provided a model of perceived similarity that could operate in this setting. It was developed to account for overt similarity judgments between two stimuli, but could be extended to explain the relative similarity of an object to two categories. Work would need to be done, however, to explain how the cognitive system manages the feature matching process, how it keeps track of the relative match exhibited by each of the two categories, and how it decides to terminate the matching process and make the judgment.

Continious Rating Scale Format.

Researchers committed to the dimensional perspective may have great difficulty in imagining how the information processing approach could account for responses on a continuous rating scale. By a continuous scale, I refer to scales that present the respondent with an unbroken line to mark, or with a set of categories sufficient in number to allow the respondent to communicate all important subjective discriminations (often accomplished with as few as seven to nine categories).

The psychophysical metaphor has for so long been the only way researchers have thought about scale responses that it becomes almost heresy to even hint at the existence of an alternative conceptualization. How would it be possible for a person to mark a continuous scale (the response continuum) if that person did not have a continuous subjective representation of that scale (the judgment continuum)? How would it be possible for a person to select one category on a scale ranging from +5 to -5 unless that person had a subjective representation of those eleven ordered categories? The "all-or-none" conception of cognition seems incapable of guiding a response on continuous scales.

One alternative to the dimensional approach is suggested by the random walk model (Stone, 1960). The approach described here was originally developed by John Lingle (personal communication). For purposes of illustration, let us take the case where a scale running from +5 (conservative) to -5 (liberal) is given to the respondent.

The random walk model assumes that people randomly "walk" through their cognitive representation; that is, they randomly sample items from their cognitive representation in a serial manner. In the present example, respondents would sample beliefs from their representation of the president. These beliefs would then be compared to the conservative and liberal schemas to determine whether they implied a conservative or liberal categorization. The model contains a parameter regarding the number of beliefs that must be sampled before the respondent concludes in favor of one or the other category.

Up to this point, the random walk model would apply equally well to the two-category case and to the continuous scale case. To deal with this added complexity, we postulate that the respondent decomposes the continuous scale (or the +5 to -5 scale) into two (or possibly three) categories. The respondent may decide to split the scale into a conservative category (covering scale positions from +1 to +5) and a liberal category (covering scale positions from zero to -5). If the original categorization was "conservative," then the respondent has reduced the possible scale responses from eleven to two.

How does the respondent select from the remaining scale categories? Several possibilities exist. The respondent may simply sample several more beliefs from the representation and if the first several were uniformly conservative, select +5. If none were conservative, select +1. And if there was a mixture of conservative and liberal, arbitrarily choose +2, +3, or +4.

An alternative (and perhaps more plausible) strategy depends on whether the person has subcategories corresponding to levels of extremity. Some people think only in bipolarities and do not recognize shades of grey. These people would not necessarily understand why five choices remained. There are no gradations of conservatism, you either are one or you are not. Consequently, such persons may select arbitrarily from among the five response alternatives, or may simply select one of the five (e.g., +5) and use it for rating all objects on this scale.

Other people may well differentiate the overall conservative category into two or more subcategories. Subjects possessing subcategories corresponding to levels of extremity would sample again from their representation and use the random walk process to determine which extremity category best characterized their impression.

Upon selecting an appropriate subcategory, these persons would have to decide which scale responses coincided with the assigned extremity category. If one of the extremity categories was the "conservative zealot," assignment of the target stimulus into that category might well lead to a rating of +5. All other objects might be labeled as "moderate conservative," in which case the respondent could arbitrarily select from among the remaining four conservative scale categories.

The analysis offered in this section makes it clear that bipolar scales need not yield the same results as ratings on the constituent unipolar scales. There is no reason to expect that presentation of one polar label (e.g., conservative) will automatically activate the other (e.g., liberal). Unlike the unidimensional approach, it is not even necessary that ratings on one of the unipolar scales be negatively correlated with ratings on the other unipolar scale. The unidimensional approach has great difficulty exlaining findings of near zero correlations and nonlinear relations between ratings on the two unipolar scales (e.g., Green & Goldfried, 1965; Semin & Rosch, 1981).

The viewpoint argued here is that people have a problem to solve when given a continuous (or an extensive multicategory) rating scale. They find it an awkward and unnatural language through which to express the contents of their cognitive representation. This is because their representation has an all-or-none, categorical structure, while the response scale presumes the existence of a subjective continuum. It is argued that respondents solve this communication problem by decomposing the survey researcher's response scale into a categorical form, one that is congruent with the respondent's own subjective thinking about the stimulus object.

## CONCLUSION

The information processing conceptions outlined in this chapter were quite rudimentary in form. They represented the most general kinds of structural features that are prominent at the point in time when a response is being generated. No mention was made of issues concerning perception, language, encoding, inference, or cognitive architecture. No mention was made of the cognitive dynamics by which people access and operate on these structures. It is clear that the complexities involved at the time of generating a survey response are only part (and perhaps a minor part) of the broader set of problems we face in understanding the cognitive system as a whole.

These complexities can be described in general terms using natural language (e.g., English or German), as has been done in this chapter. However, natural language is probably not the best symbol system to use in conceptually articulating the detailed operation of the cognitive system as it focuses on the problem of question answering. Natural language has neither the precision nor the capacity to accommodate the interaction between iterative, cyclical, cognitive systems. A much more promising symbol system for theory construction is provided by the propositional languages employed in artificial intelligence, such as LISP. Some work has already been done using artificial intelligence models (e.g., Lehnert, 1978), and this will doubtlessly be the preferred approach in the future.

This chapter has demonstrated that the information processing perspective views the process of going from cognition to action as being very complicated. The simplicities inherent in the dimensional approach, while convenient, intuitively appealing, and pervasively accepted by survey researchers, are firmly and unequivocally rejected. These new complexities carry with them many unanswered questions, questions that are vital if we are to fully understand the meaning of respondent's answers to our survey items. We have a multi-faceted research agenda before us, the extensiveness of which is at present only dimly recognized.

## ACKNOWLEDGMENT

I am pleased to acknowledge the thoughtful commentary provided on an earlier draft of this chapter by M. Brickner, R. Fuhrman, J. Krosnick, N. Schwarz, C. Tsedikedes, and R. Wyer.

## REFERENCES

Anderson, N.H. (1981). Foundations of information integration theory. New York: Academic Press.

Devine, P. G., & Ostrom, T. M. (1985). Cognitive mediation of inconsistency discounting. Journal of Personality and Social Psychology, 49, 5-21.

Devine, P. G., & Ostrom, T. M. (in press). Dimensional vs information processing approaches to social knowledge: The case of inconsistency management. In D. Bar-Tal, & A. Kruglanski (Eds.), The social psychology of knowledge. Cambridge, MA: Cambridge University Press.

Fishbein, M., & Ajzen, I. (1975). Belief, attitude, intention, and behavior. Reading, MA: Addison-Wesley.

Graesser, A. C., & Clark, L. F. (1985). Structure and procedures of implicit knowledge. Norwood, NJ: Ablex.

Green, R. F., & Goldfried, M. R. (1965). On the bipolarity of semantic space. Psychological Monographs, 79, No. 6.

Guilford, J. P. (1954). Psychometric methods. New York: McGraw-Hill.

Helson, H. (1964). Adaptation-level theory: An experimental and systematic approach to behavior. New York: Harper & Row.

Kelly, G. A. (1955). A theory of personality: The psychology of personal constructs. New York: Norton.

Lehnert, W. G. (1978). The process of question answering: A computer simulation of cognition. Hillsdale, NJ: Erlbaum Associates.

Lingle, J.H., Altom, M.W., & Medin, D.L. (1984). Of cabbages and kings: Assessing the extendibility of natural object concept models to social things. In R.S. Wyer, Jr., & T.K. Srull (Eds.), Handbook of social cognition. Vol.1. Hillsdale, NJ: Erlbaum.

Lingle, J. H., & Ostrom, T. M. (1979). Retrieval selectivity in memory-based impression judgments. Journal of Personality and Social Psychology, 37, 180-194.

McCloskey, M., & Glucksberg, S. (1979). Decision processes in verifying category membership statements: Implications for models of semantic memory. Cognitive Psychology, 11, 1-37.

Osgood, C. E., Suci, G. J., & Tannenbaum, P. H. (1957). The measurement of meaning. Urbana, IL: University of Illinois Press.

Ostrom, T. M. (1981a). Theoretical perspectives in the analysis of cognitive responses. In R. Petty, T. Ostrom, & T. Brock (Eds.), Cognitive responses in persuasion. Hillsdale, NJ: Erlbaum Associates.

Ostrom, T. M. (1981b). Attribution theory: Whence and whither? In J. Harvey, W. Ickes, & R. Kidd (Eds.), New directions in attribution theory. Vol. 3. Hillsdale, NJ: Erlbaum Associates.

Ostrom, T. M., & Upshaw, H. S. (1968). Psychological perspective and attitude change. In A. Greenwald, T. Brock, & T. Ostrom (Eds.), Psychological foundations of attitudes. New York: Academic Press.

Parducci, A. (1965). Category judgment: A range-frequency model. Psychological Review, 72, 407-418.

Semin, G. R., & Rosch E. (1981). Activation of bipolar prototypes in attribute inferences. Journal of Experimental Social Psychology, 17, 472-484.

Stone, M. (1960). Models for choice reaction time. Psychometrica, 25, 251-260.

Thurstone, L. L. (1927). A law of comparative judgment. Psychological Review, 34, 273-286.

Thurstone, L. L. (1931). The measurement of attitudes. Journal of Abnormal and Social Psychology, 26, 249-269.

Thurstone, L. L., & Chave, E. J. (1929). The measurement of attitude. Chicago, IL: University of Chicago Press.

Torgerson, W.S. (1958). <u>Theory and methods of scaling.</u> New York: Wiley.

Tversky, A. (1977). Features of similarity. <u>Psychological Review</u>, <u>84</u>, 327-352.

Tversky, A., & Gati, I. (1982). Similarity, separability, and the triangle inequality. <u>Psychological Review</u>, <u>89</u>, 123-154.

Wegener, B. (1982). <u>Social attitudes and psychophysical measurement.</u> Hillsdale, NJ: Erlbaum Associates.

# 5 ANSWERING SURVEY QUESTIONS: THE ROLE OF MEMORY

Gerhard Strube
Max Planck Institute for
Psychological Research, Munich

Many survey questions make more than neglegible demands on the respondent's memory. Not only do they tap semantic knowledge (required to understand what the interviewer is saying), or "world knowledge" (e.g., who is President), but they draw on episodic or biographical memory as well. "When did you last visit a medical doctor?" asks for a date, which usually has to be supplied from memory — not from a notebook where most people write dates down so that they do not have to bother their memory with them. A similar question from the US National Health Interview Survey is even harder, although it only asks for an approximate answer: "During the past 12 months, about how many times did you see or talk to a medical doctor?" Ideally, the respondent should skim through memory as though it were a calendar, picking relevant episodes, and estimating the one-year span. Obviously, real respondents just cannot do that without making errors, although they try. Most try a "past-to-present" strategy, which seems the second best way to get accurate results (Fathi, Schooler, & Loftus, 1984).

Demands on memory imply errors of memory. Some of those errors may surface as underreporting (because some relevant occurrences have been forgotten), or as overreporting (mostly because incidents are reported that happened before the reference period, an effect known as "forward telescoping"). Accuracy, or "veridicality" of recall, has therefore become a major concern in survey methodology (Bradburn & Danis, 1983; Loftus, Fienberg, & Tanur, 1985; Tourangeau, 1983).

## SOURCES OF INFLUENCE ON VERIDICALITY OF RECALL

The memory model proposed here as a guideline for the discussion of veridicality in recall is consistent with widely shared views of memory functioning, and distinguishes various points of possible influence of general or differential developmental factors upon the structure and content of individual memories (Figure 1, time scale running from above to below), as shown in Figure 1.

In the following, this model will be discussed in some detail.

Figure 1: Sources of Influence

| Stimulus ("outside") | Process ("inside") | Sources of Influence ("process variables") |
|---|---|---|

AT TIME OF EXPERIENCE:

event ------------ (encoding)-----------then existing schemata, context, expectations, etc.

(restructuring of representation)-----interfering influences

AT TIME OF INTERVIEW:

question ----------(understanding)-----current schemata, context, and expectations

(retrieval & re-construction)-------(ditto), and search strategies

(judgment & de-cision)-------------strategies, heuristics, and combination rules

response      (editing)----------intentional self-presentation

Encoding

Whenever we experience some specific event, we have to "capture" that event within the frame of knowledge that we have activated at that time, in order to perceive, understand, and store it for future retrieval.

Strict behavioral observation is a difficult technique to learn because our natural understanding of behavior and of events in general proceed at a higher, more global, more inferential level. Therefore, the meaning of an event, or even the boundaries of an event in the continuous stream of experience are, to a considerable extent, determined by what we expect to happen at a given time. Webb, Campbell, Schwartz, and Sechrest (1966), in their classic work on unobtrusive methods, provide an example of applying a frame: When

Chicago university students, for purposes of collecting data on interracial contacts, took up their observation posts in a Chicago shopping street, shop owners called the police because they thought they were being spied on with the intention of burglary. Obviously, this was not the frame intended by the researchers. However, business people are more ready to adopt a "crime planning" frame than a "research" frame, the former being directly related to their everyday experience and general knowledge.

Frames often refer to specific situations, for instance places like a restaurant (see Schank & Abelson, 1977, on scripts), or to a sequence of actions appropriate in that context. Developmental psychologists have also proposed that "action frames", that is, cognitive schemata that are derived from stereotypical actions, are at the very core of our information processing. It seems that children's knowledge of general event schemata comes prior to their memory of specific instances of such events (Hudson & Nelson, in press). Novel experiences become quickly generalized, and later provide the basis of experiencing similar events (Hudson, 1983). Script knowledge guides what we understand, and sometimes even what we see (or miss), as we know from the psychology of eyewitness testimony.

The passing of some coins on the counter, for example, usually occurs in the action frame of paying for goods or services. What a dime looks like is therefore not in the focus of attention – compare this to paying in a foreign country! Accordingly, subjects have been found to perform badly when asked to reproduce what is on a dime (Nickerson & Adams, 1979). We should also expect subjects to be grossly inaccurate when asked how often they have used a specific coin or bill for payments during some specified period.

The encoding of an event at the time we experience it, is certain to determine future possibilities of retrieving that event from memory. This is because retrieval from memory, as we shall see, is heavily dependent on the encoding of events. Retrieval cues must make use of what has been encoded, and the variability of encoding demonstrated in restricted verbal learning tasks (e.g., Tulving & Thomson, 1973) is still greater for real events in everyday life. Encoding therefore has been granted the status of the "truly central concept in modern theories of memory" (Bower, 1972). Its practical importance for the survey methodologist lies in its uncontrollability: Unlike retrieval strategies, which may be influenced by the interviewer (e.g., through question wording or by means of direct

instruction), encoding has happened some time ago. Therefore, research on habits of encoding for everyday events could give us hints
on how to tap people's memories. Unfortunately, research on everyday
memory is new as a major field of study (see Neisser, 1983, for an
overview).

## Events Affecting Stored Information

Apart from spectacular accidents like traumata that cause am-
nesia, and which are more of clinical interest, there are the less
obtrusive, everyday vicissitudes that befall memory traces between
storage and recall. Two cases seem of special importance here: (1)
experiencing similar events, and (2) remembering an event in the
meantime, or listening to accounts of others, often accompanied by
discussions of the event in question.

An experience, by virtue of its being similar to the original
event, obviously has many features, or characteristics in common with
the originally stored event. The result is that the memory representations of both events tend to get blurred into each other
(Wickelgren, 1976). This leads to what has been described as
"retroactive inhibition" in verbal learning as early as 1900 by
Müller and Pilzecker. Similar processes may effect what Neisser
(1981), in his analysis of John Dean's testimony before the Senate
"Watergate" Committee, termed "repisodic" memory, that is, recall
that tends to draw on a mixture of event representations, thereby
producing something correct at a more general level.

Frequent experience of similar events seems to foster generation
of more "semantic", that is, knowledge-like representation, which
lacks specific time or location indicators. Many psychologists, from
different viewpoints, have been speculating on how such
"decontextualization" may turn episodic memory contents into semantic
knowledge (e.g., Nelson, 1983; Strube, 1984; Tomkins, 1980). As
Bahrick and Karis (1982, p.429) put it: "... generalized knowledge is
rooted in episodic experiences. However, the identity of these roots
is gradually lost, and eventually most meanings and general knowledge
become disassociated from the context in which they were acquired."
There are, of course, more direct ways of acquiring general
knowledge.

Recollecting an event, pondering over causes and consequences,
or discussing an experience with others will certainly give rise to
secondary event representations of highest similarity. A major threat

against the integrity of personal recollections is what others tell us about the events we experienced - from their point of view, of course. Traces of one's own encoding of the original experience may become fused with, if not extinguished by, the vivid, elaborate, or for some other reason convincing accounts of others because of the high degree of similarity in almost all aspects concerning the event in question.

To summarize, the original representation of some event in memory may be reworked from someone else's perspective, or may become merged with some similar episodes into a "repisode" memory, or may even become totally devoid of episodic content, thus gaining the status of general knowledge, or what has often been termed a "schema." Schematic distortion of episodic memories is a well known phenomenon since Bartlett's (1932) classic study, and of considerable practical importance in court (Loftus, 1979; Yarmey, 1979), or in surveys whenever information about specific events is requested, (instead of general impressions, beliefs, or attitudes).

Determinants of Accurate Retrieval

At retrieval time, there are at least four different types of influences threatening veridicality of recall. I will not discuss the voluntary, deceptive self-presentation towards the interviewer. I shall also refrain from a discussion of the judgment and decision processes that usually transform recollections into some suitable response, but will take up part of the issue again when discussing frequency and time dating events. For now, there remain the aspects of reconstruction, and of cueing.

Reconstruction has been the most prominent aspect of recall in recent discussions among researchers, especially in the Bartlett-Gibson tradition (e.g., Bransford and his associates, see Bransford, 1979). As mentioned above, cognitive schemata acquired up to the time of recall, often guide retrieval and lead to a schema-conforming reconstruction of the memorized event (see Alba & Hasher, 1983, for an integrative review). More generally, though, cognitive schemata not even specifically related to the event in question, may have similar effects. Schemata of self-evaluation and attitudes in general provide instances of that. People remember past events so as to be consistent with their present attitudes (e.g., Goethals & Reckmann, 1973). They also "rewrite personal history" in order to arrive at a somewhat consistent biography (e.g., Epstein, 1973; Greenwald, 1980).

Cueing, especially the effect of contextual cues, has also been in the focus of research for some ten years. Tulving (who summarices his work in his 1983 book), Bower (1981), or Godden and Baddeley (1975) have provided spectacular examples of cues at work, emphasizing the importance of both internal (moods, intentions, physical states) and external context factors for recall accuracy. In all those cases, it was found that a recall-time context, concordant with context factors present at encoding time, facilitated remembering. The striking fact is that seemingly unrelated and totally unimportant contextual cues are quite efficient. For instance, in the Godden and Baddeley study, marine divers had to learn and recall word lists both on the shore and in deep water, and this situational difference was found to affect memory performance significantly.

In surveys, cues are usually provided through the context and wording of a question. (I may add that the wording of a question also provides respondents with criteria for the evaluation of recollections. Often someone remembers an event that will not be told to the interviewer because the person believes it is not a "valid" answer.) Cues guide what subjects are looking for in their memory. If encoding establishes what may be retrieved at all, cueing may be interpreted as the attempt to "hit" the proper encodings: If the features of the memory representation and of the (now also encoded) cue fit, retrieval will be successful.

I suggest that what is usually called cueing actually comprises two aspects of selection during recall. The first aspect is a broader one, resulting from contextual cues: the general course of the interview, the respondent's belief about the interviewer's intentions, and the field of content, or segment of the respondent's knowledge that is being probed by the interviewer's questions. This amounts to a general preselection of what is to be considered relevant. It bears resemblance to what was once called "set" or "orientation" in the older psychology of volitional processes (e.g., Ach, 1905). I should like to call it a "perspective" for subsequent processing. The second aspect is the cue proper, that is, the encoding of the current question (which in turn depends on the perspective currently established). This theoretical distinction provides a useful tool of explanation for the differential, context-dependent effects of identical questions (e.g., issues of question order).

It may be difficult to find good cues. In our own research (Strube, Knopf, & Weinert, 1983), we interviewed kindergarten

children, trying to get them to recall special occasions at kindergarten, such as festivities, excursions, and so forth. We tried to
find an effective cue, and finally arrived at the instruction "Tell
me about some special day", which elicited more than three times as
many responses as our earlier formulations did. (Researchers like
Friedman, 1982, have suggested that a day is the natural unit of time
for children at that age.) This example suggests that sometimes a
pretesting of cues may be useful. Average number of answers elicited
is not the only hallmark of cue quality. However, there should be
some way in which to establish the validity of the answers obtained.
(In the above case, we compared answers to the kindergarten teacher's
notes.)

### An Outline of Memory Functioning

Not all memory psychologists would subscribe to the view outlined above, that there are indeed changes in the memory representation of an event possible between encoding and retrieval.
Therefore, I shall present a sketch of a theory of memory that links
the various aspects together, and will show how such changes occur
and why cues are essential for successful recall. An extensive treatment of the theory can be found in Strube (1984).

Recall, in my view, involves processes at two distinct levels.
The first and basic level is a parallel associative memory of the
type that is described in Kohonen (1984). Such a memory store is
addressable by content, and therefore memory search is determined by
the principle of similarity: An assembly of cues called the "key" at
the input side of the associative store will evoke a response at the
output side, which contains features of the memory representations
most similar to the key. The mode of storage itself is a distributed
one; all memory representations overlay one another, and new encodings by necessity interfere with already stored ones, thus allowing
for the changes in the memory trace described above.

Success of recall from the associative store depends on how well
the retrieval cues have been specified. This is a feature that the
model shares with more traditional ones like the well-known one by
Raaijmakers and Shiffrin (1980). Both models also have in common a
stage of evaluation to some criteria after "raw" recall has occurred.
The goal of this evaluation is in detecting answers already given in
the recall protocol and the inhibiting of answers not considered
appropriate for the task given.

In order to direct cue assembly and to set criteria for the evaluation stage, processes on a second, higher level of cognitive functioning are assumed. These processes set a "strategic perspective" for subsequent recall by activating a subset of the features present in the memory representations for recall by similarity. Here is where the factors operating at recall time come in.

Figure 2: A Model of Free Recall

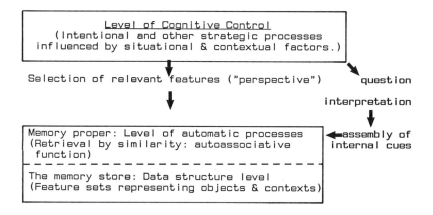

Figure 2 summarizes this model, which has already been demonstrated to account well for free recall from natural categories (Strube, 1984), and does so better than the Raaijmakers and Shiffrin model (Walker & Kintsch, 1985).

## Some Aspects of Veridicality in Surveys

In surveys, it is usually not possible to assess the correctness of subjects' answers. Indeed, were it is feasible to gain more reliable information from other sources than interviews and questionnaires, survey techniques would not be used as frequently as they are. We may, however, try to point out which questions are prone to memory failure and which ones are less likely to suffer from this cause.

The more specific the cue provided, the easier it will be for the subject to remember a suitable instance - if there is any. However, there may be issues of availability (see below) and of wording involved. Asking customers if they ever experienced trouble with a certain kind of machine, obviously will evoke answers that are a function of both the machine's performance, and of what the customer regards as trouble. But generally, questions of the "have you ever" type are better than questions of the "how often" or "when did you last" type. Assessing the frequency of repeatedly experienced events, or time dating of events, are probably among the most difficult tasks that we present subjects. In addition to memory load, they require a complicated judgment step.

Judgments of frequency

Judgments of the frequency of experienced events or of one's own actions are among the most commonly used questions in surveys. As prominent researchers have noted, frequency judgments, which by necessity rely on subject's memories, pose difficulties that are not easily amenable to correction (Bradburn, private communication). First of all, subjects tend to overestimate the frequency of rare events and to underestimate occurrence of events that happen frequently. This is what Lichtenstein, Slovic, Fischhoff, Layman and Combs (1978) have termed "primary bias," and this is compared to "secondary bias." The latter term refers to overestimation of "sensational events" (Lichtenstein et al., 1978, p. 575) which are commonly assumed to result in especially strong memory traces and have been shown to be unusually vividly recalled (e.g., the so-called "flash-bulb memories" surrounding events like being notified of President Kennedy's assassination: Brown & Kulik, 1977; Yarmey & Bull, 1978).

The apparent failure of people to correctly assess the frequency of past events or the probability of future happenings (cf. Kahneman, Slovic, & Tversky, 1982) is similar to what subjects can do in laboratory tasks like guessing how frequently they were presented with a specific word pair in a typical paired-associate learning experiment (Hintzman, 1969; Hasher & Chromiak, 1977).

In the laboratory some sources of distortion have been identified. Johnson, Taylor, and Raye (1977) showed that frequency of presentation interacted with frequency of recall even when the recall task was so modified as to avoid reproduction (e.g., constructing an image instead of writing down the word). While this still could be interpreted as confounding two types of frequency information, each valid in itself, this interpretation will not hold for the observed influence of context variation. In two experiments, Hintzman and Stern (1978) found that repetition of a word or of the name of some well-known person with the same context (semantic-differential scale for the words, sentences for the names), resulted in higher judgments of frequency than presentation of those words and names in different contexts, while context variability lead to better recall and recognition. An experiment by Rowe (1974) adds the insight that context effects are limited to what is encoded; varying the appearance of words by presenting them in different types of print did not have any effect on frequency judgments. It seems difficult to generalize from these results to the kind of memories that are of interest to the survey designer. In natural settings, greater differences exist in context variation, and there are also more variations in encoding. Both factors may boost biases in frequency judgments. On the other hand, same vs. different context might show different effects with personal recollections and with the far larger time span typical in survey applications.

A most problematic issue about errors in frequency judgments is that they seem to be robust against precautioning. Hasher and Chromiak (1977) found that informing their subjects of a subsequent frequency judgment task produced significantly, yet not substantially better judgments (for example, mean judgments of 1.39 instead of 0.95 when the actual frequency had been 4!). Lichtenstein et al. (1978, Experiment 5) tried to caution their subjects against the possible causes of distortions, and still got no improvement in their judgments. They explain the phenomenon in terms of "availability."

The concept of availability was advanced by Tversky and Kahneman (1973) who claim that ease of remembering (e.g., availability) provides the base of frequency judgment. "The easier some instances of the event category in question come to mind, the more frequently things like that must have happened" seems to be the logic of the respondent who relies on availability. While frequency and availability certainly correlate in many cases (a fact well established by verbal learning research), there may also be cases where rare events stand out and are highly available. This also constitutes a well-established result of experimental research: the "Restorff effect" (see von Restorff, 1933). Indeed, Tversky and Kahneman report that overestimation of the frequency of rare events is a common error.

Hintzman and Stern (1978) argue that availability is a questionable explanation because context variability both decreases judged frequency and increases recall (surely a measure of availability). I feel that the primary bias of underestimating frequent and overestimating rare events may well be due to ceiling or regression-to-the-mean effects (and indeed has been so interpreted by Lichtenstein et al., 1978). The secondary bias of overestimating the frequency of salient events is a result of availability judgment and has never been questioned as such.

What can be done to improve frequency judgments? According to the foregoing discussion of memory workings, availability should be a function of both what is stored in memory and by which cues we try to recall it. Therefore, some cues may lead to better judgments than others. This is what I feel Beyth-Marom and Fischhoff (1977) demonstrated when they required their subjects to produce specific examples from memory for some time (about 2 to 3 min) before judging the frequency of a class of events. This approach worked well with the category "names of countries starting with letter Aleph (Kuf, Yud)." Unaided frequency judgments (i.e., without previous recall) were significantly worse, and correlated with measures of availability (median time to produce first instance, and median number of instances produced in the first 5 s). The same technique was, however, not successful with names of kibbutzim in Israel, a failure that may be due to the peculiar linguistic structure of many kibbutz names (where first letters have no more significance than the "New" in "New York"). Therefore, first names were bad cues for kibbutz names, but better cues for the country category. In sum, the results suggest "that at least some bias induced by relying on the availability heuristic can be eliminated by using that heuristic properly" (Beyth-Marom & Fischhoff, 1977, p. 237).

Another technique has been proposed by Armstrong, Denniston, and Gordon (1975) under the name of the decomposition principle. They try to substitute guessing by strict and stepwise reasoning, as in the following example: "How many packs of Polaroid color films do you think were used in the United States in 1970?" (p. 258). The decomposed version of this question is: "How many people do you think were living in the U.S. in 1970? - In 1970 what do you think was the size of the average family living in the U.S.? - In 1970 what PERCENTAGE of the families do you think owned cameras? (etc. etc.)" (p. 259). Estimates from subjects who used the decomposed questions were significantly better (by a factor of about two) than estimates given to the simple questions. (All subjects were given sufficent time; five problems and 151 subjects were used.) Apparently, this technique works best for categories or event classes that lack a natural definition. Thus, the decomposed questions guide the subject on how to construct the required judgment from knowledge that is more readily available.

Let me suggest another variant of a decomposition technique, which I feel is better suited to typical survey questions. In many cases, instead of asking "how often do you drink beer" or some refined version of that question, we could instead provide subjects with a selection of common situations (seeing friends, watching TV, having dinner, meeting business people, etc.) and have them assess the frequency of those situations and whether or what they drink in those situations. Judging the frequency of certain situational frames (i.e., the foci around which our knowledge of what-usually-happens is organized) should be easier (and more exact) than a direct judgment of the frequency. This line of reasoning applies especially to an action like "drinking beer", which is often not encoded because it is plain and unimportant. You may well remember an event as a discussion with friends without having encoded the same event as "consumption of alcoholic beverage." The kind of procedure just described requires judgments about events, and thus should lead to more accurate judgments, from which general frequency information may be computed about actions that lack event character. In this way, frequency items could be made more valid, although the procedure is more tedious, and might be too time-consuming to be widely used.

Time dating of events

Survey questionnaires often ask for the date of some event, or judgments of temporal extension. Frequency judgments may be combined with time specifications, as "How often did this and that happen to you within the last three months?" Apart from inaccuracies due to misjudgment of frequency, errors may be introduced because of subjective distortions of the temporal scale. The most common of these errors is "forward telescoping," that is, assuming that the event in question occurred more recently, and the "squish effect" (Brown, Rips, & Shevell, 1983), which means that when subjects are asked to place events on a time scale with boundaries they tend to do both "telescoping" for older and the opposite for recent events.

Concerning the representation of an event in memory, it may safely be assumed that the exact date will usually not be among the features encoded. If features related to the date are encoded at all, then more perceptual aspects of the context will be encoded, like time of day, or the temporal relation to some other memorable event, or where it happened. If this is the case, people will have to resort to some strategy in order to reconstruct the exact time and day. As Baddeley, Lewis, and Nimmo-Smith (1978) show, their subjects used perceptual cues as above, and made use of their mastery of time scales to guess the date from those cues. Young children, however, cannot profit from their already established knowledge of seasons and holidays, but are able to order well-remembered autobiographical events in time (Strube et al., 1983). Comparing two events with respect to which one happened earlier, then seems the more basic achievement.

This explains why telescoping can be minimized through the use of "landmarks," as a study by Loftus and Marburger (1983) shows. In interviews with nearly 1700 subjects, they found that incident rates reported for victimizations within the last six months were lower for those subjects that were given some landmark for comparison. Public memorable events (the Mount St. Helen's eruption in this case) proved to be equally efficient as an important personal event (which the subjects had to think of before they were questioned), or an outstanding date (e.g., New Year's day). A nonsignificant date like December 16, however, produced as many answers as the "six months" wording, which was used as the base-line of telescoping, did.

A further strategy to minimize telescoping could be devised along the same lines as the situational context strategy for better frequency judgments: If contextual features are usually part of the memory representation of an event, while time of event is not, the latter might be derived by inferences from the context. For example, subjects might be asked to compute a time interval from context cues like place of residence ("That happened in xyz-town, to which we moved in 19xx, and which we left in 19yy"), or children ("Our youngest one had not been born then, so this must have happened before 19xx"), or other long-term context factors.

Let me try to summarize the suggestions I have made for successful survey questions. (1) If possible, make use of singular or otherwise outstanding events, which will be least likely to be forgotten. (2) Try to think of different ways in which an event can be encoded, and provide the appropriate cues. (3) If your interest is in what actually happened, aim at sampling through very specific questions; general questions reveal more of people's attitudes and beliefs. While there is nothing especially new in these guidelines, I hope to have shown their connection with the workings of human memory. It is good to have valid methods, and better still to know why they work.

# REFERENCES

Ach, N. (1905). Über die Willenstätigkeit und das Denken. Göttingen: Vandenhoeck. Alba, J. W., & Hasher, L. (1983). Is memory schematic? Psychological Bulletin, 93, 203-231.

Armstrong, J. S., Denniston, W. B., & Gordon, M. M. (1975).The use of the decomposition principle in making judgments. Organizational Behavior and Human Performance, 14, 257-263.

Baddeley, A. D., Lewis, V., & Nimmo-Smith, J. (1978). When did you last...? In M. M. Gruneberg, P. E. Morris & R. N. Sykes (Eds.), Practical aspects of memory. London: Academic Press.

Bahrick, H. P., & Karis, D. (1982). Long-term ecological memory. In C. R. Puff (Ed.), Handbook of research methods in human memory and cognition. New York: Academic Press.

Bartlett, F. C. (1932). Remembering: A study in experimental and social psychology. Cambridge: Cambridge University Press.

Beyth-Marom, R., & Fischhoff, B. (1977). Direct measures of availability and frequency judgments. Bulletin of the Psychonomic Society, 9, 236-238.

Bower, G. H. (1972). Stimulus-sampling theory of encoding variability. In A. W. Melton & E. Martin (Eds.), Coding processes in human memory. New York: Wiley.

Bower, G. H. (1981). Mood and memory. American Psychologist, 36, 129-148.

Bradburn, N. M., & Danis, C. (1983). Potential contributions of cognitive sciences to survey questionnaire data. Paper presented at the Conference on Cognitive Aspects of Survey Methodology, St. Michael's, MD.

Bransford, J. D. (1979). Human cognition: Learning, understanding, and remembering. Belmont, CA: Wadsworth.

Brown, R., & Kulik, J. (1977). Flashbulb memories. Cognition, 5, 73-99.

Brown, N., Rips, L. J., & Shevell, S. K. (1983). Temporal judgments about public events. Unpublished manuscript.

Epstein, S. (1973). The self-concept revisited: Or a theory of a theory. American Psychologist, 28, 404-416.

Fathi, D. C., Schooler, J. W., & Loftus, E. F. (1984). Moving survey problems into the cognitive psychology laboratory. Paper presented at the Meeting of the American Statistical Association, Philadelphia.

Friedman, W. J. (1982). The developmental psychology of time. New York: Academic Press.

Godden, D. R., & Baddeley, A. D. (1975). Context-dependent memory in two natural environments: On land and underwater. British Journal of Psychology, 66, 325-331.

Goethals, G. R., & Reckmann, R. F. (1973). The perception of consistency in attitudes. Journal of Experimental Social Psychology, 9, 491-501.

Greenwald, A. (1980). The totalitarian Ego. Fabrication and revision of personal history. American Psychologist, 35, 603-618.

Hasher, L., & Chromiak, W. (1977). The processing of frequency information: An automatic mechanism? Journal of Verbal Learning and Verbal Behavior, 16, 173-184.

Hintzman, D. L. (1969). Apparent frequency as a function of frequency and the spacing of repetitions. Journal of Experimental Psychology, 80, 139-145.

Hintzman, D., & Stern, L. D. (1978). Contextual variability and memory for frequency. Journal of Experimental Psychology, 4, 539-549.

Hudson, J. (1983). Scripts, episodes, and autobiographic memories. Paper presented at the Meeting of the Society for Research in Child Development, Detroit.

Hudson, J., & Nelson, K. (in press). Repeated encounters of a similar kind: Effects of familiarity on children's autobiographic memory.

Johnson, M. K., Taylor, T. H., & Raye, C. (1977). Fact and fantasy: The effects of internally generated events on the apparent frequency of externally generated events. Memory and Cognition, 5, 116-122.

Kahneman, D., Slovic, P., & Tversky, A. (1982). Judgment under uncertainty: Heuristics and biases. Cambridge: Cambridge University Press.

Kohonen, T. (1984). Self-organisation and associative memory. New York, Heidelberg, Berlin: Springer.

Lichtenstein, S., Slovic, P., Fischhoff, B., Layman, M., & Combs, B. (1978). Judged frequency of lethal events. Journal of Experimental Psychology: Human Learning and Memory, 4, 551-578.

Loftus, E. (1979). Eyewitness testimony. Cambridge: Harvard University Press.

Loftus, E. F., Fienberg, S. E., & Tanur, J. M. (1985). Cognitive psychology meets the National Survey. American Psychologist, 40, 175-180.

Loftus, E. F., & Marburger, W. (1983). Since the eruption of Mt. St. Helens, has anyone beaten you up? Memory and Cognition, 11, 114-120.

Müller, G. E., & Pilzecker, A. (1900). Experimentelle Beiträge zur Lehre vom Gedächtnis. Zeitschrift für Psychologie, Ergänzungsbd. 1.

Neisser, U. (1981). John Dean's memory: A case study. Cognition, 9, 1-22.

Neisser, U. (1983). Memory observed. San Francisco: Freeman.

Nelson, K. (1983). The derivation of concepts and categories from event representations. In E. K. Scholnick (Ed.), New trends in conceptual representation: Challenges to Piaget's theory? Hillsdale: Erlbaum.

Nickerson, R. S., & Adams, M. J. (1979). Long term memory for a common object. Cognitive Psychology, 11, 287-307.

Raaijmakers, J. G. W., & Shiffrin, R. M. (1980). SAM: A theory of probabilistic search of associative memory. In G. H. Bower (Ed.), The psychology of learning and motivation, 14. New York: Academic Press.

Restorff, H. von (1933). Über die Wirkung von Bereichsbildung im Spurenfeld. Psychologische Forschung, 18, 297-342.

Rowe, E. J. (1974). Depth of processing in a frequency judgment task. Journal of Verbal Learning and Verbal Behavior, 13, 638-643.

Schank, R. C., & Abelson, R. P. (1977). Scripts, plans, goals and understanding. Hillsdale, New Jersey: Lawrence Erlbaum Associates.

Strube, G. (1984). Assoziation. Der Prozeß des Erinnerns und die Struktur des Gedächtnisses. Berlin, Heidelberg, New York: Springer.

Strube, G., Knopf, M., & Weinert, F. E. (1983). Development and organization of biographical memory. München: Max Planck Institute of Psychological Research, paper 8/83.

Tomkins, S. (1980). Script theory: Differential magnification of affects. In H. E. Howe, Jr. & M. M. Page (Eds.), Nebraska Symposium on Motivation, vol. 27. Lincoln: University of Nebraska Press.

Tourangeau, R. (1983). Cognitive science and survey methods. Paper presented at the Advanced Research Seminar on Cognitive Aspects of Survey Methodology, St. Michael's, MD.

Tulving, E. (1983). _Elements of episodic memory_. Oxford: Clarendon Press.

Tulving, E., & Thomson, D. M. (1973). Encoding specifity and retrieval processes in semantic memory. _Psychological Review_, 80, 352-373.

Tversky, A., & Kahneman, D. (1973). Availability: A heuristic for judging frequency and probability. _Cognitive Psychology_, 5, 207-232.

Walker, W. H., & Kintsch, W. (1985). Automatic and strategic aspects of knowledge retrieval. _Cognitive Science_, 9, 261-283.

Webb, E. J., Campell, D. T., Schwartz, R. D. Sechrest, L. (1966). _Unobtrusive measures. Nonreactive research in the social sciences._ Chicago: Rand McNally.

Wickelgren, W. A. (1976). Memory storage dynamics. In W. K. Estes (Ed.), _Handbook of learning and cognition processes_, 4. Hillsdale, New Jersey: Lawrence Erlbaum Ass.

Yarmey, A. D. (1979). _The psychology of eyewitness testimony._ New York: The Free Press.

Yarmey, A. D., & Bull, M. P. (1978). Where were you when President Kennedy was assassinated? _Bulletin of the Psychonomic Society_, 11, 133-135.

# 6 RESPONSE EFFECTS IN SURVEYS

Hans- J. Hippler
Center for Surveys, Methods and
Analysis, Mannheim


Norbert Schwarz
University of Heidelberg

Since the early 1940s, survey interviews have become the dominant method of data collection in empirical social research (Phillips, 1971; Kaase, Ott, & Scheuch, 1983). Despite the popularity of the survey interview, the processes underlying the responses to survey questions are not well understood, and a "theory of asking questions" (Hyman, 1954) has never been developed. Thus, survey methodology today is characterised by rigorous knowledge about sampling procedures on the one hand, and a surprising lack of knowledge about the "art" (sicl) of asking questions (e.g., Noelle-Neumann, 1963) on the other hand. Unfortunately, however, empirical research (e.g., Sudman & Bradburn, 1974) suggests that nonsampling error provides considerable limitations to the usefulness of survey data.

In the present chapter, we will provide a short and selective review of the current state of knowledge concerning nonsampling variation due to question wording and question context. Before we consider these issues in more detail, however, we will briefly sketch the development of research on survey methodology.

## RESEARCH ON SURVEY METHODOLOGY

The beginning of survey research in the 1940s was marked by a pronounced interest in question wording, which was reflected in a number of experimental studies (most notably Cantril, 1944; Payne, 1951). These studies, however, were mainly of an ad hoc character, and were rarely based on theoretical considerations. Frequently the authors emphasized the need for a comprehensive "theory of asking questions" (Hyman, 1954, Kahn & Cannell, 1957) -- much as researchers do today. In the absence of a proper theoretical framework it seemed that research on question wording and related factors had to begin anew with each new question asked. Not surprisingly therefore, survey researchers quickly lost interest in specific effects of specific questions.

Several factors contributed to this development. On the one hand, researchers came to accept that the specific wording of a question would affect the obtained distribution of responses, and that there was little one might do about it. Researchers emphasized that they were typically not interested in specific results based on the use of a specific question but rather in relationships between variables. One hoped that these relationships would not be affected by the idiosyncratic sideeffects of the specific question used. This became known as the assumption of "form resistant correlations" (Stouffer & De Vinney, 1949).

Accordingly, research on survey methodology by the mid 1950s moved from characteristics of the question to characteristics of the respondent (e.g., Cannell & Kahn, 1968) and to the behavior of the interviewers. These became the dominant topics of research in the 1960s and early 1970s. However, as the results of this research program accumulated, it became evident that the explanatory power of respondent and interviewer variables had been overestimated. Rather, the empirical findings suggested "that the characteristics of the task are the major source of response effects and are, in general, much larger than effects due to interviewer or respondent characteristics" (Bradburn, 1983, p. 291). For this reason, the field recently experienced a revival of interest in question characteristics, marked primarily by the work of Sudman and Bradburn (1974) and Schuman and Presser (1981).

Contributing to this revival was the insight that the assumption of form-resistant correlations was not viable. As Schuman and Duncan (1974) demonstrated, the relationship between variables does depend on the specific question asked, thus bringing question form back into focus. Moreover, social researchers became increasingly interested in developments over time, using time-series analyses with univariate distributions. This development sparked a new interest in the separation of substantive change and method effects, again drawing attention to question wording and question context. Finally, the transformation of this revived interest in question effects into an active program of experimental research was considerably facilitated by the recent development of computer assisted telephone interviewing, which provides a convenient methodology for the introduction of numerous split-sample experiments.

Whether this new research activity will prove more useful than previous attempts to deal with question effects will primarily depend on the field's ability to generate a theoretical framework for the conceptualization of the cognitive processes underlying survey responses. It is our hope that the beginning collaboration between survey researchers and cognitive psychologists will contribute to this end.

## WORDING THE QUESTION AND ASSESSING THE ANSWER

### Question Wording

#### Choice of Terms.

A large number of studies demonstrated that minor changes in the exact wording of a question can lead to major changes in the obtained responses (cf. Schuman, 1985, and Schuman & Presser, 1981, for reviews). Three sources are likely to contribute to this phenomenon.

First, changes in the wording of a question may result in changes in the question's substantive meaning. As Schuman (1985) points out, most social issues are complex, "yet individual survey questions must necessarily be kept simple" (p. 650). For this reason, different questions are likely to tap different facets of the same issue, resulting in different responses. That different facets of an issue elicit different opinions is, of course, neither surprising nor problematic for the validity of survey data. Rather, it highlights the fact that the users of survey data must be careful not to misinterpret responses to one facet of an issue as responses to the issue in general, a point that is frequently overlooked in discussing the reliability of survey data.

More problematic is the fact that the same questions may mean different things to different people (Belson, 1968; 1981). For example, Fee (1979) investigated the meaning of common political terms such as "big government" or "big business." She found that these terms had dramatically different meanings for different respondents and that it was hardly possible to determine in advance how a respondent would interpret a term. Moreover, cognitive research suggests that the interpretation of a term depends on the context in which the question is asked (cf. Strack & Martin, this volume). In addition, the meaning of terms may change over time, rendering the results of repeated measurements noncomparable.

Besides affecting the substantive meaning of a question, changes in wording may affect responses by eliciting differently loaded associations. For example, introducing a reference to "communist" activities has frequently been found to increase Americans' support for their country's military operations (e.g. Payne, 1951; Mueller, 1973; Schuman & Presser, 1981) -- presumably because the term "communist" activates cognitive schemata that are otherwise not elicited by the question text (cf. Tourangeau, this volume). For this reason, textbook knowledge urges researchers not to use "loaded" terms. Note, however, that not using loaded terms that are common in public discussion, but are considered inappropriate (namely, loaded) by the researcher, may as well elicit responses that deviate from what the respondent might spontaneously feel about the issue. Thus, it is not the use or avoidance of loaded terms per se but the match between the terms used in the question and the terms spontaneously used by respondents that is likely to be the crucial issue.

Finally, changes in question wording may affect what the respondent considers to be his or her task. This may occur even for wording changes that are usually considered "nonsubstantive" (Schuman, 1985) by survey researchers. The best known of these so-called "nonsubstantive" wording changes, and the one that produced the largest wording effect documented in the literature, is the forbid-allow asymmetry originally reported by Rugg (1941). Respondents are either asked whether something should be "allowed" (yes or no) or whether it should be "forbidden" (yes or no). The general finding is that respondents are more likely to say that the behavior under investigation should not be forbidden than that it should be allowed, and are more likely to say that it should not be allowed than that it should be forbidden. Thus, the negated form of each question is more likely to be endorsed than its affirmative form, even though the two forms appear logically equivalent.

A recent analysis of the cognitive processes underlying this phenomenon (Hippler & Schwarz, 1986) suggests that respondents define their task differently depending on the form of the question. Most importantly, respondents focus on the implications of doing what they are asked about, namely forbidding or allowing something, rather than on the implications of not doing it. For this reason, indifferent respondents respond "no" to both question forms because they neither want to support the issue by allowing something, nor do they want to oppose the issue by forbidding something. Accordingly, 73.3 % of the respondents who were considered "indifferent" on the basis of previous questions said that the target issue should not be allowed while 81.2 % said that it should not be forbidden. Thus, a "nonsubstantive" change in question wording focused respondents' attention on the implications of different acts, namely forbidding or allowing. Moreover, respondents did not consider the implications of the absence of these acts, namely that not forbidding amounts to allowing and vice versa, thus exhibiting a well-known cognitive bias termed the "feature positive effect" in the cognitive literature (cf. Fazio, Sherman, & Herr, 1982).

In summary, our discussion suggests that changes in question wording may always be considered "substantive" because they change the meaning of the question in one of three ways: (a) by refering to different facets of an issue; (b) by activating concepts that affect the respondents' interpretation of the question, or (c) by presenting different cognitive tasks to the respondent. What renders this area of research particularly frustrating is that insight into the general cognitive processes underlying question comprehension is of limited utility to survey researchers. No matter how well cognitive psychologists may come to understand the general dynamics underlying wording effects in the long run, survey researchers will be mostly interested in how respondents interpret the particular question asked. To this extent, research may indeed have to start anew with each new question asked, and general principles may not provide much more than useful guidelines for pretesting specific questions.

Question Length vs. Question Simplicity.

Traditional textbook knowledge has maintained that researchers should keep questions as short as possible (e.g., Payne, 1951). Recent research challenged this assumption (e.g., Marquis & Cannell, 1971; Laurent, 1972; Blair et al., 1977; Cannell et al., 1977; 1981). Specifically, increasing question length with the addition of redundant fillers was found to result in longer and more detailed answers and in more frequent reports of past behaviors.

Again, several processes may contribute to these findings. First, respondents may consider the length of the question to indicate its importance, resulting in more detailed reports in response to presumably more important questions. Second, the addition of redundant fillers may provide a richer set of retrieval cues, thus facilitating recall from memory. Finally, longer questions leave respondents with more time to think about the answer and to retrieve the relevant information. Future research should attempt to explore the relative contributions of these processes for different types of questions. In this regard, a comprehensive review of question-length effects (Sudman & Bradburn, 1974) suggests that the length of questions or of their introductions does not increase reporting for all questions. Most importantly, they found no general effects for length in face-to-face interviews but did find higher reports in response to longer questions in self-administered questionnaires. This suggests that some of the discussed processes, for example, question length as an indicator of question importance, may be shortcut by interviewer behavior and may be more likely to affect respondents in self-administered questionnaires where the question text is the only cue available.

The addition of nonredundant words, on the other hand, increases the complexity of the question and may therefore result in an increased variation in how respondents interpret the question's meaning, with different respondents responding to different facets of the same question (Belson, 1968; Holm, 1974). Thus, the "new" recomendation is not to "keep questions short," but rather to "keep questions simple."

**Assessing the Answer**

Open- vs. Closed-Response Formats.

The advantages and disadvantages of open- and closed-response formats have been the topic of considerable debate in survey research since its early days (e.g., Lazarsfeld, 1944; Krech & Crutchfield, 1948). As J. Converse (1984) recently pointed out, these debates were, however, primarily based on "enlighted common sense, in-house experience, and practical constraints" (p. 279) rather than solid experimental studies. Thus, the actual data base is surprisingly small given the popularity of the issue.

The available data converge on the finding that open- and closed- response formats may yield considerable differences in the marginal distribution as well as the ranking of items (e.g., Schuman & Presser, 1977). On the one hand, any given opinion is less likely to be volunteered in an open-response format than to be endorsed in a closed-response format if presented. On the other hand, opinions that are omitted from the set of response alternatives in a closed format are unlikely to be reported at all, even if there is an "other" category, which respondents in general rarely use (Bradburn, 1983;

Molenaar, 1982). Several processes are likely to contribute to this finding.

First, precoded response alternatives may remind respondents of options that they may otherwise not consider. From a cognitive perspective, open-response formats present a free-recall task to respondents whereas closed formats present a recognition task. As in other domains of research, recognition tasks result in higher degrees of recall. For example, when asked "What are the most important problems facing the country today?", a precoded list of response alternatives may direct respondents' attention to issues that may otherwise not have come to mind. But when reminded of it, respondents may endorse the issue as important. Accordingly, Schuman and Presser (1977) found that "security" was mentioned 13 % less often as an important feature of a job when respondents were asked in an open rather than a closed format. Thus, open-response formats are more adequate when the investigator is interested in the salience of an issue, where the order in which a respondent retrieves different issues and the total number of respondents who retrieve a particular issue are of primary interest (cf. Bodenhausen & Wyer, this volume). Closed formats, on the other hand, are more appropriate when the investigator is interested in a fairly complete evaluation of a large set of issues to determine their relative importance.

Second, respondents are unlikely to spontaneously report, in an open-answer format, information that seems self-evident or irrelevant. In refraining from these responses they follow the conversational maxime that an utterance should be informative (Grice, 1975; see the discussion by Strack & Martin, this volume). This results in an underreporting of presumably self-evident information that is eliminated by closed-response formats, where the explicit presentation of the proper response alternative indicates the investigator's interest in this information.

Moreover, respondents may frequently be uncertain if information that comes to mind does or does not belong to the domain of information the investigator is interested in. Again, closed formats may reduce this uncertainly, resulting in higher responses. This differential complexity of open and closed formats is reflected in higher no-response rates in the open form, in particular among less educated respondents (Schuman & Presser, 1981).

These processes are likely to result in an "underreporting" of opinions and knowledge in an open-response format as compared to a closed format. For behavioral reports, on the other hand, the pattern may reverse under some conditions. Specifically, Blair, Sudman, Bradburn, and Stocking (1977) found pronounced underreporting in response to threatening behavioral questions with a closed-answer format. This effect is most likely mediated by the informative function of response alternatives discussed by Schwarz and Hippler (this volume; see also Schwarz et al., 1985). That is, the range of the response alternatives provides a salient frame of reference and respondents may be reluctant to report frequencies at the extreme range of the scale because these frequencies presumably deviate from the "usual" behavior, which is assumed to be represented by the middle range of the scale. In contrast, no frame of reference is suggested in an open-response format, resulting in less constraints and a fuller range of reports. Accordingly, undesirable behaviors are underreported in closed formats (Blair et al., 1977), while desirable behaviors may be overreported, though data on this latter assumption are not available.

Let us now turn to a consideration of various types of closed-response formats.

Response Categories.

The most frequently used closed format is the presentation of discrete response alternatives. A considerable number of studies investigated whether one or two sides of an issue should be presented, whether the introduction of a middle alternative affects the distribution, and how the likelihood of endorsement is influenced by the order in which the response alternatives are presented.

Regarding the balance issue -- that is, whether one side (e.g., favor - yes or no) or two sides (e.g., favor or oppose) should be presented -- the findings suggest that this makes little difference as long as the alternatives are formal opposites such as "yes" or "no" or "favor" or "oppose" (Schuman & Presser, 1981). If the terms have different connotations, however, such as "forbid" and "allow" for example, dramatic response differences may arise (e.g., Rugg, 1941; Hippler & Schwarz, 1986), as discussed in the question wording section of the present chapter. To be on the safe side, researchers may in general be advised to use balanced alternatives.

The inclusion of a middle alternative between two extreme responses has been the topic of some debate. In general, the data indicate that explicitly offering the logically possible middle-alternative will produce a considerable increment in the percentage of respondents that will endorse it (Molenaar, 1982) as compared to conditions where the middle-alternative has to be volunteered.

Moreover, offering a middle alternative is likely to reduce the rate of "don't know" responses. Regarding the impact of middle alternatives on the endorsement of polar opposites, the findings are mixed. While Schuman and Presser (1981) found that the introduction of middle alternatives did not change the substantive conclusions drawn from the endorsement of the opposites, Bishop (in press) reported a series of studies where the introduction of middle alternatives affected the substantive conclusions. The conditions that determine whether middle alternatives draw similar or dissimilar numbers of respondents from both sides of the attitude continuum, thus affecting or not affecting the substantive conclusions, need further investigation.

In general, the inclusion or omission of response alternatives changes the task of the respondent and is likely to result in different proportions, as well as different rankings of several proportions (McNemar, 1946; Schuman, 1985) because "most respondents seem to assume that the rules of the game call for working within the categories offered" (Schuman, 1985, p. 648).

Moreover, the order in which response alternatives are presented may affect their likelihood of endorsement. In this regard, most studies demonstrated primacy effects, that is, higher endorsements for items presented early in the list, especially if the list is long (e.g., Payne, 1951; Mueller, 1970; Brook & Upton, 1974; Krosnick & Alwin, in press). As Krosnick and Alwin (in press) point out, primacy effects are likely to be obtained when the items are presented visually because the items presented early in the list are the subject of more extensive cognitive processing. Moreover, the items presented early may establish a frame of reference for evaluating the later items, thus rendering them particularly salient.

Recency effects, on the other hand, seem to be rare though they have occasionally been demonstrated (e.g., Payne, 1951; Schuman & Presser, 1981). Recency effects may be particularly likely to occur when the items are presented orally, thus taxing the respondent's memory. Despite these speculations, the conditions that foster primacy or recency effects are not well understood and attempts to draw parallels to the psychological memory literature have been of limited success.

Finally, special problems arise with the use of precoded response alternatives for the assessment of behavioral frequencies. Because these are discussed in detail by Schwarz and Hippler in the present volume, they will not be elaborated here.

Rating Scales.

Beside discrete response categories, rating scales are ubiqui-
tous in social research, particularly in attitude measurement. Dawes
and Smith (1985) provide a careful discussion of their properties,
and of the empirical and psychological justifications for their use.
Leaving concerns about their psychometric properties aside (cf.
Nunnally, 1978), rating scales with labeled endpoints do not seem to
be very controversial. Respondents are able to use these scales
consistently, even in telephone interviews without visual aids (cf.
Hormuth & Brueckner, 1985). Seven-point scales seem to be best in
terms of reliability , percentage of undecided respondents, and
respondents' ability to discriminate between the scale values (Cox,
1980). Thus, seven plus or minus two is the usual recommendation.

Researchers should be aware, however, that both the terms used
to label the endpoints, and the terms used to designate the separate
values of verbal rating scales, affect the obtained distribution
(Rohrmann, 1978; Wegner, Faulbaum, & Maag, 1982; Wildt & Mazis,
1978). This is particularly problematic for self-anchoring scales
(e.g., Kilpatrick & Cantril, 1960) where the respondent supplies
individual end-anchors. Recent research (Hippler, 1986) on left-right
self-placements suggests that the selection of anchors is particularly susceptible to variations in the question context, resulti-
ing in systematic shifts in the rating scores.

Rank-Ordering Scales.

Rank-ordering tasks are more difficult and taxing for respondents than rating tasks, and take about three times longer to complete (Munson & McIntyre, 1979). In particular, ranking more than
five to six items may result in an overly difficult task for many
respondents (Bradburn & Sudman, 1979). Accordingly, primacy effects
are likely to be obtained with longer lists even under conditions
that keep the ranking task itself rather simple. For example,
Krosnick and Alwin (in press) asked respondents to pick the three
most important values from a list of 13 (the three chosen were to be
ranked later), and found that items presented early in the list were
disproportionately more likely to be selected. Moreover, this primacy
effect was more pronounced among less educated respondents and it
affected the correlations between items (though not the nature of the
latent value dimension).

In addition to problems with the rank-ordering task itself,
rank-orderings may bias respondents' use of subsequent rating scales.

In a series of studies, Schwarz and Wyer (1985) found that rank-ordering a set of six items from the "most" to the "least" important (or trivial) resulted in pronounced differences in subsequent ratings of related as well as unrelated items. Specifically, respondents who began the ranking with the "most" important (or trivial) item subsequently assigned higher ratings than respondents who began the ranking with the "least" important (or trivial) item. This finding generalized across various ranking and rating dimensions as well as across the content dimension of the items. For example, environmental issues were rated as more important when respondents had previously ranked a number of attributes desired in a potential marriage partner from the most to the least, rather than from the least to the most important. In general, beginning the ranking task at the "high" ("most") end of the ranking dimension resulted in assignments of higher values in subsequent ratings, a finding that reflects the well-known anchoring bias reported by Tversky and Kahneman (1974). Accordingly, rank-ordering tasks may render the absolute values of subsequent ratings uninterpretable and may limit the comparability of ratings across surveys.

The Assessment of "No Opinion."

In general, respondents are more likely to report not having an opinion on an issue when this alternative is explicitly offered than when it has to be volunteered (cf. Schuman & Presser, 1981; Molenaar, 1982, for reviews). Moreover, the increase in "no opinion" responses depends on the form of the filter used. Generally, the use of a so-called quasi-filter, that is, offering a no opinion option as part of a precoded set of response alternatives, results in smaller increases than the use of a full filter, where respondents are explicitly asked whether they have an opinion on the issue before the interviewer procedes to ask the question proper. In the latter case, the increase depends on the strength of the wording of the filter question, with stronger wordings resulting in higher rates of no opinion responses (e.g., "Do you have an opinion on this?" vs. "Have you thought enough about this to have an opinion?"). Several processes are likely to contribute to these findings.

First, from the perspective of conversational norms, the mere fact that a person is asked a question presupposes that the person can answer it (cf. Clark, 1985; Grice, 1975; Belnap & Steel, 1976). Thus, responding that one has no opinion is an illegitimate answer to an opinion question that respondents are unlikely to give unless the

question indicates its legitimacy. Moreover, this effect of communication norms is likely to be enhanced in survey interviews by
respondents' assumption that they have to work within the set of
response alternatives provided to them (Schuman, 1985). Note,
however, that conversational norms do not account easily for the
differential impact of different forms of filters because any filter
should be sufficient to render no opinion responses legitimate.

Regarding the differential impact of filters, Bishop et al.
(1983) suggested that full filters encourage don't know responses
more strongly than quasi-filters, and to a greater degree the more
strongly they are worded. While this assumption describes the findings very well, it seems to us that a slightly different focus
accounts better for the underlying process. Specifically, we want to
suggest that full filters, in particular when they are strongly
worded, discourage substantive responses because they suggest to
respondents that considerable knowledge is required to answer the
question. For example, respondents who are asked, "Have you thought
enough about this issue to have an opinion on it?" may assume that
this question is particularly important to the researcher and that
they should only answer it when they have a well-considered opinion
based on sound knowledge of the facts. Moreover, respondents may
assume that this filter question leads into a series of detailed
questions that require considerable knowledge about the issue. Both
of these assumptions may prevent respondents from offering a substantive opinion even though they may have a general preference for one
or the other side of the issue, which they would report in response
to a global question with "favor"/"oppose"/"no opinion" response
alternatives. Recent research on respondents' assumptions about the
degree of knowledge needed to answer a given question that is paired
with differently worded filters supports this analysis (Trometer,
unpublished data).

If this analysis is correct, full filters -- in particular when
strongly worded -- may screen out respondents that may well have an
opinion on which they may act in everyday life but which they are
unlikely to report based on their inferences about the potential
demands of the task. To this extent, the use of full filters is
likely to result in a considerable underestimation of the proportion
of respondents who hold an opinion.

Accordingly, the finding that "floaters" (Schuman & Presser,
1981), that is, respondents who give an opinion to an unfiltered
question but would not give one to a filtered question, do not

provide random responses is not surprising. According to the present analysis, floaters do have a global opinion but are prevented from reporting it by the implications of the filter, which suggest that a global response may be insufficient.

## STRUCTURING THE QUESTIONNAIRE

So far, we have mainly considered single questions in isolation. In the actual interview, however, questions are arranged in a fixed sequence which "is determined by the demand to make the interview schedule as logical, coherent and smooth as possible" (Molenaar, 1982, p. 77). The order in which questions are asked may affect responses in a variety of ways that are not yet well understood. Because most of these effects are treated in detail by Strack and Martin in the present volume, we will limit ourselves to a short review of the potential effects.

### Motivational Considerations

Some of the effects of question order discussed in the survey literature are primarily of a motivational nature. To increase respondents' collaboration, the questions asked early in the interview should be easy and interest provoking and should communicate to respondents that participating in the interview is a worthwile endeavor (cf. Sudman & Bradburn, 1983). This interest- provoking quality of the early questions is particularly important for mail surveys where the interviewer, who could potentially handle a lack of respondent motivation, is not present (Dillman, 1978). Moreover, researchers are advised to place difficult or threatening questions in later parts of the interview, to allow the development of a good rapport between interviewer and respondent (cf. Dijkstra & Van der Zouwen, this volume) and to prevent early break-offs. In fact, Sudman and Bradburn (1974) and others found higher reports in response to threatening questions placed at the end rather than at the beginning of the interview. On the other hand, fatigue effects may arise in the course of lengthy interviews, resulting in more superficial and incomplete responses to later questions (Bradburn, 1983). Moreover, respondents' decreasing attention is likely to increase the vulnerability of later questions to response effects.

Cognitive Considerations

In contrast to the rather straightforward motivational effects of question order, its cognitive effects are considerably more complex. Most importantly, these effects need to be conceptualized within a general process model of answering questions as proposed by Strack and Martin (this volume). The mere enumeration of possible effects, as is characterized by large parts of the survey literature, on the other hand, is likely to distract from the similarity of the underlying processes, some of which have already been discussed.

Generally speaking, preceding questions will direct respondents' attention to a certain set of information, thus increasing this information's cognitive accessibility later (cf. Hastie or Bodenhausen & Wyer, this volume). Therefore, respondents are more likely to consider this information in forming later judgments than they would otherwise. The exact effect, however, depends on the specific characteristics of the question context.

For example, preceding questions may increase the salience of an issue, resulting in a larger number of respondents who will comment on that issue later on. Thus, questions about a specific social issue may increase the likelihood that this issue is reported as one of the major problems facing the country. On the other hand, respondents may feel that they would repeat themselves if they reiterated something they said before. This, in turn, may result in decreased reports in an attempt to avoid redundancy (e.g., Bradburn & Mason, 1964). Whether "saliency" or "redundancy effects" are likely to be obtained is probably a function of the similarity of the relevant questions, with redundancy effects being more likely the more similar the questions are.

Moreover, if the activated information is used in forming a judgment it may be used in various different ways. On the one hand, respondents may consider the direct implications of the information for the judgment at hand. For example, respondents may infer from their inability to answer a series of questions requiring political knowledge that they are not very interested in politics after all (see Bishop, this volume). Similarly, the preceding questions may activate a certain norm that bears on subsequent judgments. This seems to underlie the well-known communist reporter item, where respondents are more likely to support freedom of the press for communist reporters in the U.S. if they have previously supported the same freedom for American reporters in communist countries (Schuman &

Presser, 1981). On the other hand, the activated information may be used as a standard of comparison resulting in contrast effects. In a study of food images, for example, Noelle-Neumann (1970) found that potatoes were considered to be more typically "German" when they were preceded by rice than when they were not. As predicted by Ostrom and Upshaw's (1968) perspective theory, these contrast effects tend to be asymmetric, with the more extreme stimuli affecting the less extreme ones but not vice versa (Schwarz & Münkel, 1986).

The exact manner in which previously activated information is used in forming subsequent judgments is currently a popular area of research in social information processing and considerable progress may be expected in the coming years (see Bodenhausen & Wyer and Strack & Martin, this volume, and Schwarz & Strack, 1986, for elaborations).

## MODE OF ADMINISTRATION

Survey questions may be asked in face-to-face interviews, telephone interviews, or self-administered questionnaires. These forms of administration differ along two dimensions: their degree of impersonality and the cognitive demands they place on the respondent.

Regarding the degree of impersonality, self-administered questionnaires provide more anonymity than face-to-face interviews -- with telephone interviews somewhere in-between. The more anonymous methods are likely to encourage fuller reports in response to threatening and sensitive questions. The available data by and large support this assumption (e.g., Hochstim, 1962, 1967; Thorndike et al., 1952; Knudsen et al., 1967) but differences by method disappear for very threatening questions, which are always substantially under-reported (Bradburn & Sudman, 1979). With regard to the cognitive demands placed on the respondent, things are more complex. On the one hand, self-administered questionnaires allow respondents to use as much time to answer a question as they may wish. On the other hand, an interviewer who could provide clarification and encouragement is not available. Depending on the nature of the question, these factors may offset one another, resulting in the finding that "contrary to the common belief favoring face-to-face interviews, there is no clearly superior method that yields better results for all types of questions" (Bradburn, 1983, p. 294; see also Sudman & Bradburn, 1974; Dillman, 1978).

Telephone interviews, on the other hand, are likely to place a higher burden on respondents than either face-to-face interviews or self-administered questionnaires. Most importantly, respondents may be less likely to take their time in thinking about a question. In a face-to-face interaction, pauses in the conversation can be bridged by nonverbal communication that indicates that one is thinking about the issue. The use of these signals is severely limited on the phone, thus rendering pauses more disruptive. To keep the conversation flowing, respondents are therefore likely to avoid pauses, which limits their time to think about the question asked, resulting in increased time pressure in telephone interviews. In addition, visual aids cannot be administered on the phone, thus placing additional burden on respondents' memory.

While the memory burden may be reduced through the avoidance of long lists and difficult questions, the time-pressure issue is potentially more troublesome. Specifically, research in cognitive psychology (e.g., Kruglanski, 1980; Strack, Erber, & Wicklund, 1982) suggests that "top of the head" phenomena increase with increasing time pressure. That is, the less time respondents have to form a judgment the more likely they are to base their judgment on the first piece of information that comes to mind. Under this condition, response effects due to question wording or question context should be particularly likely to be obtained.

The limited empirical data available (Bishop & Hippler, 1986; Bishop, Hippler, Schwarz, & Strack, in preparation) support this possibility. For example, the inclusion of a middle alternative, as well as the position of the middle alternative, resulted in more pronounced differences in telephone interviews than in self-administered questionnaires. Similarly, replications of the well-known abortion items, as well as items of the already discussed communist reporter type (Schuman & Presser, 1981), resulted in stronger order effects in the telephone interview than in the self-administered form.

Moreover, recency effects were obtained with a moderately long list of response alternatives in the telephone interview but not in the self-administered questionnaire, and responses to open-ended questions were more detailed in the latter than in the former form. Finally, leaving respondents more time to think about the question by means of adding redundant filler words increased the percentage of respondents who could correctly date the war over the Falkland

Islands in a telephone interview. In the self-administered questionnaire, on the other hand, no effect of question length was obtained,
presumably because respondents could use as much time as they wanted,
independent of question wording.

In summary, these results suggest that telephone interviews may
be more susceptible to effects of question wording and question
context because they place respondents under a certain time pressure
that increases the likelihood of the top-of-the-head phenomena.

A detailed understanding of the underlying processes will require additional research efforts in controlled laboratory settings
as well as in surveys. Pursuing these research issues is likely to
increase not only our insight  into the dynamics of the survey interview but also our understanding of basic cognitive processes.

## ACKNOWLEDGMENT

Preparation of this chapter was supported by a Feodor Lynen
Fellowship from the Alexander von Humboldt Stiftung to the second
author. The helpful comments of Fritz Strack and Seymour Sudman on a
previous draft are gratefully acknowledged.

# REFERENCES

Belnap, D.(Jr.), & Steel B.(Jr.) (1976). _The logic of questions and answers_. New Haven: Yale University Press.

Belson W.A. (1968). Respondent understanding of survey questions. _Polls, 3_, 1-13.

Belson, W.A. (1981). _The design and understanding of survey questions_. Aldershot, Hants: Gower.

Bishop, G., & Hippler, H.J. (1986). _Response effects in self-administered and telephone surveys: An experiment in Germany and the United States_. Paper presented at the Annual Conference of the American Association for Public Opinion Research (AAPOR), St. Petersburg, Florida.

Bishop, G.F. (in press). Experiments with the middle alternative in survey questions on policy issues. _Public Opinion Quarterly._

Bishop, G.F., Oldendick, R.W., & Tuchfarber, A.J. (1983). Effects of filter questions in public opinion surveys. _Public Opinion Quarterly, 47_, 528-546.

Bishop, G., Hippler, H.J., Schwarz, N., & Strack, F. (1986). _Response effects in telephone interviews and self-administered questionnaires: A comparative study_. (in preparation)

Blair, E., Sudman, S., Bradburn, N.M., & Stocking, C.B. (1977). How to ask questions about drinking and sex: response effects in measuring consumer behavior. _Journal of Marketing Research, 14_, 316-321.

Bradburn, N.M. (1983). Response effects. In P.H. Rossi, & J.D. Wright (Eds.), _The handbook of survey research_. New York: Academic Press.

Bradburn, N.M., & Mason, W.M. (1964). The effect of question order on responses. _Journal of Marketing Research, 1_, 57-61.

Bradburn, N.M., & Sudman, S. (1979). _Improving interview method and questionnaire design_. London: Jossey-Bass.

Brook, D., & Upton, G.J.G. (1974). Biases in local government elections due to position on the ballot paper. _Applied Statistics, 23_, 414-419.

Cannell, Ch.F., & Kahn, R.L. (1968). Interviewing. In G. Lindzey, & E. Aronson (Eds.), _The handbook of social psychology, Vol.II._ Reading, MA.: Addison-Wesley.

Cannell, Ch.F., Marquis, K.H., & Laurent, E. (1977). A summary of studies of interviewing methodology: 1959-1970. _Vital and Health Statistics, Series 2_, No. 69, 1-78.

Cannell, Ch.F., Miller, P.V., & Oksenberg, L. (1981). Research on interviewing techniques. In S. Leinhardt (Ed.), _Sociological Methodology 1981_. San Francisco: Jossey-Bass.

Cannell, Ch.F., Oksenberg, L., & Converse, J.M. (1977). Striving for response accuracy: experiments in new interviewing techniques. _Journal of Marketing Research, 14_, 306-315.

Cantril, H. (Ed.) (1944). _Gauging public opinion_. Princeton: Princeton University Press.

Clark, H.H. (1985). Language use and language users. In G. Lindzey, & E. Aronson (Eds.), _Handbook of social psychology_. Vol. II. New York: Random House.

Converse, J.M. (1984). Strong arguments and weak evidence: the open/closed questioning controversy of the 1940s. _Public Opinion Quarterly, 48_, 267-282.

Cox, E.P. (1980). The optimal number of response alternatives for a scale: a review. _Journal of Marketing Research, 17_, 407-422.

Dawes, R.M., & Smith, T. (1985). Attitude and opinion measurement. In G. Lindzey, & E. Aronson (Eds.), _Handbook of social psychology, Vol. II_. New York: Random House.

Dillman, D.A. (1978). Mail and telephone surveys - The total design method. New York: Wiley.

Fazio, R.H., Sherman, S.J., & Herr, P.M. (1982). The feature positive effect in self-perception process: Does not doing matter as much as doing? Journal of Personality and Social Psychology, 42, 404-411.

Fee, J. (1979). Symbols and attitudes: How people think about politics. Unpublished doctoral dissertation, University of Chicago.

Grice, H.P. (1975). Logic and conversation. In P. Cole, & J.L. Morgan (Eds.), Syntax and semantics 3: speech acts. New York: Academic Press.

Hippler, H.J. (1986). Urteilsprozesse in Befragungssituationen: Experimentelle Studien zu Frageeffekten. Unpublished doctoral dissertation, University of Mannheim.

Hippler, H.J., & Schwarz, N. (1986). Not forbidding isn't allowing: The cognitive basis of the forbid-allow asymmetry. Public Opinion Quarterly, 50, 87-96.

Hochstim, J.R. (1962). Comparison of three information-gathering strategies in a population study of sociomedical variables. In Proceedings of the American Statistical Association, Social Statistics Section.

Hochstim, J.R. (1967). A critical comparison of three strategies of collecting data from households. Journal of the American Statistical Association, 62, 976-989.

Holm, K. (1974). Theorie der Frage. Koelner Zeitschrift fuer Soziologie und Sozialpsychologie, 26, 91-114.

Hormuth, S.E., & Brueckner, E. (1985). Telefoninterviews in Sozialforschung und Sozialpsychologie. Ausgewaehlte Probleme der Stichprobengewinnung, Kontaktierung und Versuchsplanung. Koelner Zeitschrift fuer Soziologie und Sozialpsychologie, 37, 526-545.

Hyman, H.H. (1954). Interviewing in social research. Chicago: The University of Chicago Press.

Kaase, M., Ott, W., & Scheuch, E.K. (Eds.) (1983). Empirische Sozialforschung in der modernen Gesellschaft. Frankfurt: Campus Verlag.

Kahn, R.L., & Cannell, Ch.F. (1957). The dynamics of interviewing. New York: Wiley.

Kilpatrick, F.P., & Cantril, H. (1960). Self-anchoring scaling: a measure of individuals unique reality worlds. Journal of Individual Psychology, 16.

Knudsen, D.D., Pope, H., & Irish, D.P. (1967). Response differences to questions on sexual standards: An interview-questionnaire comparison. Public Opinion Quarterly, 31, 290-297.

Krech, D., & Crutchfield, R.S. (1948). Theory and problems of social psychology. New York: McGraw Hill.

Krosnick, J.A., & Alwin, D.F. (in press). An evaluation of a cognitive theory of response order effects in survey measurement. Public Opinion Quarterly.

Kruglanski, A.W. (1980). Lay epistemologic process and contents: Another look at attribution theory. Psychological Review, 87, 70-87.

Lazarsfeld, P.F. (1944). The controversy over detailed interviews-an offer for negotiation. Public Opinion Quarterly, 8, 38-60.

Marquis, K.H., & Cannell, C.F. (1971). Effect of some experimental techniques on reporting in the health interview. Vital and Health Statistics. National Center for Health Statistics. DHEW Publication No. 1000, Series 2, No. 41. Washington, D.C.: U.S. Government Printing Office.

McNemar, Q. (1946). Opinion-attitude methodology. Psychological Bulletin, 43, 289-374.

Mueller, J.E. (1970). Choosing among 133 candidates. Public Opinion Quarterly, 34, 395-402.

Mueller, J.E. (1973). War, presidents and public opinion. New York: Wiley.

Munson, J.M., & McIntyre, S.H. (1979). Developing practical procedures for the measurement of personal values in cross-cultural marketing. Journal of Marketing Research, 16, 48-52.

Noelle-Neumann, E. (1963). Umfragen in der Massengesellschaft. Reinbek bei Hamburg: Rowohlt.

Noelle-Neumann, E. (1970). Wanted: Rules for wording structured questionnaires. Public Opinion Quarterly, 34, 191-201.

Nunnally, J.C. (1978). Psychometric theory. New York: McGraw Hill.

Ostrom, T.M., & Upshaw, H.S. (1968). Psychological perspective and attitude change. In A. Greenwald, T. Brook, & T.M. Ostrom (Eds.), Psychological foundations of attitudes. New York: Academic Press.

Payne, S.L. (1951). The art of asking questions. Princeton: Princeton University Press.

Phillips, D.L. (1971). Knowledge from what? Theories and methods in social research. Chicago: Rand McNally.

Rohrmann, B. (1978). Empirische Studien zur Entwicklung von Antwortskalen fuer die sozialwissenschaftliche Forschung. Zeitschrift fuer Sozialpsychologie, 9, 222-245.

Rugg, D. (1941). Experiments in wording questions: II. Public Opinion Quarterly, 5, 91-92.

Schuman, H., & Kalton, G. (1985). Survey methods. In G. Lindzey, & E. Aronson (Eds.), Handbook of social psychology. Vol. I. New York: Random House

Schuman, H., & Duncan, O.D. (1974). Questions about attitude survey questions. In H.L. Costner (Ed.), Sociological Methodology 1973/1974. San Francisco: Jossey-Bass.

Schuman, H., & Presser, S. (1977). Question wording as an independent variable in survey analysis. Sociological Methods and Research, 6, 151-176.

Schuman, H., & Presser, S. (1981). Questions and answers in attitude surveys. Experiments on question form, wording and context. New York: Academic Press.

Schwarz, N., & Muenkel, T. (1986). Asymmetric context effects: A perspective theory analysis. Unpublished manuscript: Universitaet Heidelberg.

Schwarz, N., & Strack, F. (1986). How respondents answer satisfaction questions. A judgement model of subjective well-being. Paper presented at the Annual Conference of the American Association for Public Opinion Research (AAPOR), St. Petersburg, Florida.

Schwarz, N., & Wyer, R.S. Jr. (1985). Effects of rank ordering stimuli on magnitude ratings of these and other stimuli. Journal of Experimental Social Psychology, 21, 30-46.

Schwarz, N., Wyer, R.S. Jr., & Kruglanski, A.W. (1982). Effekte von Rangordnungsaufgaben auf nachfolgende Bewertungen. Paper presented at 24. Tagung Experimentell Arbeitender Psychologen, Trier, April 1982.

Stouffer, S.A., & DeVinney, L.C. (1949). How personal adjustment varied in the army-by background characteristics of the soldiers. In S.A. Stouffer, E.A. Suchman, L.C. DeVinney, S.A. Star, & R.M. Williams (Eds.), The American soldier: Adjustment during army life. Princeton: Princeton University Press.

Strack, F., Erber, R., & Wicklund, R. (1982). Effects of salience and time pressure on ratings of social causality. Journal of Experimental Social Psychology, 18, 581-594.

Sudman, S., & Bradburn, N. (1974). Response effects in surveys: A review and synthesis. Chicago: Aldine.

Thorndike, R.L., Hagen, E.H., & Kemper, R.A. (1952). Normative data
obtained in the house-to-house administration of a psychosomatic
inventory. Journal of Consulting Psychology, 16, 257-260.

Trometer, R. (1986). Meinungslosigkeit in der Umfrageforschung.
Unpublished Diplomarbeit, University of Mannheim.

Tversky, A., & Kahneman, D. (1974). Judgment under uncertainity:
Heuristics and biases. Science, 85, 1124-1131.

Wegner, B., Faulbaum, F., & Maag, G. (1982). Die Wirkung von
Antwortvorgaben bei Kategorialskalen. ZUMA-NACHRICHTEN, 10, 3-
20.

Wildt, A.R., & Mazis, M.B. (1978). Determinants of scale responses:
label versus position. Journal of Marketing Research, 15, 261-
267.

# 7

## THINKING, JUDGING, AND COMMUNICATING: A PROCESS ACCOUNT OF CONTEXT EFFECTS IN ATTITUDE SURVEYS

Fritz Strack
University of Mannheim


Leonard L. Martin
University of Georgia

The central goal of asking questions in a survey is to obtain reliable information about characteristics of the respondent. Asking, and consequently answering questions, however, never occurs in a vacuum. Rather, it occurs in a specific social and cognitive context that may influence responses in undesired ways (e.g., Schuman & Presser, 1981). Thus, a change in the answer to a particular question may not necessarily reflect an attitude change on the part of the respondent but simply may be the influence of a different context. Schuman, Presser, and Ludwig (1981), for example, found that divergent responses toward abortion, as measured in two consecutive surveys, were caused not by a change of opinion over time but by the presence or absence of a particular question before the target question.

While the effects of context as "irrelevant" determinants of respondents' reactions have been frequently demonstrated by survey researchers, these researchers "often cannot predict when such effects will occur or explain them when they do occur" (E.Martin, 1984; p. 279). This may be because there is still little systematic understanding of the psychological mechanisms that underlie these influences. Identification of psychological mechanisms that are relevant in survey situations may eventually contribute to a better understanding of context effects in general, because "survey artifacts represent systematic psychological phenomena that do not exist only in surveys" (E.Martin, 1984; p. 279).

In the present chapter, we will first describe several cognitive and judgmental processes that we feel play an important role in context effects (cf. Tourangeau, 1984; Abelson, 1984) and then we will outline a theoretical model that takes these processes into account. The purpose of this model is to provide a convenient and coherent way of conceptualizing context effects and to suggest some directions for future thinking and research in the area.

## THE MULTIPLE TASKS OF ANSWERING A SURVEY QUESTION

Before the different influences of context are discussed in detail, we shall outline a typical sequence of cognitive tasks that a survey respondent has to go through. This psychological framework of survey responding contains four distinct cognitive tasks, which may be performed roughly in sequence (see Figure 1).

First, respondents have to interpret a question to understand what is meant. Second, they have to generate an opinion on the issue. Third, they must fit it into the response format that has been provided. Forth, the respondents may edit their overt answer as a function of particular motives that may arise in the survey situation.

We argue, then, that interpreting the question, generating an opinion, formatting the response, and editing are the main psychological components of a process that starts with respondents' exposure to a survey question and ends with their overt response. How context influences may come into play at each of these stages will now be discussed in more detail. To illustrate this process with a concrete example, it will be assumed that a respondent is given the following question: "How satisfied are you with Ronald Reagan's performance?". The answer has to be given on a response scale from 0 to 10 where 0 means "very unsatisfied" and 10 means "very satisfied."

### Interpretation of the Question

The first step in this sequence is to understand what is meant. On a very basic level, a person must, of course, know the semantic meaning of the words used in the question. As in all linguistic contexts, the respondent must find out what this word means in a particular survey question. That is, the respondent to our example question who is familiar with the concept "performance," still has to identify what exactly "performance" means in this question.

Figure 1: Model of information processing in a survey situation

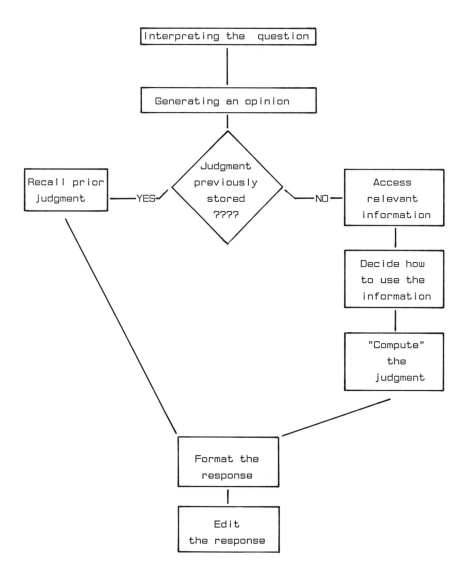

Psychological research suggests that there are two types of processes that may influence the interpretation of information. The first type of process is passive and automatic in nature and may occur without the respondent's control (cf. Schneider & Shiffrin, 1977; Shiffrin & Schneider, 1977). The second type involves active inferences by the respondent and may be seen as a kind of problem solving. Both processes, however, may be elicited by information that was primed or activated earlier, for example, by a preceding question. In this prototypic situation the preceding question will be called the context question and the subsequent question is the target question.

The first automatic influence of a context question on the interpretation of information is a function of the ambiguity of the target information and the activation of a concept in terms of which the target information can be encoded or interpreted. The answer to a context question may have a priming effect because exposure to a certain content in a prior question may increase the ease and the likelihood with which the same or a similar content comes to mind at a later time (Higgins & King, 1981; Wyer & Srull, 1981; cf. Bodenhausen & Wyer, this volume). As a consequence, ambiguous information in subsequent questions may be interpreted in terms of the concepts that are most accessible to the respondent at that moment. It has been shown, for instance, that individuals asked to respond to information that is open to more than one interpretation were likely to respond in a manner that was consistent with the implications of concepts that had been recently activated (Higgins, Rholes, & Jones, 1977; Srull & Wyer, 1979, 1980). Applied to a survey situation, this suggests that when the interpretation of the target question is unclear, respondents may rely on concepts primed by the context to disambiguate the target.

As an example, suppose that respondents are asked how much they agreed (or disagreed) with the statement "In this town, it is difficult to buy drugs." The word "drugs" is ambiguous and has two meanings: narcotics and pharmaceuticals. The respondents' answers to a question containing such an ambiguous word will certainly depend on their interpretation of the word. On the basis of the reported research, unambiguous and applicable concepts that have been activated before the target question may render one interpretation more likely than the other. Thus, if the context had been concerned with criminal activity in the neighborhood, for example, then the target might be interpreted as referring to the purchase of narcotics. If the context had been concerned with medical practices, then the target might be interpreted as referring to the purchase of prescription drugs. More generally, exposure to the context may increase the accessibility of one concept relative to another, and thus determine how ambiguous targets will be interpreted. As noted before, this type of influence may occur without the respondent being aware of it. Bargh and Pietromonaco (1982) for instance, have demonstrated that even information, that was not attended to by the respondent affected the interpretation of subsequent information.

While such ambiguities can be easily avoided by unambiguous wording, another type of question interpretation that occurs at this stage is open to context influences. Frequently, more general words are interpreted by substituting them with a more specific instance. A "container," for example, that holds apples is different from a "container" that holds cola; and "holding" apples is different from "holding" a thief or someone's attention (cf. Anderson & Ortony, 1975; Anderson et al., 1976). In our survey example, for the inter- pretation of "performance" it is necessary to decide that it is the performance of a head of state that has to be evaluated, and not the performance of an actor. In the first case, "performance" is inter- preted as setting policies, enacting laws, and so forth, and in the second case as delivering lines, following choreography, and so forth. This type of ambiguity arises in part out of the necessity to understand what the interviewer or the survey researcher wants to know when he or she asks a particular question. Let us assume a person who has just seen the Reagan movie "Law and Order" is asked about Ronald Reagan's performance. Here, the second interpretation of the word would be appropriate.

The need to understand not only the semantic meaning of the words but also the intended meaning of the underlying concepts originates from the respondent's desire to cooperate in a type of social situation in which the respondent is expected to provide information. In principle, any ambiguity the respondent is aware of could be resolved by asking for clarification. In surveys, however, further explanation is typically not available and providing it may even be discouraged for the sake of standardization (cf. E.Martin, 1984; p.280). In this situation, the respondent may use other avail- able information to infer what the survey researcher wants to know.

There are three sources of information that the respondent may use to infer the intended meaning of a question. First, there is the content of the question itself. Second, the response scale may serve as a basis for inferences, and third, the preceding questions may provide information. These possibilities will now be discussed in turn.

The Content of the Question.

In a straightforward sense, the question itself provides information that allows respondents to use their general knowledge to infer what the question means. As mentioned earlier, the narrow context of a sentence may be used by the respondent to infer the exact interpretation of particular words. Since this problem is not unique to survey questions but is present in the comprehension of words and sentences in general (e.g., Bransford, 1979), we shall not discuss it further here.

The Response Scale.

A source of information for the interpretation of questions that is unique to surveys is the response scale that may accompany a question. This is because the available response alternatives set the range for possible instantiations of more general terms used in the question. Because the questioner provides the alternatives, the respondent may legitimately use this information to infer what is meant by the question.

Assume a survey respondent is asked how often a situation occurs in which he or she feels "really annoyed" -- a term that may refer to a wide range of specific instances on the dimension of annoyance. Of course, in a natural conversation, the respondent could ask what the researcher means by "really annoyed." In a survey situation, however, such a request is generally precluded. The respondent may therefore use the frequency range of the provided response scale to infer the intended degree of annoyance. More specifically, a response scale with a range of frequencies that is low would suggest to the respondent a higher degree of annoyance for the target items than a response scale with a frequency range that is high. This exactly was the result of an experiment in which the response range determined the perceived annoyance level of the experiences that the respondents used as the basis for judging how often they experienced annoying situations (For a more detailed description, see Schwarz & Hippler, this volume).

This finding supports the contention that response scales may provide information for the interpretation of survey questions. In the reported study, the respondents in the low frequency conditions may have concluded that annoying experiences, where frequency of occurrence was supposed to fall into the range between "less than once a year" to "more than every three months" were probably asking for more severe cases than they would have spontaneously thought. As a consequence, "really annoying" situations are interpreted as severe experiences.

The Preceding Questions.

For the task of interpreting a target question, the preceding questions may serve several functions. First, they may activate concepts that facilitate the interpretation of ambiguous terms. As elaborated earlier, the word "drugs" may be interpreted as a pharmaceutic if the preceding question asked about prescriptions. The ambiguous word would be more likely to be interpreted as "narcotic" if a preceding question asked about street crimes. This may be understood as one example for an assimilation effect. Assimilation refers to a shift in the judgment of a target toward the implications of the context.

Such an assimilation effect, as a consequence of interpreting ambiguous words in terms of previously activated concepts, may be particularly likely when respondents are presented with "fictitious issues." Bishop, Tuchfarber, and Oldendick (1986), for instance, found that various fictitious issues differed with respect to "no opinion" answers. "No opinion" responses were less frequent, however, when the target issue was similar to an actually existing issue with which the respondents were familiar. This observation suggests that respondents try to interpret the meaning of these issues and succeed at this task if they can apply a concept that they have used before. As a consequence, one might expect preceding questions, which activate applicable concepts, to have a similar effect.

Preceding questions may serve a second function for the interpretation of a target question. They may inform the respondent about what the questioner already knows. This is important because the survey situation may be controlled by similar norms of cooperation as a natural conversation (cf. Grice, 1975; Clark 1985). In natural conversations, questioners are expected to ask for information they do not yet have and respondents are expected to make their contribution as informative as is required by the situation. Most important, the respondent's contribution is expected to be nonredundant with respect to the questioner's degree of knowledge.

One strategy of inference is based on the so-called "given-new contract" (Clark & Haviland, 1977; Clark, 1985), that is, implicitly formed between two cooperating conversants. According to this contract, respondents are informative if they add new information to what the questioner already knows.

To illustrate, let us assume that a survey in your hometown asks "where" you are going to spend your vacation. Your answer "Greece" may be completely appropriate if that is where you are planning to go. When you have arrived at your vacation spot, however, and are asked the same question, the response "Greece" would be uninformative, or redundant. Rather, you would probably respond by giving the name of the specific city or hotel in which you are staying. The reason for this variation in answers lies in the different degrees of informativeness under different circumstances. In each case, the respondent has to make an inference about what the questioner exactly means by "where." On the basis of what the location is when the question is asked, the respondent may infer which information is given and which information is new to the researcher and may then interpret the question using the assumption that questioners do not ask for information they already have.

In a more subtle way, preceding questions and answers may give similar information. One example is the case in which a specific question is asked immediately before a more general one such that both are perceived as belonging together. For instance, a survey question may require respondents to indicate whether they "think it should be possible for a pregnant woman to obtain a legal abortion if there is a strong chance of a serious defect in the baby?" (Schuman et al., 1981). Imagine that a respondent answers affirmatively to this question (as 84% of the respondents did), and is then asked whether abortion should be "generally available for married women." How does a cooperating respondent interpret the latter question? What does the researcher want to know?

Obeying the given-new contract, the respondent would assume that the researcher asks for new information, that is, for information the respondent has not yet provided in the answer to the preceding question. More specifically, respondents would interpret the more "general" question as not including the more "specific" one that they had just answered. So, "abortion in general" would then be interpreted as "abortion under circumstances other than when a defect in the baby is expected." However, since allowing abortion under these more lenient conditions is less likely to be supported, one would expect less respondents to assent to the general question when it follows the more specific one. This is exactly what Schuman et al. (1981) found. In their sample, the proportion of respondents who reacted affirmatively to the general question was drastically reduced from 60.7% to 48.1% when the specific question was asked first. The answer to the specific question, however, was not influenced by prior answering of the general one. This is consistent with the given-new contract because the answer to a general question is usually not informative regarding the answers to specific questions. That is, the respondent has not yet provided the requested information and the prior answer to the general question has no effect. Such influences have been obtained for different issues and have been labeled "part-whole contrast" effects (Schuman & Presser, 1981).

Similar contrast effects have been found in surveys that as-sessed both people's happiness with their life in general and with their marriage in particular (cf. Schuman & Presser, 1981). Respondents who first evaluated their marital happiness (about two-thirds were "very happy" with their marriage) gave subsequently lower "general" happiness ratings than when the general happiness question was asked first. Following our earlier argument, it is reasonable to assume that the interpretation of the general happiness question differed as a function of the information that was elicited by the previous, more specific question.

Strack and L. Martin (1986) conducted a study to find the condi-tions under which a part-whole contrast or an assimilation effect would occur. In this American student sample, characteristics of their "love life" (boyfriend/girlfriend and frequency of dating) showed the highest correlation with measures of subjective well-being (cf. Emmons & Diener, 1985). They gave students a two-page question-naire about "student issues," in which questions about dating and general happiness were embedded in a series of questions about university issues. The respondents were asked both how happy they were with life in general, and how happy they were with their dating. Answers had to be given on a scale from 1 (not so happy) to 11 (extremely happy). The experimental manipulation consisted of the order of the two questions and whether they were to be perceived as belonging together or not.

Interestingly, Strack and L. Martin found a substantially higher correlation between reports of general happiness and of happiness with dating when the specific question was asked before the general question than when the two questions were asked in the reverse order. It is assumed that priming information about this specific domain of happiness will increase its subsequent availability. Other things being equal, the probability that the general judgment will be based on the more specific information will be increased (this mechanism will be discussed later in more detail). If situational norms, however, preclude the use of this information, the availability effect should be neutralized. That is, no increase in the correlation should be observed. Activating the conversational norm of the "given-new contract" would have exactly the effect of preventing already "given" information from being communicated a second time. If the respondents want to obey the implicit norms of this contract, they must try to communicate "new" and nonredundant information to the researcher. Applied to the present situation, the answer to the general happiness question should not be based on the primed specific information.

In the Strack and L. Martin study, the conversational norm of being informative was activated by creating a context in which the two questions would be perceived as belonging together. It was assumed that an important feature of a natural conversation is that its components are related to one other, such that the meaning of a question can be inferred on the basis of the question that was asked before. The elements of a survey questionnaire, however, are often unrelated and the conversational norms may therefore have not always been effective. To establish this perceived relationship, the general and specific happiness questions were introduced in the following way:

> "Now, we would like to learn about two areas of life that may be important for people's overall well-being:
> > a) happiness with dating, and
> > b) happiness with life in general."

Subsequently, the two happiness questions were asked in the specific-general order. As expected, the correlation between the two measures was significantly reduced. This suggests that although the specific information was highly available when the general question was to be answered, this information was not used. In the condition where the conversational context was established, the interpretation of the general question may have been influenced by the preceding specific question, meaning something other than the activated content.

Generating an Opinion

After the respondents completed the interpretation of the question, they generated an opinion on the issue. Often, respondents may recall an opinion they have already stored in memory. Assume, for example, that respondents have previously evaluated Reagan's achievements as President. Then they may recall their judgment and use it as the basis for their answer to the question about Ronald Reagan's performance. The likelihood that a respondent has already formed an opinion on which he or she can subsequently draw may depend on several determinants. First, important issues may be more likely to elicit opinions than unimportant ones. Second, a person must form an opinion about targets that require action, like buying a new car or casting a vote. Third, having been explicitly asked before for an opinion will induce a respondent to evaluate the issue and increase the probability that this opinion is later recalled. The respondent may use this opinion whenever it is accessible, at the time of judgment (cf. Lingle & Ostrom, 1979). One implication of this is that respondents may answer a question not by reviewing the original information on which the question is based, but by retrieving the prior judgment. Thus, if this prior judgment is influenced by a particular context, subsequent judgments will be similarly affected (Carlston, 1980; Higgins & McCann, 1984; see also Bodenhausen & Wyer, this volume).

Frequently, however, respondents have not previously evaluated the issues on the dimension of the survey question. In this case, the opinion has to be generated at the time of the interview. Assume that our survey question was directed not at the President's performance but at that of the Secretary of State. Although the respondents may have accumulated information about particular activities of this target person, they may not have yet formed an opinion on the secretary's overall performance. Thus, they must first generate an opinion before they can answer the question. For the successful performance of this task, the respondents must access information from memory that is relevant for the judgment. An exhaustive search of memory, however, is not possible and the survey situation, with its limited time allotment, may truncate the search for information even more than most natural conditions. Therefore, the relative ease of recall may determine which information will be considered. The most important determinants of the accessibility of information are the frequency and the recency of their prior activation (cf. Wyer & Srull, 1981; Bodenhausen & Wyer, this volume).

Prior questions may be regarded as the most important activators of information that is relevant for answering subsequent questions. There are several types of information that may be primed by previous questions and the respondents' answers. First, another exemplar of the category in question may come to mind. For example, respondents may think about a past president when they have to evaluate the present one. Second, respondents may think about specific features of the target. For example, the President's economic policy may be in the focus of attention rather than his foreign policy. Third, respondents may be occupied with a certain normative standard, like fairness as opposed to efficiency, that would be relevant for the judgment. Fourth, respondents may remember their own behaviors, like having voted for the President or having donated money to his election campaign. Finally, respondents may be in a mood state that may influence the judgment.

Thus, a context question may activate a particular exemplar, specific features of the target, a normative standard, specific past behaviors of the respondent, or a mood state. Once activated, they may influence the judgment. However, to predict the nature of this influence, one has to understand how this information is used.

The Priming of Another Exemplar

Thinking about another exemplar, like a past president, may have the effect that the respondent bases his or her judgment on a previous evaluation of this past president or on features the two have in common. On the other hand, the respondent may become aware of how different the target is from the primed exemplar and may base the judgment in those features on which the two differ. In the first case, the primed exemplar would lead to assimilation, in the second case to contrast.

Herr, Sherman, and Fazio (1983) found that assimilation and contrast were a function of both the ambiguity of the target stimulus and the similarity of the context stimulus. More specifically, Herr et al. demonstrated in a priming study that judgments became more consistent with the primed category (assimilation) when the context stimulus was similar to the target stimulus and the target stimulus was ambiguous. Contrast effects were found when the target stimulus was not ambiguous and with the combination of a dissimilar context stimulus and an ambiguous target. Applied to the present example, one would expect that the more information a respondent has about the President, the more likely prior thinking about another President would produce a contrast effect. That is, the target President would be judged as more different. The same should occur if the respondent has little information about the target and the context President is dissimilar. On the other hand, the target President should be judged more similar to the context if little is known about the target and the context person is similar to the target.

Herr et al. (1983) obtained these effects by presenting different context information. Similarly, one might expect that the perceived similarity between a context and a target stimulus may be a function of respondents' attention toward the common vs. the distinctive features of the stimuli. An existing belief that the present President is like a particular predecessor may direct the respondent's attention toward the features the two individuals have in common. A prior belief that the present President is unlike a particular predecessor, however, may induce the respondents to focus on characteristics the two individuals do not share, that is, the distinctive features.

This reasoning suggests that it is not only the context information available at the time of the judgment that determines assimilation vs. contrast but also how this information is used. L. Martin and Wyer (1986) asked subjects to form impressions of two stimulus persons. The initial person was described such that a certain trait concept (e.g., adventurous) was unambiguously depicted. The second person, on the other hand, was described in terms that were ambiguous regarding this initial concept (e.g., adventurous/reckless). It was assumed that reading about the first person (i.e., the context) would prime a concept that could then be used to disambiguate the information about the second person (i.e., the target). Before reading about these two individuals, however, subjects were asked to define either the commonalities or the differences between various pairs of professions. It was assumed that this task would prime subjects into thinking about people's commonalities or differences, respectively.

Consistent with this hypothesis, L. Martin and Wyer found less of a difference between the impressions of the two stimulus persons when subjects had been primed to think of differences. Interestingly, these differences were obtained only on judgmental dimensions directly related to the primed concept (e.g., adventurous/reckless). They were not obtained on dimensions only evaluatively related to this concept (e.g., dislike/like, dishonest/honest). This suggests that the relational prime did not induce a general set to perceive the stimulus persons as similar or different, but rather induced a specific use of the contextually activated concept. Thus, priming appears to be composed of at least two factors: activation of a concept and activation of a strategy in the use of that concept.

Applied to surveys, these findings suggest that the overall degree of interrelatedness of the survey items may itself be a source of information in determining how individuals respond to any given item. When the items appear generally interrelated, respondents may interpret ambiguous target items in a manner that is consistent with the implications of the context items. When the items appear generally different or unrelated, however, respondents may shift their interpretation of the target away from the implications of the context items.

## The Priming of Specific Features

Context effects may also be produced by prior activation of specific features of the target. Sears and Lau (1983), for instance, found that survey respondents who had to assess their personal income were subsequently more likely to evaluate the President's overall performance on the basis of his more specific performance in the economic domain than respondents who were not given this prior task. This is because thinking about their own economic situation may have directed the respondents' attention toward the economic situation of the nation. As a result, information about this specific domain may have been salient at the time of the judgment and more likely to be used for the global rating of the President.

Similarly, Iyengar, Kinder, Peters, and Krosnick (1984) found that watching a specific television news program that emphasized a particular political domain increased the impact of the respondents' evaluation of that dimension on their overall rating of former President Carter. Watching a news program that focussed on energy problems, for instance, increased the relationship between respondents' evaluation of Carter's handling of these problems and his global evaluation. These findings further support the notion that those features of a judgmental target that are most salient and accessible at the time of judgment may have a stronger influence on a global evaluation. If the context of a survey question activates information about such features, it is likely that they will influence a subsequent judgment.

## The Priming of Normative Standards

Attitudes and evaluations are often based on more general values and normative standards. An evaluative judgment may therefore differ depending on which normative standard is used. Respondents who hold the reduction of traffic deaths as an important goal, for example, would express a more positive attitude toward the compulsory use of safety belts than respondents for whom personal freedom is a central value. Frequently, one person may simultaneously hold several normative standards that imply different evaluations of one particular target. Here, one would assume that the most accessible norm at the time of the judgment would have the greatest impact. Again, this may be influenced by the context of the particular question. It is also possible that having previously answered a related question in a certain way may elicit standards of equal treatment, fairness, or reciprocity such that these standards determine the answer to a second question.

In an often-cited study, Hyman and Sheatsley (1950) reported strong order effects of two questions that asked in 1948 whether (a) Communist newspaper reporters should be allowed to come to the U.S. and to send back their uncensored reports and (b) whether American reporters should be allowed to report freely from a Communist country like Russia. The results showed that the Communist-reporter question elicited little agreement (36.5%) and its American counterpart very strong agreement (89.8%) when each question was asked by itself (i.e., first). However, when the same question was asked after its counterpart, the agreement with the Communist-reporter question rose to 73.1% and the agreement with the American-reporter question declined to 65.6%.

This pattern demonstrates that the second question was answered differently when it was presented in isolation (i.e., first) than when it was answered in the context of the response to the first question. As Schuman and Presser (1981) suggest, the respondents may have based their response to the first question on currently prevalent anti-Communist or pro-American sentiments. The second question in the context of the respondents' answer to the first, however, may have activated a standard of reciprocity. As a consequence, the answers to the second question became more consistent with their answers to the first.

A similar effect was reported by Cantril (1944). He reported the results of a survey in which respondents were asked during World War II whether the U.S. should permit its citizens to join (a) the French and British armies, as well as (b) the German army. It was found that the agreement to the allied-army question was higher and the agreement to the enemy-army question lower when each question was asked by itself. When the question was asked in the context of the respondents' answer to the first item, the answers became more similar to prior ones.

It is important to note that these data result from a particular behavior, that is, the response to the first question. Thus, the norm of reciprocity is based on a prior reaction of the respondent. It remains to be shown that mere cognitive activation of normative standards may produce similar effects.

The Priming of Own Knowledge and Behavior

It has long been recognized in social psychology that one's own past behavior may also provide information for attitudinal inferences (cf. Bem, 1967), and that thinking about it may influence subsequent self-judgments. This relationship has been repeatedly demonstrated. Salancik and Conway (1975), for instance, had subjects rate the frequency of their own behaviors that indicate a positive attitude toward religion, like giving donations. In one condition, the questions asked if the subjects showed this particular behavior "frequently," in the other conditions "on occasion." This different wording was intended to elicit more "yes" responses in the "on occasion" condition than in the "frequently" condition. The data revealed that. Moreover, subjects in the "on occasion" conditions rated themselves subsequently more religious than subjects in the "frequently" conditions. These data suggest that the subjects used their responses to the preceding questions as behavioral information to infer their own attitudes.

Recently, it has been shown that directing respondents' attention toward their own degree of knowledge may have similar effects. Assume that respondents are requested to indicate their interest in politics after they had failed to answer several questions on political matters. If their behavior provides information for attitudinal judgments, it is likely that the respondents in such a survey would infer their interest in politics from their difficulties in answering these knowledge questions. This is exactly the result of a study by Bishop, Oldendick, and Tuchfarber (1983). These authors found that respondents who had to answer two very difficult political questions (more than 80% of the respondents admitted their ignorance) rated themselves as less interested in public affairs than respondents who were not confronted with these questions (see Bishop, this volume).

The Priming of One's Own Mood

Like respondents' knowledge and behavior, one's own mood also has informational properties that may influence judgments. In particular, judgments for which one's mood has informational value should be affected. Global assessments of one's subjective well-being, for instance, should be a prime candidate for such influences because affect is an important component of happiness and satisfaction (cf. Andrews & McKennell, 1980). This was, in fact, found in a series of studies (Schwarz & Clore, 1983; Strack, Schwarz, & Gschneidinger, 1985) that induced good or bad mood in subjects and subsequently measured their happiness with life in general. The mood induction was achieved by having subjects imagine positive or negative events of their life. As a result of this manipulation, respondents described themselves as happier and more satisfied if thinking about the event induced a positive mood. However, when thinking about this event did not elicit a mood (like abstract thinking), a contrast effect occurred on the dimension of well-being.

## Accessibility and the Use of Information

It has been argued that primed information becomes subsequently more accessible. Typically, it has been demonstrated that the activation of relevant information leads to an assimilation of subsequent judgments toward the content of the primed information (e.g., Higgins et al., 1977; Srull & Wyer, 1979). More recently, however, it was found that a primed concept may, under specific conditions, also lead to a contrast effect (L. Martin, 1986). That is, the judgment becomes more different from the activated information. The mere accessibility of information does not therefore imply its positive influence on the judgment. What are the determinants of whether and how accessible information will influence the judgment?

L. Martin (1986) has argued that the salience of the priming episode may play an important role. He noted that assimilation effects of priming were typically obtained with subtle priming procedures. When the priming episode is more explicit, however, people may try not to use the primed information to avoid a biased judgment (cf. Kubovy, 1978). L. Martin (1986) found that activation of an applicable concept actually led to contrast when that concept had been blatantly activated in a prior task and subjects had completed their performance of that prior task. He argued that the blatantness of the priming caused the respondents to associate the increased accessibility with the prior task rather than with the target stimulus. So, in an effort to make an independent, unbiased interpretation of the target, the respondents retrieved a new concept that was distinct from the earlier one, and interpreted the target in terms of this. The result was contrast.

Interestingly, when subjects were interrupted during their performance of the priming task, the interpretation of the target stimulus was not contrasted with the implications of the primed concepts. Rather, the result was assimilation. Presumably, the interruption of the priming task causes thoughts related to that task to persevere (e.g., Zeigarnik, 1927) making it more difficult for the respondents to avoid the use of that concept. As a result, they use it to interpret the subsequent information, and judgment of the target shifts toward the implications of the context.

For surveys, these findings suggest that context questions that are obviously associated with a particular content and have clear, definitive answers may be likely to produce contrast in the judgment of a subsequent target item. Questions, however, that are more subtly worded or that respondents do not complete (i.e., do not answer to their satisfaction) may be likely to produce assimilation in the judgment of a subsequent target.

Another mechanism that mediates between assimilation and contrast is the degree of difference between the primed context and the target stimulus. It has been found that the more different the two stimuli are on the dimension of judgment, the more likely are contrast effects (e.g., Herr et al., 1983). It is also possible that differences on other dimensions may have similar consequences. Temporal distance, for example, has been found to produce contrast effects (cf. Dermer, Cohen, Jacobsen, & Anderson, 1979; Strack et al., 1985). Spatial and social distance may also increase the likelihood of contrast. A close social relationship between context and target, on the other hand, may increase the likelihood that judgments and feelings are assimilated toward the context (cf. Heider, 1958).

More generally, one might speculate that if a global classification of the context stimulus is "distinct" from the target, then this provides the basis of contrasting judgments. Such a classification may be elicited by both semantic and episodic aspects of the primed information. If the content of the context information is sufficiently different from the target, then its distinctive features may become more salient. If the priming episode is more explicit, such that it becomes associated with context information, then a respondent may actively try to avoid possible influences from the context (cf. Martin, 1986).

## Formatting the Response

Most frequently, judgments in a survey have to be reported in a format that is provided by the survey researcher. That is, the respondent may not use the categories he or she would spontaneously use. Instead, the response is given within the range of the provided possibilities and, in the case of categorical response alternatives, by choosing one of the provided options.

It has already been pointed out that the provided response range may help infer the meaning of the question. Moreover, the response range may be used to infer the average response and to derive one's relative position in a frequency distribution (Schwarz, Hippler, Deutsch, & Strack, 1985). Thus, it is not surprising that responses are influenced by such inferences (for a more detailed discussion see the chapter by Schwarz & Hippler, this volume).

Anchoring effects have been frequently demonstrated with attitude scales. These effects are influenced, in part, by the response scale that is provided. Specifically, it is assumed (e.g., Ostrom & Upshaw, 1968; Wyer, 1974) that respondents align the extreme values of the provided response range with the extreme values of the stimuli that they consider in the situation. Thus, the respondents' choice of a scale value or a verbal label of intensity and evaluation may depend on the range of the response scale.

## Editing the Response

Responses to a survey question are often part of a social interaction between the interviewer and the respondent. In these situations, social norms are likely to influence the response. Such normative influences, however, should be more likely if a response has to be uttered openly vis-a-vis the interviewer. Its influence should be less likely if the response remains private. The norm of social desirability may be among the most important determinants of public responses. That is, a respondent to a survey question may be apprehensive that his or her response will result in an unfavorable evaluation by the person who observes the reaction.

Typically, negative self-reports are considered socially undesirable. Thus, the question "How are you?" rarely elicits the answer, "Bad." This is also true for survey situations. Respondents' reports of their own happiness and satisfaction are skewed toward the positive side of the response scale. More important, this tendency

toward positiveness is more pronounced in a personal interview than
in a self-administered questionnaire. In a split sample of catholic
Americans, Sudman (cited by Smith, 1979) found that 23% of the
respondents described themselves as "very happy" in a questionnaire
as opposed to 36% when they were personally interviewed. A related
result was found by LeVois, Nguyen, and Atkisson (1981) in a different setting. These authors found that clients' reports of their
satisfaction with community health services was significantly more
positive when the questions were orally administered than with written administration.

There are situations, however, in which the norm of social
desirability operates in the opposite direction. Under specific
circumstances, social desirability also inhibits respondents from
presenting themselves in too positive a fashion. This should be the
case if one anticipates that one's self-presentation may serve as a
standard of comparison for another person. Chassein, Kern, Strack,
and Schwarz (1986) demonstrated that salient information about
a person who was severely handicapped by a chronic illness influenced
the subjects' ratings of their own well-being in the opposite
direction. Subjects for whom this information was salient described
themselves as happier and more satisfied than subjects for whom this
information was not salient. Such a contrast effect would not be
expected, however, if the self-rating has to be publicly given in the
presence of the unfortunate other person. This is because the actor
anticipates that his or her much more positive self-rating would
itself serve as a standard of comparison for the handicapped individual and thus negatively affect this person's feelings of well-
being. This prediction was tested by Wagner, Strack, and Schwarz
(1984) who studied the effect of a physically handicapped interviewer
on respondents' reports of their well-being under private and public
conditions. It was found that female subjects who had to fill out a
questionnaire rated themselves as happier and more satisfied when the
interviewer was handicapped than when not. This suggests that the
disabled person did, in fact, provide a standard of comparison for
the judgment. This contrast effect disappeared, however, when the
ratings had to be given orally, as when the comparison person himself
conducted the interview.

These results suggest that normative forces of the social situation may be a determinant of a survey response. The direction of
these influences depends on the behavioral requirements of the norm
in a specific social situation.

## METHODOLOGICAL IMPLICATIONS

It was the purpose of this chapter to demonstrate how the complex task of answering a survey question can be analyzed with the help of cognitive theory and methodology. An analysis of this type makes it possible to identify the component mechanisms involved and to bring to bear the knowledge that has been accumulated. Studying the underlying cognitive processes has recently been recognized as a promising route to a better understanding of the survey situation (e.g., Jabine, Straf, Tanur, & Tourangeau, 1984). This approach, however, is tied to a methodology that differs in some respects radically from methodological tenets of traditional survey research.

The central reason for these methodological differences is that survey researchers are mainly interested in knowledge about content whereas cognitive scientists are typically interested in knowledge about processes. That is, survey researchers want to find out what the attitudes are toward a certain issue, where they differ for various sociodemographically defined groups, and to what other attitudes or values they relate. Cognitive researchers, on the other hand, want to understand how the cognitive mechanisms operate, independent of the content that is processed. For them, the validity of specific mechanisms of survey responding even depend on their independence from the particular content of the particular attitude that is being reported.

This difference, in perspective, has important methodological implications that concern those sources of variation that are in the focus of the researchers' interest, that is, the systematic variance, and those sources of variance that may blur the result (i.e., the error variance). For the survey researcher, the error variance is generated by variations of the question form, wording, context, and mode of administration. These are influences that are largely independent of content. To avoid such "response effects" (cf. Bradburn, 1983), survey researchers try to keep these features constant when they conduct cross-sectional or longitudinal comparisons between contents. Cognitive researchers, on the other hand, want to detect response effects, and therefore, they systematically vary these influences to study the resulting cognitive processes. For them, it is the variation in content that may blur the results and obscure findings that reflect properties of the underlying cognitive mechanisms. The more heterogeneous a sample is with respect to content, the more difficult it is to detect the variation produced by the systematic variation of determinants that affect the cognitive processes in the survey situation. Therefore, homogeneity of content typically helps discover those cognitive differences. This may be achieved by using a homogeneous sample.

Such a strategy, however, violates a central methodological norm of survey research, namely the representativeness of the sample, which is typically realized along sociodemographic dimensions. From a psychological perspective, however, there is no a priori reason to expect that different cognitive mechanisms depend on social class or income. Rather, these processes may be influenced by variables like the respondents' prior knowledge, the accessibility of the schemata they have formed, and so forth. The heterogeneous sample will therefore add variance from sources that are out of the cognitive researchers' focus of interest.

Failure in reducing this type of variation has the consequence that a given mechanism can only be reliably tested if the number of respondents is substantially increased, which makes methodological research more expensive than necessary as a comparison of surveys and experiments indicates. Thus, the possibility seems worth considering that controlled experiments with a smaller but more homogeneous group of participants are perhaps a more promising route to insights about response effects than large, but heterogeneous, split-ballot surveys. This is not to say that these experiments should be confined to only one sociodemographic group. Whenever there is a theoretical reason to assume that a determinant that covaries with sociodemographic indices will exert an influence on response effects, then these indices can easily be used as a classification variable in the experiment. This way, their variance can be extracted and the response effects can be studied within the more homogeneous subgroups.

From a cognitive perspective, however, it seems more fruitful to identify the psychological determinants that are directly responsible for such influences and to vary them experimentally, rather than to group respondents on the basis of other characteristics that only have a weak relationship to the theoretical variable and that are typically confounded with other psychological determinants. It therefore seems that the understanding of response effects in surveys is best fostered if their cognitive determinants are identified. This lays the groundwork for effective consequences in survey construction and creates the potential for methodological improvements of survey research.

## ACKNOWLEDGMENT

The writing of this chapter was supported by grants Str 264/1-1 and Schw 278/2-2 from the Deutsche Forschungsgemeinschaft to Fritz Strack and Norbert Schwarz and by a NIMH postdoctoral research fellowship to Leonard Martin. The authors would like to thank Axel Bühler, Thomas Ostrom, Norbert Schwarz, and Robert S. Wyer for their helpful comments on earlier drafts of this chapter.

## REFERENCES

Abelson, R.P. (1984). Contextual influences within sets of survey questions. In C.F. Turner & E. Martin (Eds.) Surveying subjective phenomena, Vol.I. New York: Russell Sage Foundation.

Anderson, R.C., & Ortony, A. (1975). On putting apples into bottles - a problem of polysemy. Cognitive Psychology, 7, 167-180.

Anderson, R.C., Pichert, J.W., Goetz, E.T., Schallert, D.L., Stevens, K.V., & Trollip, S.R. (1976). Instantiation of general terms. Journal of Verbal Learning and Verbal Behavior, 15, 667-679.

Andrews, F.M., & McKennell, A.C. (1980). Measures of self-reported well-being. Their affective, cognitive, and other components. Social Indicators Research, 8, 127-155.

Bargh, J.A., & Pietromonaco, P. (1982). Automatic information processing and social perception: The influence of trait information presented outside of conscious awareness on impression formation. Journal of Personality and Social Psychology, 43, 437-449.

Bem, D.J. (1967). Self-perception: An alternative interpretation of cognitive dissonance phenomena. Psychological Review, 74, 183-200.

Bishop, G.F., Tuchfarber, A.J., & Oldendick, R.W. (1986). Opinions on fictitious issues: The pressure to answer survey questions. Public Opinion Quarterly, 50, 240-250.

Bishop, G.F., Oldendick, R.W., & Tuchfarber, A.J. (1983). Effects of filter questions in public opinion survey. Public Opinion Quarterly, 47, 528-546.

Bradburn, N. (1983). Response effects. In P.H. Rossi, S.D. Wright, & A.B. Anderson. Handbook of survey research. New York: Academic Press, 289-327.

Bransford, J.D. (1979). Human cognition: Learning, understanding and remembering. Belmont, CA: Wadsworth.

Cantril, H. (1944). Gauging public opinion. Princeton: University Press.

Carlston, D.E. (1980). The recall and use of traits and events in social inference processes. Journal of Experimental Social Psychology, 16, 303-328.

Chassein, B., Kern, D., Strack, F., & Schwarz, N. (1986). Befindlichkeitsurteils im sozialen Kontext: Die Rolle der Augenfälligkeit von Vergleichsinformationen. Paper presented at the 28th Tagung experimentell arbeitender Psychologen. Saarbruecken.

Clark, H.H. (1985). Language use and language users. In G. Lindzey & E. Aronson (Eds.), Handbook of social psychology, Vol.II. New York: Random House.

Clark, H.H., & Haviland, S.E. (1977). Comprehension and the given-new contract. In R.O. Freedle (Ed.), Discourse production and comprehension. Norwood, NJ: Ablex.

Dermer, M., Cohen, S.J., Jacobsen, E., & Anderson, E.A. (1979). Evaluative judgments of aspects of life as a function of vicarious exposure to hedonic extremes. Journal of Personality and Social Psychology, 37, 247-260.

Emmons, R.A., & Diener, E. (1985). Factors predicting satisfaction judgments: A comparative examination. Social Indicators Research, 16, 157-167.

Grice, H.P. (1975). Logic and conversation. In P. Cole & J.L. Morgan (Eds.), Syntax and semantics 3: speech acts. New York: Academic Press.

Heider, F. (1958). *The psychology of interpersonal relation*. New York: Wiley.

Herr, P.M., Sherman, S.J., & Fazio, R.H. (1983). On the consequences of priming: Assimilation and contrast effects. *Journal of Experimental Social Psychology*, 19, 323-340.

Higgins, E.T., & King, G.A. (1981). Accessibility of social constructs: Information-processing consequences of individual and contextual variability. In N. Cantor & J.F. Kihlstrom (Eds.). *Personality, cognition, and social interaction*. Hillsdale, NJ: Erlbaum.

Higgins, E.T., & McCann, C.D. (1984). Social encoding and subsequent attitudes, impressions, and memory: "Context-driven" and motivational aspects of processing. *Journal of Personality and Social Psychology*, 47, 26-39.

Higgins, E.T., Rholes, W.S., & Jones, C.R. (1977). Category accessibility and impression formation. *Journal of Experimental Social Psychology*, 13, 131-154.

Hyman, H.H., & Sheatsley, P.B. (1950). The current status of American public opinion. In J.C. Payne (Ed.). *The teaching of contemporary affairs*. Twenty-first Yearbook of the National Council of Social Studies, 11-34.

Iyengar, S., Kinder, D.R., Peters, M.D., & Krosnick, J.A. (1984). The evening news and Presidential evaluations. *Journal of Personality and Social Psychology*, 46, 778-787.

Jabine, T.B., Straf, M.L., Tanur, J.M., & R. Tourangeau (Eds.), (1984). *Cognitive aspects of survey methodology: Building a bridge between disciplines. Report of the advanced research-seminar on cognitive aspects of survey methodology.* Washington, DC: National Academy Press.

Kubovy, M. (1978). Response availability and the apparent spontaneity of numerical choices. *Journal of Experimental Psychology: Human Perception and Performance*, 3, 359-364.

LeVois, M., Nguyen, T.D., & Atkisson, C.C. (1981). Artifact in client satisfaction assessment. Experience in community mental health settings. *Evaluation and Program Planning*, 4, 139-150.

Lingle, J.H., & Ostrom, T.M. (1979). Retrieval selectivity in memory-based impression judgments. *Journal of Personality and Social Psychology*, 37, 180-194.

Martin, E. (1984). The question-and-answer process. In C.F. Turner & E. Martin (Eds.) *Surveying subjective phenomena, Vol.I*. New York: Russell Sage Foundation.

Martin, L.L., (1986). Set/Reset: The use and disuse of concepts in impression formation. *Journal of Personality and Social Psychology*, 51, 493-504.

Martin, L.L., & Wyer, R.S. (1986). *Declarative and procedural knowledge: Priming different uses of an activated concept in impression formation.* Manuscript under review.

Ostrom, T.M., & Upshaw, H.S. (1968). Psychological perspective and attitude change. In A.G. Greenwald & T.C. Brock (Eds.) *Psychological foundations of attitudes*. New York: Academic Press.

Salancik, G.R., & Conway, M. (1975). Attitude inference from salient and relevant cognitive content about behavior. *Journal of Personality and Social Psychology*, 32, 829-840.

Schneider, W., & Shiffrin, R.M. (1977). Controlled and automatic human information processing: I. Detection, research and attention. *Psychological Review*, 84, 1-66.

Schuman, H., & Presser, S. (1981). *Questions and answers in attitude surveys*. New York: Academic Press,

Schuman, H., Presser, S., & Ludwig, J. (1981). Context effects on survey responses to questions about abortion. *Public Opinion Quarterly*, 45, 216-223.

Schwarz, N., & Clore, G.L. (1983). Mood, misattribution, and judgments of well-being: Informative and directive functions of affective states. Journal of Personality and Social Psychology, 45, 513-523.

Schwarz, N., Hippler, H.J., Deutsch, B., & Strack, F. (1985). Response scales: Effects of category range on reported behavior and comparative judgments. Public Opinion Quarterly, 49, 388-395.

Sears, D.O., & Lau, R.R. (1983). Inducing apparently self-interested political preferences. American Journal of Political Science, 27, 223-252.

Shiffrin, R.M., & Schneider, W. (1977). Controlled and automatic human information processing: II. Perceptual learning, automatic attending, and general theory. Psychological Review, 84, 127-190.

Smith, T.W. (1979). Happiness: Time trends, seasonal variations, inter-survey differences, and other mysteries. Social Psychology Quarterly, 42, 18-30.

Srull, T.K., & Wyer, R.S. (1979). The role of category accessibility in the interpretation of information about persons: Some determinants and implications. Journal of Personality and Social Psychology, 37, 1660-1672.

Srull, T.K., & Wyer, R.S. (1980). Category accessibility and social perception: Some implications for the study of person memory and interpersonal judgments. Journal of Personality and Social Psychology, 38, 841-856.

Strack, F., & Martin, L.L. (1986). Verfügbarkeit und Verwendung selbstbezogener Informationen in der Befragungssituation. Paper presented at the 35th Kongress der Deutschen Gesellschaft fuer Psychologie. Heidelberg.

Strack, F., Schwarz, N., & Gschneidinger, E. (1985). Happiness and reminiscing: The role of time perspective, affect, and mode of thinking. Journal of Personality and Social Psychology, 49, 1460-1469.

Tourangeau, R. (1984). Cognitive sciences and survey methods. In T.B. Jabine, et al. (Eds.), Cognitive aspects of survey methodology: Building a bridge between disciplines. Report of the advanced research seminar on cognitive aspects of survey methodology. Washington, D.C.: National Academy Press.

Wagner, D., Strack, F., & Schwarz, N. (1984). Das Leid des Einen ist das Glueck des Anderen: Soziale Vergleiche und Selbstdarstellung bei der Beurteilung des eigenen Wohlbefindens. Paper presented at the 26th Tagung experimentell arbeitender Psychologen. Nuernberg.

Wyer, R.S. (1974). Changes in meaning and halo-effects in personality impression formation. Journal of Personality and Social Psychology, 29, 829-835.

Wyer, R.S., & Srull, T.K. (1981). Category accessibility: Some theoretical and empirical issues concerning the processing of social stimulus information. In E.T. Higgins, C.P. Herman & M.P. Zanna (Eds.). Social cognition: Ontario Symposium, Vol.I. Hillsdale, NJ: Erlbaum.

Zeigarnik, B. (1927) Das Behalten erledigter und unerledigter Handlungen. Psychologische Forschung, 9, 1-85.

# 8 ATTITUDE MEASUREMENT: A COGNITIVE PERSPECTIVE

Roger Tourangeau
National Opinion Research
Center, Chicago

This paper concerns attitude questions, especially artifacts in the attitude measurement process. When it comes to artifacts, one man's meat is another man's poison. For most of us -- most of the time -- artifacts are nuisances that obscure the real phenomena of interest. But sometimes it is worthwhile to take another, more charitable view toward artifacts and to treat them as interesting phenomena in their own right. As McGuire (1969) has pointed out, today's artifact is tomorrow's independent variable. In a similar vein, Schuman (1982) has argued that artifacts are in the mind of the beholder. This chapter will take both tacks, viewing artifacts as substantive meat and as methodological poison.

There are four parts to the chapter. The first part simply gives an indication of the nature of the problems that can crop up in attitude surveys. It examines two examples of response effects. In the next part, I outline the major steps in the process by which attitude questions are answered. The aim here is to deepen our under-standing of how response effects can arise. It is, of course, hard to talk about process without also talking about structure. The third part of the paper outlines a view of the structure of attitudes. Having laid a theoretical foundation, I return in the final section to the examples; I attempt to show that our conceptions of the struc-ture of attitudes and the process of answering attitude questions can explain these and similar response effects.

Before turning to the examples, I should say something about how they were selected. I chose them with three criteria in mind. First, I deliberately selected examples that were reliable and systematic. Neither example can be explained away as random error. Instead, both reflect systematic factors in the attitude measurement process. Another criterion for selection was that the examples should be typical of the measurement problems that survey researchers face. One example represents item wording effects and the other, item context effects. Both types of artifacts are common in attitude surveys. My

final criterion was that the examples should be relatively familiar
ones from the methodological literature. Although my discussion of
them is necessarily quite brief, more detailed examinations are
readily available. My own comments lean quite heavily on these earlier treatments.

## RESPONSE EFFECTS: TWO EXAMPLES

In an example cited by Bradburn and Danis (1984), both NORC and
the Gallup organization asked questions about public support for the
Korean War during the early 1950s. The two questions differed
slightly. The NORC question asked: "Do you think the United States
was right or wrong in sending American troops to stop the Communist
invasion of South Korea?" The Gallup question asked: "Do you think
the United States made a mistake in deciding to defend Korea, or
not?" The NORC results consistently indicated more support for the
war than the Gallup results. Whenever two different survey organizations produce different results, it is always tempting to write off
the discrepancy as reflecting a "house effect" or some difference in
procedure. Still, this difference is typical of the shifts that can
occur as a result of apparently minor differences in question wording
-- even when the same survey  house asks both forms of the question.
For this reason our interpretation assumes that the differences in
question wording is the key variable. The two items differ in several
ways, but it seems reasonable to assume that the critical difference
is the reference to stopping the Communist invasion in the NORC item.
(Research by Schuman & Presser, 1981, indicates that in fact this is
the key difference.) It is always difficult to be against stopping
Communist invasions, particularly in the early 1950s.

Sometimes discrepancies arise even when the identical question
is used. Turner and Krauss (1978) report such a set of results,
involving public confidence in national institutions. From 1973
through 1977, both NORC and Louis Harris and Associates asked identical questions about nine institutions (such as major companies and
the Supreme Court). The NORC questions were part of its regular
General Social Survey (GSS); the Harris questions were part of the
Harris Survey series. The two time series used similar methods -- the
results for each year are based on approximately 1,500 cases,
selected in national multistage samples. Confidence in the nine
institutions was assessed by both organizations for all five years --
yielding 45 points of comparison. In 27 cases, the difference between

the results from the two organizations is 5 % or more; a discrepancy of this size would arise from sampling error only about one time in twenty. Clearly the organizations are reporting large and reliable differences. Turner and Krauss explore a number of possible explanations for the discrepancies, including seasonal effects, the demographic representativeness of the samples and differences in sampling procedures. In each case, differences in the timing or procedures of the NORC and Harris survey cannot account for the difference in the results. Nor do differences reflect a simple pattern – neither organization consistently yields results indicating lower confidence than the other.

Turner and Krauss argue that the differences reflect differences in the contexts in which the confidence questions were embedded. The questions surrounding the confidence items changed from house to house and from year to year. In one year, the Harris confidence items immediately followed six items on political alienation. In the same year, NORC placed the confidence items first in the GSS questionnaire. Not surprisingly, the Harris results for the year indicated less confidence in all nine national institutions.

Item wording and item context effects are common in surveys that measure attitudes and opinions, although nobody really knows just how common they are. One of the reasons that we cannot say how common they are is that we know so little about why they occur; we lack an understanding of mechanisms that produce response effects. The well-developed models of measurement error in the psychometric tradition do not have much to offer the survey researcher trying to reduce or to understand response effects. Part of the problem is that the classical psychometric models, valuable as they are, focus on random errors of measurement and the response effects illustrated by the two examples are clearly not random. Another part of the problem is that the classical psychometric models are applicable across a wide range of situations precisely because they make no assumptions about the process by which responses are generated. As a result, these models are more useful for measuring errors than for predicting when they are likely to occur.

## THE PROCESS OF ANSWERING ATTITUDE QUESTIONS

Although survey researchers, sociologists, and social psychologists have been measuring attitudes for more than fifty years and have used a wide variety of measurement procedures, there has been surprisingly little research on what happens when a person answers an attitude question. This is not to say that we do not know a good deal about the determinants of attitudes -- almost all research on attitudes and attitude change gives some indication of the variables that affect the attitudes a person holds. What we do not know are the details of the attitude measurement process itself.

A common tack in cognitive psychology is to analyze a complex behavior -- and surely answering an attitude question is a complex behavior -- by breaking it down into simpler components. Following this strategy, we can reformulate a difficult question (How do we answer attitude questions?) into a somewhat easier question (What are the steps or stages in answering an attitude question?). Elsewhere (Tourangeau, 1984), I have argued that there are four major stages: we must understand the question; we must call to mind the relevant facts, beliefs, or feelings; we must use what we have recalled to render a judgment; and finally, we must formulate (or select) a response. These four stages -- comprehension, retrieval, judgment, and response selection -- all present opportunities for response effects to arise.

The literature on comprehension includes numerous studies that show that context often provides a kind of interpretive framework for new material. Many of the terms that appear in recurring opinion items -- such as the confidence items in the GSS and Harris surveys -- are inherently vague. It would hardly be surprising if a term like "big government" were interpreted one way when it was embedded in a series of items about noncontroversial government programs (such as meat inspection and public health programs) and quite another way when it was part of a series of items about the federal deficit. Fee (1979) has shown that big government has at least four different connotations for different respondents. Most of the issues that appear repeatedly in opinion surveys have this same complex and multifaceted character.

Context and subtle changes in wording influence not only the comprehension stage but the other stages as well. Recently, Bower (1981) has reviewed evidence from a number of studies that suggest that our mood can affect the ease with which we recall events: When we are in a good mood, it is easier to remember happy events than sad ones. In a similar vein, a study by Johnson and Tversky and (1983) shows that reading about one disastrous event affects judgments regarding the likelihood of unrelated events -- if we read about an epidemic, for example, we tend to see other disasters as more likely to occur. Like Bower, Johnson and Tversky interpret their results in terms of the impact of mood -- the minimal context of the epidemic story apparently affects mood and mood affects later judgments.

In addition to these mood carryover effects, a number of studies (e.g., Higgins & King, 1981) indicate that the prior use of a concept can increase the likelihood that it will be used in interpreting and answering later questions. In the terms of cognitive psychology, the concept has been "primed" by its prior use. The impact of the context provided by prior items in a survey on responses to later questions may be another example of priming.

So context can have an effect on how we interpret attitude questions, what we think about as we try to answer them, and how we render judgments on attitude issues. Context and other response effects can arise at any of these stages. And, of course, the final stage, in which a response is formulated or selected is the most widely recognized source of response effects. It is during this stage that responses are tailored to present the most favorable impression, to avoid the stigma of the socially undesirable, and to meet the subtle demands of the interviewer. Context can have an impact at this stage as well -- as when we reshape our answers in order to maintain consistency with earlier responses. I will focus on the first three stages of the questions-answering process. Survey researchers are already amply aware of the artifacts that can arise during the response selection phase.

The analysis of the processes underlying survey responses sug-gests that context effects are not the products of a simple, unitary mechanism but can arise during any of the stages of the question-answering process. The same principle is likely to hold for item wording and other response artifacts as well.

## THE STRUCTURE OF ATTITUDES

It may not seem like much of an advance to say that response effects can occur during any of the four components of the question-answering process. After all, if our aim is to reduce these effects, it does not help much to know that they can arise at any of several stages. Still, understanding is often a prerequisite to control. To deepen our understanding of response effects, it is necessary to take a closer look at each stage of the process; this closer look will require some conception of the structures that the process is operat-ing on.

## Cognitive Scripts

Cognitive psychologists have begun to recognize the importance of relatively high-level conceptual structures, referred to variously as scripts (Abelson, 1981; Schank & Abelson, 1977), schemata (Rumelhart & Ortony, 1977), and frames (Minsky, 1975). These structures are organized packages of beliefs, feelings, and knowledge about classes of situations or things. Much of the work on these higher-level cognitive structures has focussed on how people think about frequently encountered situations or roles, like going to a restaurant. By the time we are adults, most of us have a detailed conception of what cognitive and social psychologists call a script.

Like many new ideas in the social sciences, this one is, in part, an old idea -- the idea of role expectations -- dressed up in new language. What is perhaps new about the script concept is the recognition that these structures play a central role in a wide range of cognitive processes. They are seen as central to the comprehension process and to the organization of memory. In a widely cited example, Bransford and Johnson (1972) have shown that it is difficult to comprehend a passage unless we can fit the individual ideas into a coherent structure or script. Here is the passage they used:

> The procedure is quite simple. First you arrange items into different groups. Of course, one pile may be sufficient depending on how much there is to do. If you have to go somewhere else due to the lack of facilities, that is the next step; otherwise, you are pretty well set ... At first the whole procedure will seem complicated. Soon, however, it will become just another facet of life...
> After the procedure is completed, one arranges the materials into different groups again. Then they can be put into their appropriate places. Eventually they will be used once more, and the whole cycle will then have to be repeated. However, that is part of life.

Most people have a hard time understanding this passage. It is like a riddle. Each sentence is clear but the meaning of the passage as a whole remains elusive because we do not see how the sentences fit together. In terms of the recent cognitive theories, we might say that the passage makes it difficult to impose any schema or script. It turns out that the passage is also very hard to remember -- unless one knows beforehand that it is about doing the laundry. Some overall structure -- a script -- is, thus, a prerequisite to detailed comprehension and accurate retrieval.

## Scripts and Attitudes

The idea that beliefs and attitudes are organized into coherent
structures has some interesting applications in attitude measurement.
First, many attitude issues are represented cognitively as scripts.
For one person, an issue like Welfare may activate a whole set of
interrelated images, stories, and feelings involving Welfare Queens,
fraudulence, and a sense of injustice. For another person, the same
issue may activate a completely different script involving people
down on their luck and feelings of obligation. For some issues,
multiple scripts about an issue are available within a society, with
some people subscribing to one script and others to different
scripts. Since the issues that appear over and over again in surveys
of public opinion are generally subjects of enduring controversies --
topics like Welfare and big government, where a number of views are
in competition -- it should not surprise us that these issues mean
different things to different people. What the cognitive theories
tell us is that these differences in interpretation are real
phenomena, reflecting real differences in opinion.

## Scripts and the Survey Process

For the script theorist, the key step in the comprehension of an
attitude question is the activation and application of the appropriate script. The same process of script activation is also
likely to have a major impact at the next stage in answering a question, the retrieval stage. Once the question has been interpreted,
the respondent must think about the issue. Clearly, it will make a
big difference if the respondent conceives of Welfare as a kind of
institutionalized rip off or as a kind of institutionalized charity.
Whichever script is uppermost is likely to have a decisive impact on
the images, beliefs, and feelings that come to mind as the respondent
mulls the question over. Cognitive psychologists emphasize that this
mulling activity, in which memory is searched for relevant items, is
not random; rather it is guided by the same high-level structures
that organize the initial comprehension and storage of information.

The cognitive researchers emphasize another point: Several
factors determine what script is uppermost on a particular occasion.
One factor is the overall "strength" of the script; the scripts we
use frequently or that are closely related to our most important
goals are more likely to be applied than other, weakly-held scripts

(see also Bodenhausen & Wyer, this volume). But the literature on affective carryover and priming suggests that a number of more tran- sient factors -- such as mood or recent use -- can influence the selection and application of a script as well.

How we think about an attitude issue is determined in large part by the script we apply. Our thoughts provide the raw material for the next stage in the question-answering process, the judgment stage. Almost all attitude and opinion items require some form of judgment: Are we pro or con? In favor or opposed? Do we agree or disagree? Often the judgment to be made must be rendered on some quantitative scale; we must decide not only _whether_ we are positive or negative but _how_ positive or negative we are. Different types of questions require different kinds of judgments. One of the basic distinctions among opinion items is between questions assessing belief and ques- tions assessing favorability. For example, an item about Welfare might be couched as a statement that Welfare reduces the incentive to work; respondents are then supposed to say whether (or how much) they agree with the statement. A different kind of item might ask whether the amount of money spent on Welfare programs should be increased or decreased.

According to a recent study by Wyer and Hartwick (1984), the judgment process may be very different for the two kinds of items. In deciding whether we agree with a statement, we tend to focus on antecedent events that would make the statement more or less likely to be true. In deciding whether we support a proposed course of action, we focus on the likely consequences of the course of action - - we ask ourselves what would be likely to happen if Welfare spending were increased. Whether the question forces us to search for antece- dents or consequents, the search will be guided by the script that organizes our thoughts on the topic.

Sometimes the question and the underlying script it evokes will fit each other nicely. The person who views Welfare programs as a rip off, for example, will not require much time to think in order to say that he or she opposes increased Welfare spending. The contents of the script and the form of the question can interact to make the judgment stage quick and simple or slow and complicated.

## Scripts and Affect

Scripts and other cognitive structures thus guide comprehension, organize the search for relevant beliefs and feelings, and, along with the form of the question, shape the process of rendering a judgment. There are two additional points to make about the relationship between scripts and attitudes. The first is that scripts not only organize our beliefs about an issue -- they organize our feelings as well. The emotional component of scripts is particularly clear with issues that are the focus of "symbolic attitudes" (Kinder & Sears, 1981). These attitudes are distinguished by their marked affective tone and by their relative imperviousness to practical considerations. Kinder and Sears have argued that attitudes about school busing are less a reflection of such objective factors as whether the respondent's children are likely to be bused than of deep seated feelings about black people. Similarly, we cannot expect people who see abortions as murder to respond to persuasive appeals based on the costs to society of unwanted children -- whatever the costs, abortion is, for these respondents, still murder. When attitudes are tied so closely to deeply felt values, it is hard for us to respond to attitude and opinion items dispassionately. Our scripts for the issue link our beliefs and our feelings into a single inseparable package.

## Multiple Scripts

The second point to be made about scripts is that, to a greater or lesser degree the scripts competing for the allegiance of society also tend to compete within each person. Except for the most extreme partisans, most of us subscribe with varying strengths to more than one script for controversial issues. We are capable of seeing Welfare both in terms of the obligations of the prosperous toward the impoverished and in terms of the opportunities for fraud. Both scripts are available to us, even if one script predominates most of the time. When the circumstances are right, the secondary script may become our primary response.

There are, I think, two basic principles that determine which of several competing scripts is activated by an issue. The first principle is the principle of relative strength. Most cognitive theorists assume that the use of a cognitive structure on one occasion tends to lower the threshold for its activation on the next occasion. For extremists on any issue, the strength of one script will greatly exceed those of its rivals; the issue tends to be seen in the same terms regardless of the occasion. For the rest of us, a second principle comes into play, the principle of availability. The ease with which a cognitive structure is activated is affected in the short run by situational factors, such as mood or the recent activation of material that is closely related to the script. In the language of cognitive psychology, we say that a script can be "primed." Most of us are aware, perhaps subliminally, of this priming effect. Politicians tailor their discussions of issues in order to encourage their listeners to apply one script -- the one that is most favorable to their position -- over others. President Reagan's discussions of El Salvador are peppered with references to Cuban-backed insurgents, the threat of Communism, and the plight of democracy, which serve to invoke a script about Communist takeovers of democratic countries. Context, phasing, and mood all have a role to play in determining how an issue strikes us, what script it triggers.

## Summary

The main contours of the argument are, I hope, clear by now. When we answer an attitude item, we take several steps. We interpret the question by activating the relevant script. We think about the issue by retrieving from memory the beliefs and feelings organized by the script. We render a judgment and select our response using as raw materials the contents of the script brought to mind during the retrieval phase. The form of the question and the form of the scripted material interact to make the judgment hard or easy. When the form of the question fits the contents of the script, we can simply "read off" our answer. The contents of the script include not only beliefs but feelings and emotions as well. Several scripts may be available for a particular issue embodying alternative views that compete within society and within individual respondents. Which script is invoked on any occasion depends on the relative strength and situational availability of the alternative scripts.

## REEXAMINING THE EXAMPLES

I began my chapter with two illustrative response effects. It is time now to see whether the theoretical notions I have sketched out can help to explain response effects observed in practice. One of the examples involved two items about the Korean War. The NORC item ("Do you think the United States was right or wrong in sending American troops to stop the Communist invasion of South Korea?"), with its reference to stopping the Communist invasion, produced higher levels

of support for the war than the Gallup items, which had no comparable
reference. The view I have sketched suggests that the two items may
have invoked an anti-Communism script to differing degrees. The NORC
item invites respondents to view the issue in terms of a Communist
takeover of a legitimate government -- a powerful script both then
and now. Of course, the Gallup item does not prevent respondents
from seeing the issue in terms of the same script but it simply does
not encourage it to quite the same degree. It is difficult from our
vantage point to say what rival scripts the items may have invoked. I
suspect the main competitor to the anti-Communism script may have
been an isolationism script that emphasized the cost of American
involvement in foreign wars. This view was embodied in the slogan
that we should not get bogged down in an Asian land war, a notion
revived during the Vietnam War. But whatever the alternatives to the
anti-Communism script, the Korean War was controversial and the
controversy took place within individuals as well as in the society
at large. The NORC wording apparently tipped the balance for
respondents; it made the anti-Communism script temporarily more
available than its rivals.

The second example involved two parallel times series dealing
with confidence in nine national institutions. Here the critical
variable appeared to be item context rather than item wording. In one
year, the Harris confidence items immediately followed six questions
on political alienation; the Harris results indicated lower confidence in all nine institutions than the corresponding NORC results
for the same year. As with the previous example, this one may illustrate the operation of the principle of availability. Just as the
reference to a Communist invasion in the NORC item may have increased
the availability of an anti-Communist script, the Harris political
alienation items have temporarily raised the availability of a
political cynicism script. (The time period for this example included
both the Watergate scandal and the collapse of the South Vietnamese
government.) Thus, the political alienation items may have encouraged
a cynical mind-set in some respondents. Once this script was invoked,
it may have carried over to the confidence items. We should not
ignore the possibility that it was not so much the content of the
alienation items as their affective tone that carried over into the
confidence items. Scripts encompass both feelings and beliefs; if the
context invoked either portion of the script's contents it increases
the chances that the script will be invoked in its entirety.

Affective carryover effects are potentially a very general phenomenon.

Both examples reflect the effects of variables -- such as item wording and item context -- that affect the short-term availability to attitudinal scripts. What makes them measurement artifacts from the point of view of most survey researchers is that attitude items are not supposed to measure availability; instead, they are intended to measure more stable properties of attitudes, such as their strength. From another point of view, they represent an important characteristic of some respondents -- the fact that some respondents do not have a single viewpoint on an issue. These respondents have two or more scripts for the issue and they vacillate between them. Their reported attitude on any occasion reflects the relative strength and relative availability of rival scripts; their responses are based on the temporary winner of an ongoing competition. For these vacillating respondents it may make more sense to refer to their attitudes as "non-attitudes" (Converse, 1964, 1975) because their responses lack the stability presupposed in most of the classi- cal definitions of attitude.

Both examples illustrate a second theoretical point. It can be difficult to disentangle interpretation from judgments in attitude questions. Abstract items, like "big government" and "Welfare," can receive different interpretations from different respondents and they evoke different judgments. The theoretical point is that part of what it means to have an attitude is to have a propensity to interpret an issue in a particular light. When an issue invokes different scripts in different respondents, the respondents differ not only in their judgments of the object but also in the objects of their judgment. Although the use of inherently vague terms may promote response effects, the ambiguity may be necessary if an item is to tap the full range of views on a controversial issue.

My main theme has been that response effects are theoretically interesting phenomena in their own right, reflecting important properties of the processes and structures underlying responses to attitude items. In one sense, this analysis does not offer much consolation to survey researchers. It suggests how difficult it is to reduce or eliminate response effects, since they are rooted in the underlying attitudes (or non-attitudes) themselves. It will be hard to throw out this bath water without also throwing out the baby too. But, in other senses, our analysis holds out hope on a number of points. It suggests that response effects may be limited to some issues and some respondents. It reemphasizes the usefulness of random probe techniques to determine how respondents interpret a given item. And it suggests that we should develop methods to identify respondents whose attitudes are likely to vacillate because they hold several scripts weakly rather than one script strongly. Our analysis opens the way for new lines of substantive investigation and for new lines of methodological work as well.

To give the flavor of these new lines of research, let me close by describing very briefly some of my own work, currently in progress. One implication of our analysis is that response effects should be more prevalent for some issues than for others. For relatively vague and abstract issues (such as big government or Welfare), quite a large number of scripts are likely to be seen as relevant; for more concrete issues (such as abortion), only a few scripts are likely to be seen as relevant. This suggests that response effects will be more common for questions concerning abstract issues than for concrete ones; in addition, it suggests that multi-item scales addressing specific aspects of multi-faceted issues may produce less artifactual data than single items couched in abstract terms. Our goal is to delimit the kinds of issues and items that are susceptible to response effects. On a more substantive level, we are attempting to develop methods for identifying the scripts underlying attitudes on several issues. We have experimented with a variety of techniques including unstructured interviews with small numbers of respondents, open-ended follow-up probes to standard attitude items, and ratings of the similarity of different attitude statements. Our results have been encouraging. Millions of dollars are spent each year to ascertain the public's opinions. Our research on cognitive scripts may give a clearer picture of what these opinions are about.

# REFERENCES

Abelson, R. (1981). The psychological status of the script concept. American Psychologist, 36, 715-729.

Bower, G. (1981). Mood and memory. American Psychologist, 36, 129-148.

Bradburn, N., & Danis, C. (1984). Potential contributions of cognitive research to survey questionnaire design. In T. Jabine, M. Straf, J. Tanur, & R. Tourangeau (Eds.), Cognitive aspects of survey methodology: Building a bridge between disciplines. Washington DC: National Academy Press.

Bransford, J., & Johnson, M. (1972). Contextual prerequisits for understanding: Some investigations of comprehension and recall. Journal of Verbal Learning and Verbal Behavior, 11, 717-726.

Converse, P. (1964). The nature of belief systems in mass publics. In D. Apter (Ed.), Ideology and discontent. New York: Free Press.

Converse, P. (1975). Public opinion and voting behavior. In F. Greenstein & N. Polsby (Eds.), Handbook of political science (Vol. 4). Reading, MA: Addison-Wesley.

Fee, J. (1979). Symbols and attitudes: How people think about politics. Unpublished doctoral dissertation: University of Chicago.

Higgins, E.T., & King, G. (1981). Accessibility of social constructs: Information-processing consequences of individual and contextual variability. In N. Cantor & J. Kihlstrom (Eds.), Personality, cognition, and social interaction. Hillsdale, NJ: Lawrence Erlbaum.

Johnson, E.J., & Tversky, A. (1983). Affect, generalization, and the perception of risk. Journal of Personality and Social Psychology, 45, 20-31.

Kinder, D., & Sears, D. (1981). Prejudice and politics: Symbolic racism versus racial treats to "the good life." Journal of Personality and Social Psychology, 40, 414-431.

McGuire, W. (1969). Suspiciousness of experimenter's intent. In R. Rosenthal, & R. Rosnow (Eds.), Artifact in behavioral research. New York: Academic Press.

Minsky, M. (1975). A framework for representing knowledge. In P. Winston (Ed.), The psychology of computer vision. New York: McGraw-Hill.

Rumelhart, D., & Ortony, A. (1977). The representation of knowledge in memory. In R. Spiro, & W. Montague (Eds.), Schooling and the acquisition of knowledge. Hillsdale, NJ: Lawrence Erlbaum.

Schank, R., & Abelson, R. (1977). Scripts, plans, goals, and understanding. Hillsdale, NJ: Lawrence Erlbaum.

Schuman, H. (1982). Artifacts are in the mind of the beholder. The American Sociologist, 17, 21-28.

Schuman, H., & Presser, S. (1981). Questions and answers in attitude surveys: Experiments on question form, wording and context. New York: Academic Press.

Tourangeau, R. (1984). Cognitive science and survey methods. In T. B. Jabine, M.L. Straf, J.M. Tanur, & R. Torangeau (Eds.), Cognitive aspects of survey methodology: Building a bridge between disciplines. Washington DC: National Academy Press.

Turner, C., & Krauss, E. (1978). Fallible indicators of the subjective state the nation. American Psychologist, 33, 456-470.

Wyer, R., & Hartwick, J. (1984). The recall and use of belief statements as bases for judgments: Some determinants and implications. Journal of Experimental Social Psychology, 20, 65-85.

# 9 WHAT RESPONSE SCALES MAY TELL YOUR RESPONDENTS: INFORMATIVE FUNCTIONS OF RESPONSE ALTERNATIVES

Norbert Schwarz
University of Heidelberg


Hans-J. Hippler
Center for Surveys, Methods
and Analysis, Mannheim

One of the most extensively discussed (though not most exten-sively researched, see Converse, 1984) issues in the literature on survey methodology is the choice between an open - or a closed - response format. Researchers are usually advised to use open-ended questions sparingly because they are time consuming, expensive, and difficult to analyze (e.g., Sheatsley, 1985; Sudman & Bradburn, 1983). In fact, "despite a few exceptions, the results of social surveys today are based mainly on what are varyingly called closed, fixed-choice, or precoded questions" (Schuman & Presser, 1981, p. 79). According to textbook recommendations, the construction of precoded questions should be based on the responses to open-ended questions obtained during pilot studies.

However, "such sensible-sounding advice is perhaps more often preached than practiced -- and even where practiced is usually com-promised by the small, unrepresentative, und hurried nature of much pretesting" (Schuman & Presser, 1981, p. 80). As a result, the con-struction of response alternatives is in fact left to the researchers assumptions and intuitions about the phenomena under investigation.

As methodological research testifies, survey researchers are well aware of some of the problems associated with this state of affairs. Specifically, split-ballot experiments demonstrated that open-and closed-answer formats may result in different distributions. Moreover, the results obtained in a closed-answer format may depend on the number of response alternatives provided, the inclusion of a middle alternative, and the order in which the alternatives are presented (see Payne, 1951; Schuman & Presser, 1981, and Sudman &

Bradburn, 1974 for reviews). Most of this research, however, concentrated on biases in response to the particular open- or closed-ended questions under study and did not explore whether the specific set of response alternatives presented may affect responses to subsequent related questions. Moreover, this research did not provide a theoretical rationale for conceptualizing the cognitive processes underlying the obtained effects.

In the present chapter, we will raise some of the neglected issues with regard to a specific type of precoded question: questions designed to assess quasi-objective data such as frequency of church attendance, hours of television watched, and the like. Specifically, we will explore the impact of the range of response categories on respondents' identification of the target behavior, the behavioral reports, and subsequent related judgments. For the time being we will set aside the more complicated issues involved in precoding attitude and knowledge questions, and will concentrate on the simpler issue of assessing quasi-objective data (but see Strack & Martin, this volume).

Central to the present information processing perspective is the assumption that response scales are not simply passive "measurement devices" that respondents use to report their behaviors. Rather, response scales may also serve as a source of information for the respondent. Specifically, respondents may consider the range of behaviors described in the response alternatives to reflect the researcher's knowledge of or expectations about the distribution of these behaviors in the "real world". If so, respondents may use the range of behaviors described in the response alternatives as a frame of reference in estimating and evaluating their own behavior. Thus, the range of the response alternatives may affect behavioral reports as well as respondents' assumptions about the behavior of others, and judgments to which such assumptions are relevant. Moreover, the range of response alternatives may influence the respondents' understanding of what the question refers to. Let us now consider each of these possibilities, and the evidence bearing on them, in more detail.

## BEHAVIORAL REPORTS AND COMPARATIVE JUDGMENTS

### Behavioral Reports

When respondents are asked to report how frequently they engage in certain behaviors they may use one of two strategies to arrive at an answer. If the question refers to discrete behaviors that occur with a low frequency, such as buying a new car or beginning a new job, for example, they may try to recall all instances of that behavior. In that case, the accuracy of their reports will depend on the accuracy of their memories, raising the problems discussed by Strube in the present volume. For more frequent and mundane behaviors, however, such as buying coffee, smoking cigarettes, or watching TV, respondents have no choice but to provide an _estimate_ of their behavioral frequencies, using whatever information is available at the time of judgment. In computing this estimate they may use the range of the response alternatives as a frame of reference.

Figure 1: Response Scales

LOW CATEGORY RANGE                     HIGH CATEGORY RANGE


up to 1/2 hour                         up to 2 1/2 hours
1/2 to 1 hour                          2 1/2 to 3 hours
1 to 1 1/2 hours                       3 to 3 1/2 hours
1 1/2 to 2 hours                       3 1/2 to 4 hours
2 to 2 1/2 hours                       4 to 4 1/2 hours
more than 2 1/2 hours                  more than 4 1/2 hours


Suppose respondents are asked to estimate the amount of television they watch daily along a scale that ranges, in half-hour steps, either (a) from "up to 1/2 hour" to "more than 2 1/2 hours" or (b) from "up to 2 1/2 hours" to "more than 4 1/2 hours," as presented in Figure 1. It seems plausible that respondents may assume that the range of values specified in the scale reflects the researcher's knowledge of, or expectations about the typical use of television. If this assumption is made, the scale may affect respondents' estimates in various ways. On the one hand, respondents may not even try to recall how much TV they watch but may rather use their biographical knowledge to locate themselves in the distribution suggested by the scale. Thus, a person who considers him or herself an "average viewer" may endorse a response alternative in the middle part of the scale without spending too much effort on reviewing his or her actual TV consumption. On the other hand, respondents may compute an estimate based on some review of their behavior but may then be influenced by the scale when they try to report their estimate by checking the proper alternative. In particular, they may be reluctant to report behaviors that seem unusual in the context of the response scale -- for example behaviors that constitute the extreme categories and/or are lumped into undifferentiated "other" categories. In both cases, it seems likely that respondents report less television watching along the scale ranging from "up to 1/2 hour" to "more than 2 1/2 hours" than along the scale ranging from "up to 2 1/2 hours" to "more than 4 1/2 hours." Thus, respondents' behavioral reports should be a function, in part, of the frequencies reflected in the response categories.

The first split-ballot experiment to test this hypothesis was carried out in March/April 1983 as part of a larger survey with a quota sample of 132 German adults (see Schwarz, Hippler, Deutsch, & Strack, 1985, Experiment 1, for details). Respondents were asked to report how many hours a day they spend watching TV. They had to provide their reports either on the low - or on the high-frequency range scales presented in Figure 1. While previous research indicated that the average daily TV consumption in the Federal Republic of Germany is slightly more than 2 hours (Darschin & Frank, 1982), we may expect respondents' reports to be influenced by the range of the scale. Specifically, it was hypothesized that respondents, presented the high-category range beginning with "up to 2 1/2 hours," would report a higher TV consumption than respondents presented the low-category range beginning with "up to 1/2 hour."

Respondents' reports on these scales were coded to reflect an estimate of either (a) 2 1/2 hours or less, or (b) more than 2 1/2 hours. As expected, the range of the response scales affected the obtained reports. Specifically, only 16.2 % of the respondents who were presented the low category range reported watching TV for more than 2 1/2 hours while 37.5 % of the respondents presented with the high category range did so, chi square(1)=7.7, $p < .005$. Thus, the range of the response alternatives provided to the respondents affected their frequency estimates -- a finding that has meanwhile been replicated over a wide range of different issues, including less mundane behaviors such as frequency of sexual intercourse (Schwarz & Scheuring, 1985).

Comparative Judgments

    In addition to serving as a frame of reference for estimating
the frequency of one's own behavior, the range of the response alternatives may also be used to infer which behavior is "usual." It seems
plausible that respondents may assume that the behavior of the
"average" person is represented by the values stated in the middle
range of the response scale, at least as long as these values do not
appear obscure in the context of the respondents' naive theories.

    In line with this assumption, respondents of the television
study just described estimated the average TV consumption of German
citizens to be higher  when they reported their own behavior on the
high rather than the low frequency range scale ($\underline{M}$'s = 3.2 hr vs. 2.7
hr, assessed in an open-ended format, $\underline{F}(1,127)$ = 8.8, $\underline{p}<.004$). Thus,
respondents' inferences about presumably "usual" behavior were in-
fluenced by the specific values stated in the response scales.

    This being the case, the range of response alternatives may also
be  expected to affect a wide range of subsequent judgments. Most
importantly, checking one from an ordered set of response alternatives may be considered as determining one's own location in a
distribution. For example, respondents given the scale ranging from
1/2 hour to 2 1/2 hours may assume that most people watch little TV.
They may therefore perceive themselves to watch more TV than is
"typical." For this reason, they may consequently judge TV to be more
important in their own life than respondents who were given the high-
frequency range scale, which suggested to them that most people watch
a lot of TV. Thus, respondents may use the information about the
presumably "typical" behavior extracted from the range of the
response categories (however incorrectly) as a standard of comparison
in making subsequent judgments to which comparison information is
relevant (cf. Suls & Miller, 1977). If so, the range of the response
alternatives may not only determine the responses given to that
particular question, but may influence subsequent answers as well.

    To test these considerations, respondents in the TV study were
asked to evaluate how important a role TV plays in their own life
along a scale from 0 (not at all important) to 10 (very important).
As predicted, respondents reported a higher importance of TV in their
own life when the low-frequency range scale suggested a low TV consumption to be typical ($\underline{M}$ = 4.6) than when the high-frequency range

suggested that most people watch a lot of TV ($\underline{M}$ = 3.8), $\underline{F}$(1,127) = 7.92, $\underline{p}$<.006. Note that this was true even though the former respondents reported watching $\underline{less}$ TV than the latter.

In a later study (Schwarz et al., 1985, Experiment 2) we found that the range of the response scale used to report one's own TV consumption affected respondents' subsequent evaluation of their leisure time even under conditions where the crucial response scale and the leisure time question were separated by several buffer items. In this study, respondents reported higher satisfaction with the variety of things they do in their leisure time when they had previously reported their own TV consumption on the high-frequency range scale, which suggested to them that they watch less TV than average, than when they had given their report on the low-frequency range scale. Thus, it seems that the impact of the range of the response categories on subsequent comparative judgments is rather robust.

## Assessing One vs. Two Behaviors

So far we have considered the effects of assessing $\underline{one}$ behavior on behavioral reports and comparative judgments. Under this condition, respondents are likely to use the range of the response alternatives as a convenient frame of reference in making $\underline{social}$ comparisons, that is, comparisons of their own behavior with the assumed behavior of others.

Frequently, however, researchers may assess not only one behavior but instead a set of several related behaviors using either the same or different response scales. If several behaviors are assessed, two potentially conflicting standards of comparison may become salient. On the one hand, respondents may use the information provided by the scale as a basis for comparing their own behavior with the assumed behavior of others. We will refer to this as the use of a $\underline{social}$ comparison standard. On the other hand, they may compare the frequency with which they themselves engage in the various related behaviors with one another. We will refer to this possibility as the use of an $\underline{intraindividual}$ comparison standard.

Under some conditions, social comparisons and intraindividual comparisons may result in different judgments. We suggest that respondents will engage in social comparisons if only $\underline{one}$ behavior is assessed, but will prefer intraindividual comparisons if $\underline{several}$ $\underline{related}$ behaviors are assessed. The basis for this hypothesis is the

well-documented finding from research on the use of base-rate information that individuals prefer concrete information over abstract
information bearing on the distribution of a behavior (cf. Nisbett,
Borgida, Crandall, & Reed, 1976).

This hypothesis was tested in two surveys of male college students, in Germany, using self-administered questionnaires (Schwarz &
Scheuring, 1985). In the first study, only one behavior was assessed,
namely respondents' frequency of masturbation or their frequency of
sexual intercourse. Respondents reported their behavior either on the
high- or on the low-frequency range scale shown in Figure 2.
Respondents' satisfaction with their current sexual relationships was
assessed as the major dependent variable along a rating scale ranging
from 1 (not at all satisfied) to 11 (very satisfied).

Figure 2: Response Range

LOW FREQUENCIES                          HIGH FREQUENCIES


less than once a year                    several times a day
about once every six month               about once every day
about once every three months            two or three times a week
more frequently                          less frequently


The results replicated our previous findings. Respondents
reported lower satisfaction with their current relationship when the
low-frequency response scale suggested to them that they masturbate
more frequently than "average" ($M = 7.3$) than when the high-frequency
scale suggested that they masturbate less frequently than average ($M = 9.8$), $F(1,43) = 5.31$, $p < .03$. The frequency range of the intercourse
question, on the other hand, did not affect respondents' judgments.
This asymmetry in the results is probably due to the fact that,
according to implicit theories of sexuality, the satisfaction derived
from intercourse is not a function of its sheer frequency. A high
frequency of masturbation, on the other hand, suggests that something
is "missing" in the relationship, reflecting the compensatory nature
of masturbation that is prevalent in naive theories of sexual behavior (Simon, 1973). In summary, respondents, who reported their
frequency of masturbation, engaged in social comparisons to evaluate

their satisfaction with their relationship when only <u>one</u> behavior was assessed.

In a subsequent study, male German college students were asked to report <u>both</u> their frequency of masturbation and their frequency of sexual intercourse using either high- or low-frequency response scales. Following a 2x2 factorial design, some respondents reported both behaviors on either low- or high-frequency response scales, while others reported one behavior on a low-frequency and the other behavior on a high-frequency scale.

Let us consider the different predictions generated by the social and intraindividual comparison hypotheses. If respondents engage in social comparisons, as was the case when only one behavior was assessed, the results should mirror our previous findings. That is, respondents should report lower satisfaction when the low- frequency response scale suggests to them that they masturbate more frequently than average. The frequency range of the intercourse question, on the other hand, should show no effect. A totally different picture should emerge when respondents engage in <u>intraindividual</u> comparisons, that is, when they compare their <u>own</u> reported frequency of masturbation with their own reported frequency of intercourse. In this case, they should report the highest satisfaction when the high-frequency intercourse scale induces them to estimate a high frequency of intercourse while the low-frequency masturbation scale leads them to estimate a low frequency of masturbation. When these conditions are reversed -- low-frequency intercourse scale and high-frequency masturbation scale -- they should report the lowest satisfaction. The remaining conditions should result in similar frequency estimates for intercourse and masturbation, and should therefore also result in judgments of intermediate satisfaction.

Respondents' ratings of their satisfaction with their current relationship as well as their ratings of their interest in sexual contacts with other partners (along 11-point bipolar scales) clearly support this prediction. Specifically, respondents reported the highest satisfaction with their current relationship ($\underline{M}$ - 8.9), and the lowest interest in sexual contacts with other partners ($\underline{M}$ - 4.8), when the combination of the high-frequency intercourse and low-frequency masturbation scales suggested to them that they masturbate <u>less</u> frequently than they have intercourse. Respondents who reported their behavior on the reversed combination of scales, suggesting to them that they masturbate <u>more</u> often than they have intercourse, on the other hand, reported the lowest relationship satisfaction ($M =$ 7.3) and the highest interest in sexual contacts with other partners ($M = 7.1$), $t$'s (58) = 2.17 and 2.08, $p < .05$, respectively, for the differences between both groups. The remaining conditions, which suggested similar frequencies of masturbation and intercourse, fell between these extremes.

In summary, then, these findings suggest that respondents use the range of the response scale to infer a social standard of comparison if only one behavior is assessed. Under these conditions, the information provided by the scale is the most salient standard available. However, if several related behaviors are assessed, respondents are more likely to compare the frequency with which they engage in each of these behaviors intraindividually. To the extent that the frequency range of the response scales affects respondents' frequency estimates of their behavior, these intraindividual comparisons will, in part, be a function of the frequency range of the response alternatives.

In addition, these results demonstrate that the impact of precoded response alternatives is not limited to behavioral reports and judgments that may seem unimportant to respondents, thus being little involving, such as watching TV, or assessing the importance TV has in one's life. Rather, the range of the response scales may also affect reports about more involving behaviors as well as judgments that are central to an individual's subjective well-being.

What, then, are the limits? On theoretical grounds one can assume that the impact of the response alternatives is limited to behaviors about which the respondents have little other information. Therefore, the respondents' assumptions about "private" behaviors such as sexual activities or watching TV are most likely to be affected. Given the lack of information about other people's behavior in these areas, respondents are likely to use whatever information is available to them at the time of judgment. The impact of the response alternatives should be much weaker, however, when respondents have reliable comparison information from other sources, for example when the behavior under investigation is highly visible.

And How About the Researcher?

So far, we have seen, that the range of the response alternatives is likely to affect respondents' comparative judgments. The use of the response scale as a frame of reference in making comparative

judgments is not limited to the respondent, however. Rather, potential users of the respondent's report are also likely to be affected
by the response scale in their interpretation of the reported
behavior. In a first exploration of this possibility (Deutsch &
Schwarz, unpublished), we found that advanced students of medicine
were more likely to assume that having a given physical symptom once
a week requires medical attention when this frequency was reported on
a low- rather than a high-frequency range scale. Thus, the same
frequency report was evaluated differently depending on the context
provided by the response scale.

Similarly, the users of survey data may be influenced by the
range of the response categories presented in a summary table. This
possibility deserves further investigation.

## UNDERSTANDING THE QUESTION

In addition to affecting respondents' behavioral reports and
comparative judgments, the range of the response alternatives may
also determine how respondents define the target behavior that is to
be reported (see also Strack & Martin, this volume).

Let us assume that respondents are asked to indicate how frequently they were "really irritated" recently. Before the respondent
can give an answer, he or she must decide what the researcher means
by "really irritated." Does this refer to major irritations such as
fights with one's spouse or does it refer to minor irritations such
as having to wait for service in a restaurant? If the respondent has
no opportunity to ask the interviewer for clarification, he or she
might pick up some pertinent information from the questionnaire. One
such piece of information may be the frequency range provided by the
scale. For example, respondents who are asked to report how often
they are irritated on a scale ranging from "several times daily" to
"less than once a week" may consider instances of less severe irrita-
tion to be the target of the question than respondents who are
presented a scale ranging form "several times a year" to "less than
once every three months." If so, the type of annoying experiences
that respondents are likely to report would be determined by the
frequency range of the response alternatives in combination with
respondents' general knowledge rather than by the wording of the
question per se. In the present example, the general knowledge that
respondents might bring to bear is the assumption that extreme experiences are less frequent than less extreme ones. Obviously,

respondents' definition of the target behavior would also determine their responses to subsequent related questions.

This possibility was explored in a study that is only partially reported in the present chapter (for a full report see Schwarz, Strack, Müller, & Deutsch, 1985). Fourty-three respondents reported, in a self-administered questionnaire, how frequently they felt "really annoyed" using either an open-answer format or one of two sets of precoded response alternatives. The first set ranged from "several times a day" to "less than twice a week," and the second set from "more than once every three months" to "less than once a year." While the second set provides considerably lower frequencies than pretest subjects reported in an open-answer format, the first set is roughly equivalent to these reports.

Following their behavioral reports the respondents were asked, on the next page of the questionnaire, to describe a typical example of the annoying situations they experienced. If the respondents use the range of the response alternatives to determine what the researcher might mean by "annoying," they should report more extreme experiences when they were previously presented the low- rather than the high-frequency range scale. Moreover, because more extreme experiences occur less frequently and are likely to receive more attention, one might also expect that they are represented in memory in more detail. For this reason, the descriptions provided by respondents who were presented the low-frequency range scale may also be more concrete than the descriptions provided by the other respondents.

To test these hypotheses, two independent judges, who were blind to conditions, rated the degree of annoyance of respondents' examples (11 = extremely annoying) and the concreteness of their descriptions (11 = very concrete). Interrater agreement was high, $r$ = .87 for ratings of annoyance, and $r$ = .92 for ratings of concreteness.

The results confirmed both predictions. Specifically, respondents who had reported the frequency with which they feel really annoyed on the low-frequency scale, suggesting to them that the question concerns rare events, described more extreme annoyances ($M$ = 4.4) than respondents who were presented the high-frequency response alternatives ($M$ = 3.5), $t(40)$ = 2.01, $p<.05$. In addition, the descriptions provided by the former respondents, who reported more extreme events, were also more concrete than the descriptions provided by the latter respondents, $M$'s = 2.7 vs. 4.1, $t(40)$ = 2.68, $p<.02$.

Not surprisingly, comparisons of the open-answer format condition with both precoded conditions indicated that the examples
provided by control group respondents did not differ from the examples provided by respondents who were presented with the high-
frequency range scale. As noted previously, the high-frequency range
scale was designed to match the behavioral frequencies reported in an
open-answer format. The control group's examples ($M = 3.5$ for an-
noyingness and 3.3 for concreteness) did differ as predicted,
however, from the examples reported in the low-frequency range
condition. Thus, using a precoded response scale rather than an open-
answer format affected respondents' examples only when the range of
the response alternatives deviated from the range of respondents'
spontaneous behavioral reports.

In summary, the results of the present study demonstrate that
the range of the response alternatives helps respondents to determine
the specific referent of the question. Thus, the same question combined with different response alternatives assesses <u>different</u> behaviors because the target behavior is not determined by the wording
of the question per se but by the question and the frequency of the
response alternatives in combination.

## THE INFORMATIVE FUNCTIONS OF RESPONSE SCALES:
### IMPLICATIONS FOR QUESTIONNAIRE CONSTRUCTION

The findings reviewed in the present chapter demonstrate that
response alternatives may serve a variety of informative functions
for the respondent.

First, respondents may use the response alternatives to determine the meaning of the question. While survey researchers have been
aware of this possibility with regard to some questions -- for example, questions about household income where the response alternatives may help to define what to consider as "income" (cf. Sudman &
Bradburn, 1983) -- this possibility has been overlooked for other
types of questions, in particular questions designed to assess the
frequency of behaviors and experiences. Theoretically, the impact of
the response alternatives should be more pronounced the less clear
the target behavior is defined. For this reason, questions about
subjective experiences may be particularly sensitive to the impact of
response alternatives because researchers usually refrain from
providing a detailed definition of the target experience so as not to

interfere with its subjective nature. Ironically, assessing a behavior's frequency with precoded response alternatives may result in
doing just what is avoided in the wording of the question.

Second, respondents may use the frequency range suggested by the
response alternatives as a frame of reference in estimating the
frequency of their own behavior. To this extent, their behavioral
reports will be a function, in part, of the range of the response
categories provided to them. This should be more likely the more
frequent and mundane the behavior is and the more difficult respondents find it to evaluate its frequency on the basis of recalled
instances. How strongly the scale biases respondents' reports will
depend upon how much the scale deviates from respondents' actual
behavioral frequencies. Theoretically, a precoded scale that matches
respondents' behavior may, for the same reason, be expected to increase the validity of the obtained reports. Note, however, that the
effects of a given response scale may be different for different
subpopulations. To the extent that the actual frequency of a behavior
varies across subpopulations, a set of response alternatives constructed on the basis of pretest data is unlikely to match the actual
behavior of extreme groups that were underrepresented in the pretest.
Because the range of the scale may be used by all respondents as a
frame of reference in estimating behavioral frequencies, it may tend
to reduce the reported differences between subpopulations.

So far we have discussed the assessment of frequent and mundane
behaviors, the frequency of which is difficult to reconstruct from
memory. The assessment of rare and highly salient events, on the
other hand, may be based on respondents' recollections. For this
reason, respondents' _private_ assessment of these events or behaviors
is less likely to be affected by the range of the scale.
Nevertheless, the response alternatives may influence respondents'
_public_ reports under these conditions because they may suggest that
the respondents' behavior is unusual, for example because the proper
response alternative constitutes the extreme category in the list. An
example of this possibility has been discussed by Bradburn, Sudman,
and Associates (1979). They found that estimates of beer consumption
given in an open-answer format were about 60 % greater than those
given in a precoded response format that ranged from "1" to "6 or
more" glasses of beer at one time. As Bradburn and Davis (1984)
speculate, this difference may be due to the reluctance of respondents to place themselves in the highest category. Thus, in the
present example, precoding a question about an undesirable behavior

may have resulted in underreporting. Similarly, precoding questions about socially desirable behaviors may result in overreporting relative to an open-answer format. Note, however, that for many people drinking beer is a rather mundane and frequent behavior. For this reason it seems likely that respondents may also have used the range of the response alternatives as a frame of reference in estimating their behavior in the first place.

Finally, respondents may extract information about a presumably "usual" behavior from the values stated in the scale, and they may use this information as a social comparison standard in making comparative judgments. Theoretically, the impact of the response alternatives on comparative judgments should be more pronounced the less reliable comparison information is easily available from other sources. In addition, one may speculate that the influence of the response scale is more pronounced when the scale is visually presented on a card or in a self-administered questionnaire. Checking one from a list of ordered response categories is indeed the same as locating oneself in a hypothetical distribution, and clearly informs respondents about their relative placement. Respondents may be less likely to pick up the comparison information if the response alternatives are read to them without visual presentation, as is the case in telephone interviews. For this reason, the impact of response scales on comparative judgments may be less pronounced in telephone interviews, a possibility that deserves further investigation.

In addition, researchers should be aware that precoded response alternatives may bias respondents' comparative judgments even under conditions where the set of response alternatives perfectly matches the actual distribution of behavior, thus introducing little bias in behavioral reports. While individuals who were not exposed to the response scale may use varying standards of comparison (e.g., based on their reference group), exposure to a given response scale may result in the use of the salient comparison information provided by the scale. To this extent, judgments obtained from a sample that was exposed to the response scale may differ from judgments prevailing in the population to which one wants to generalize the obtained results.

The issue of comparative judgments is finally complicated by the fact that respondents may use social as well as intraindividual standards of comparison. That is, they may either compare their own behavior with the behavior of others, or they may compare the frequency with which they themselves engage in various related behaviors intraindividually. Both comparisons may be affected by the frequency range of the response scales, and the findings reported in the present chapter suggest that social comparisons are likely when only one behavior is assessed, while intraindividual comparisons are likely when several related behaviors are assessed.

In combination, these findings indicate that both the question <u>and</u> the response alternatives should be considered together. Providing precoded response alternatives affects respondents' understanding of the question and their behavioral reports as well as related judgments. Moreover, changes in the response alternatives undermine the comparability of the obtained results. Researchers may therefore be well advised to use open-answer formats to obtain data on behavioral frequencies. As Sudman and Bradburn (1982, p. 115) noted, "there is no difficulty in coding such responses, since the data are numerical and can easily be processed without need for additional coding." For this reason, the major disadvantages of the open-ended format -- time, cost, interviewer variability, coding, and analytical problems -- are not of considerable concern in the assessment of frequencies. Precoding the responses, on the other hand, may introduce systematic bias because response scales are not only "measurement devices" but serve informative functions as well.

### ACKNOWLEDGMENT

The reported research was supported by grant Schw 278/2 from the Deutsche Forschungsgemeinschaft to N. Schwarz and F. Strack, and the preparation of this chapter was supported by a Feodor Lynen Fellowship from the Alexander von Humboldt Stiftung to the first author. We want to thank Fritz Strack, Brigitte Chassein, and Bettina Scheuring for their helpful comments on a previous draft.

## REFERENCES

Bradburn, N., & Davis, C. (1984). Potential contributions of cogni-
    tive research to survey questionnaire design. In T.B. Jabine,
    M.L. Straf, J.M. Tanur, & R. Tourangeau (Eds.), Cognitive
    aspects of survey methodology: Building a bridge between dis-
    ciplines, Washington, DC: National Academy Press.

Bradburn, N., Sudman, S., & Associates (1979). Improving interviewing
    methods and questionnaire design. San Francisco, CA: Jossey-
    Bass.

Converse, J.M. (1984). Strong arguments and weak evidence: The
    open/closed questioning controversy of the 1940s. Public Opinion
    Quarterly, 48, 267-282.

Darschin, W., & Frank, B. (1982). Tendenzen im Zuschauerverhalten.
    Teleskopie-Ergebnise zur Fernsehnutzung im Jahre 1981. Media
    Perspektiven, 4, 276-284.

Mueller, A. (1980). Einstellungen der Fernsehzuschauer zur weiteren
    Entwicklung des Mediums Fernsehen. Media Perspektiven, 3, 179-
    186.

Nisbett, R.E., Borgida, E., Crandall, R., & Reed, H. (1976). Popular
    inductions: information is not always informative. In J.
    Carroll, & J. Payne (Eds.), Cognition and social behavior.
    Potomac, MD.: Erlbaum.

Payne, S.L. (1951). The art of asking questions. Princeton, NJ:
    Princeton University Press.

Schwarz, N., Hippler, H.J., Deutsch, B., & Strack, F. (1985).
    Response categories: Effects on behavioral reports and compara-
    tive judgements. Public Opinion Quarterly, 49, 388-395.

Schwarz, N., & Scheuring, B. (1985). Inter- und intraindividuelle
    Vergleichsprozesse als Funktion der Antwortvorgabe in
    Frageboegen. Paper presented at the 2nd Fachtagung
    Sozialpsychologie, Landau, FRG, February.

Schwarz, N., Strack, F., Mueller, G., & Deutsch, B. (1985). The
    range of the response alternatives may determine the meaning of
    the question. Manuscript under editorial review.

Schuman, H., & Presser, S. (1981). Questions and answers in attitude
    surveys. Experiments on question form, wording, and context. New
    York: Academic Press.

Sheatsley, P.B. (1985). Questionnaire construction and item writing.
    In P.H. Rossi, J.D. Wright, & A.B. Anderson (Eds.), Handbook of
    survey research. New York: Academic Press.

Simon, W. (1973). The social, the erotic, and the sensual: The
    complexities of sexual scripts. In J.K. Cole, & R. Dienstbier
    (Eds.), Nebraska Symposium on Motivation, Vol.21, Lincoln, NE:
    University of Nebraska Press.

Sudman, S., & Bradburn, N.M. (1974). Response effects in surveys.
    Chicago: Aldine.

Sudman, S., & Bradburn, N.M. (1982). Asking Questions. San Francisco
    CA: Jossey-Bass.

Suls, J.M., & Miller, R.L. (Eds.) (1977). Social comparision
    processes: Theoretical and empirical perspectives. New York:
    Hemisphere Publishing.

# 10 CONTEXT EFFECTS ON SELF-PERCEPTIONS OF INTEREST IN GOVERNMENT AND PUBLIC AFFAIRS

George F. Bishop
University of Cincinnati

Previous experiments have shown that when people are asked a question about how interested they are in politics, their answers can be significantly affected by the context in which the question is asked. When asked, for example, how much they "...follow what's going on in government and public affairs...," people are much less likely to say they follow such matters "most of the time" if they are asked about it immediately after being unable to answer some rather difficult questions about their United States Congressman's record than if they are asked about it before such questions (see Bishop et al., 1982, 1984b). Similarly, when asked how interested they were "...in following the political campaigns...," people were significantly more likely to say they were "very interested" when asked about it immediately after, rather than before, giving answers to several questions about the 1980 presidential election campaign, answers that implied that they were quite interested in following the political campaigns that year (see Bishop, Oldendick, & Tuchfarber, 1982, 1984a). Such is the influence of question order and context on people's self-perceptions.

The results of such experiments suggest that people's answers to survey questions are, in large part, the product of what Wyer and Hartwick (1980) call a conditional inference process (see also Wyer and Srull, 1981):

> "...when a person is asked to report his belief in a target proposition, he typically does not engage in an exhaustive search of memory for information bearing on it. Rather, he searches only until he encounters a piece of information (i.e., another proposition) that he considers relevant, and bases his judgement primarily on (a) the implications of its being true and (b) the implications of its being false, without taking into account other information that may also bear on the validity of the target proposition... this process implies that the person's reported belief in a target proposition may be influenced greatly by factors that affect which of several alternative pieces of information he happens to retrieve in his search of memory." (pp.244-45)

When people are asked, for instance, how much they "follow what's going on in government and public affairs," they do not try to think of everything they have ever said or done that has to do with politics. Instead, they probably think about it only as long as it takes for something to come to mind that seems relevant to answering the question and then they answer it largely on the basis of what that information implies about their interest in government and public affairs, without considering other pieces of information from their past experience with politics that might be equally, if not more relevant to answering the question. A respondent, for example, may answer the question by saying he or she follows what's going on in government and public affairs "only now and then" because what comes to mind, which seems relevant to answering the question, is their answer to a previous question in which the respondent indicated to the interviewer that he or she didn't remember too much about what the Congressman had done for the district or how he or she had voted on any legislation (see Bishop et al., 1984b). And because this respondent believes that if people don't know anything about what their Congressman is doing, they must not follow too much what's going on in government and public affairs, it is infered, therefore, that they must follow such matters "only now and then."

In answering the question, then, they may not consider other information about their political experience, which is equally relevant to answering the question, such as the fact that they vote in all or nearly all elections, that they read the editorial page and syndicated political columns nearly every day in the newspaper, and that they watch the national and local news on television just about every night, all of which would imply that they follow what is going on in government and public affairs "most of the time." But if they do happen to think of some of these other indicators of their inter-est in politics when answering the question, they may say that they follow what's going on "some of the time" because they must somehow reconcile the implications of the information about their previous experience with the implications of the most recent information about their inability to answer the question(s) about what their Congressman has been doing. Respondents may not of course consider both sources of information to be equally relevant; they may indeed regard the fact that they cannot answer some difficult questions about their Congressman's record as irrelevant to answering the more general question about how much they follow what's going on in government and public affairs because they consider that sort of

information to be trivial and because they know from previous experience that they do follow what's going on "most of the time."
Respondents therefore disregard the more recent information about
their lack of knowledge and answer the question by saying they follow
what's going on "most of the time." Such an inference process seems
quite plausible when we look at the results from previous experiments
(see Bishop et al., 1982, 1984b) which show that many respondents
will say they follow what's going on in government and public affairs
"most of the time," though they cannot think of anything at all that
their Congressman has done or voted on. This finding suggests that
their answers to such questions may depend more upon the relevance of
the information that comes to mind than on its recency. As Wyer and
Hartwick (1980) would put it, people use that subset of relevant
information that has most recently been deposited in the appropriate
memory bin (e.g., the "politics bin"). Some evidence for this
hypothesis comes from a recent set of experiments conducted by the
Behavioral Sciences Laboratory at the University of Cincinnati.

## EXPERIMENTS ON BUFFER EFFECTS

Evidence from our recent experiments indicates that the context
effect created by asking people how much they follow what's going on
in government and public affairs immediately after asking them what
they know about their Congressman's record cannot be eliminated or
significantly reduced merely by asking the question about following
public affairs in a separate part of the interview after a "buffer"
of questions on unrelated topics (see Bishop et al., 1984b; cf.
Schuman, Kalton, & Ludwig, 1983). The buffer in these initial experiments, however, was relatively small, consisting of a little less
than thirty items, which took anywhere from 5-10 minutes for interviewers to administer, depending upon the number of questions asked
of a particular respondent. Perhaps a larger buffer, we reasoned,
would be more effective in reducing or erasing the effect of context.
A forty- or fifty-item buffer, for example, should reduce or erase a
context effect more effectively than a twenty-item buffer, because
respondents have more time to forget how they failed to answer correctly the questions asked earlier in the interview about their
Congressman's record when they are asked later in the interview how
much they follow what's going on in government and public affairs.

But it may not be the amount of time, per se, that matters so
much as the content of the questions that are included in the buffer.

Because the short-term memory of an answer to a survey question is not likely to last much more than thirty seconds or so (see Loftus and Loftus, 1976, Chapter 3), the answers people give to the questions about their Congressman's record must be stored in long-term memory (or in an intermediate store that lasts at least through most of the interview) and then retrieved from memory later in the interview when they are asked how much they follow public affairs. Otherwise, we would have found that the context effect was absent or significantly smaller when a buffer was used than when it was not. This reasoning suggests that such context effects will last throughout an interview, regardless of the size or duration of the buffer, and that the only way in which the effect can be undone, in whole or in part, is if the respondent is asked another question about government and public affairs, the answer to which implies that he or she is more knowledgeable than the failure to answer the previous question about the Congressman's record would indicate. The effect, in other words, will last until the respondent has an experience that changes his or her self-perception, either during the interview or afterwards. People's self-perceptions can thus be changed in the process of measuring them (cf. Bem, 1978).

Consider, for example, a male respondent who is unable to answer correctly either of the two difficult questions about his Congressman's record. If he is not given an opportunity, subsequently, to answer a question on politics about which he does know something (e.g., the name of his Congressman or Senator), he is likely to infer that he does not follow what's going on in government and public affairs "most of the time" when he's questioned about it later in the interview, but rather that he follows such matters just "some of the time," "only now and then," or "hardly at all." And this will be the case regardless of how many other questions have been asked as part of the buffer or how long it has been since he was asked the difficult questions about his Congressman. On the other hand, if he is asked an easier question about politics, after being asked about his Congressman's record, and he answers it correctly and thus in a way that implies that he is somewhat knowledgeable, then he should be more likely to infer that he follows what's going on in public affairs if not "most of the time," at least "some of the time," when he's asked about it later on in the interview. In the language of conditional inference his answer should be based largely on the implications of the most relevant, recent information that comes to mind, namely how he answered the easier question about his

183

Figure 1: Summary of Experimental Conditions and Design

| Form A-1 | Form A-2 | Form B | Form C-1 | Form C-2 | Form D |
|---|---|---|---|---|---|
| Know what U.S. rep. has done for district | Know what U.S. rep. has done for district | Interest in govt. and public affairs | Know what U.S. rep. has done for district | Know what U.S. rep. has done for district | Know name of governor |
| Know how U.S. rep. has voted | Know how U.S. rep. has voted | Know what U.S. rep. has done for district | Know how U.S. rep. has voted | Know how U.S. rep. has voted | Interest in govt. and public affairs |
| Interest in govt. and public affairs | "Buffer" | Know how U.S. rep. has voted for district | Know name of governor | "Buffer" | Know what U.S. rep. has done for district |
| Know name of governor | Interest in govt. and public affairs | Know name of governor | Interest in govt. and public affairs | Know name of governor | Know how U.S. rep. has voted |
| Other questions | Know name of governor | Other questions | Other questions | Interest in govt. and public affairs | Other questions |

knowledge of politics. A more recent set of experiments on the effects of buffering made it possible to test this conditional inference hypothesis more directly.

Research Design

All of the experiments were designed as part of the Greater
Cincinnati Survey, a multipurpose, random-digit-dialed telephone
survey that is conducted twice a year by the Behavioral Sciences
Laboratory at the University of Cincinnati. As a multipurpose survey,
it contains many questions that are purchased by various public and
private organizations. Because most of these questions usually have
nothing to do with government and public affairs, we have been able
to use them as "buffer" material in our experiments on context
effects. The content of the questions purchased by these outside
organizations, however, will generally vary from one survey to the
next, which means that the nature and size of the "buffer" will also
vary. Though this represents a disadvantage, in that the buffer
cannot be exactly replicated from one experiment to the next, this
"natural" variation makes it possible to test whether the effects we
have observed hold up under different conditions, in different surveys, and at different times, which represents a powerful advantage
from the standpoint of being able to generalize the results. Let me
now describe the experiments and replications.

Experiment I

This first experiment was completed in May and June of 1983 as
part of the Greater Cincinnati Survey, which consisted of telephone
interviews with 1133 respondents (1), each of whom was randomly
assigned to one of six question orders and buffer conditions (see
Figure 1).

Form A-1. Respondents in this condition were asked the following
sequence of questions at the beginning of the interview, the first
three of which were adapted from items used in the American National
Election Studies (see Miller, 1978).

1. "Do you happen to remember anything special that your U.S.
representative has done for your district or for the people in
your district  while he has been in congress?" (IF YES): "What
was that?"
2. "Is there any legislative bill that has come up in the house
of  representatives, on which you remember how your Congressman
has voted  in the last couple of years?" (IF YES): "What bill
was that?"

3. "Now, some people seem to follow what's going on in government and public affairs most of the time, whether there's an election going on or not. Others aren't that interested. Would you say you follow what's going on in government and public affairs most of the time, some of the time, only now and then, or hardly at all?"

4. "Do you happen to know the name of the Governor of Ohio?" (IF YES): "What is it?"

Form A-2. In this condition respondents were also asked the first two questions about their Congressman's record, but unlike Form A-1, the question about interest in government and public affairs and the following question about knowing the name of the governor were not asked until later in the interview, after a buffer of 33 questions on various topics (see below).

Form B. Respondents in this group were asked, first, about their interest in government and public affairs, next about their Congressman's record, and last about the name of the governor.

Form C-1. Here respondents were asked, first, as in Form A-1, about their Congressman's record. But, in contrast to Form A-1, they were asked next about the name of the governor and last about their interest in government and public affairs (see Figure 1).

Form C-2. As in Form C-1, these respondents were asked, first, about their Congressman's record. They were not asked about the name of the governor and their interest in government and public affairs, however, until later in the interview after the 33-item buffer.

Form D. These respondents were asked, first, about the name of the governor, then about their interest in government and public affairs, and finally about their Congressman's record.

The questions about the respondents' Congressman and their interest in government and public affairs are identical to those used in our previous experiments (Bishop et al., 1984b). We constructed the question about the name of the governor to give respondents an "easy" item to answer, though as we shall see, it was not as easy as we assumed it would be. The buffer in this experiment included the following sets of questions: a block of items concerning the respondent's use of the local metropolitan bus company; a series of questions about the respondent's awareness, knowledge, and impressions of Cincinnati Technical College; items measuring the respondent's awareness, knowledge, and impressions of the Cincinnati Metropolitan Housing Authority, as well as their perceptions and use of the housing authority for assistance; questions about the respondent's awareness and knowledge of a health maintenance plan sponsored by Blue Cross; questions about whether the respondent or anyone else in the household had ever been diagnosed as having any type of cancer; questions about whether the respondent had been laid off or involuntarily unemployed during the previous 24 months; a question about whether the respondent had ever had any children, either by birth or by adoption, and about the difficulty of that decision; a question on the respondent's perception of racial problems in the neighborhood; and a pair of items asking whether the respondents subscribed to Warner Amex Cable Television, and if yes, a question about their perception of the quality of service provided by the company (2). As indicated, there was a total of 33 items in the buffer. On the average, it took 7.8 minutes for respondents to answer these questions. The time varied of course, depending upon the number of questions for which a respondent was eligible or able to answer. Suffice it to say that this buffer was just slightly larger than those that were used in our previous experiments (27-28 items).

Figure 1 shows a summary of the six experimental conditions and the design used in this and the subsequent experiments. With the exception of the question about knowing the name of the governor, Forms A-1, A-2, and B are exact replications of the forms used in our earlier studies (Bishop et al., 1984b). We should therefore expect to replicate the results of those studies if the buffer is of little or no consequence in eliminating the context effect created by the sequence of the questions asked in Form A-1. Respondents receiving Form B, in other words, should be significantly more likely to say they follow what's going on in government and public affairs "most of the time" than those administered either Form A-1 or Form A-2. But if the buffer is effective, we should find no significant differences in the results between Form B and Form A-2.

Form C-1 allows us to test whether asking respondents an easy question about the name of the governor, which most people can answer, will eliminate the context effect that is created by asking them first the more difficult questions about their Congressman's record. If respondents base their answer to the question about their interest in government and public affairs largely on the implications of their answer to the question about the name of the governor (i.e., the most relevant, recent information that comes to mind), then we should expect to find that people receiving Form C-1 should be sig- nificantly more likely to say they follow what's going on in govern- ment and public affairs than those who are given Form A-1, in which the question about the name of the governor is not asked until _after_ the question about interest in government and public affairs.

Form C-2 provides a test of the combined effects of the buffer and answering the easy question about the name of the governor. This form should be most effective in erasing, or reducing the magnitude of the context effect produced by the inability of most respondents to answer correctly the first two questions concerning their Congressman's record.

Finally, a comparison of Forms B and D makes it possible for us to assess the effect of being asked the easy question about the name of the governor, alone, on respondents' self-perceptions of their interest in government and public affairs.

## Experiment II

We repeated the experiment in the Greater Cincinnati Survey of November and December, 1983, which was based on interviews with 1259 respondents (3). The only difference between this experiment and the previous one (other than the date of the study) was that the buffer in this experiment was somewhat larger, and different in content. Covered in the buffer were the following topics: questions about the respondents' use, perceptions, and awareness of the local bus company; their awareness and impressions of a local hospital system; their smoking habits; and their use and perceptions of cable television (4). There was a total of 40 items in the buffer which took 10.6 minutes to answer, on the average, depending upon the number of questions for which a respondent was eligible to answer.

## Experiment III

The experiment was repeated once again in May and June of 1984 as part of the Greater Cincinnati Survey, this time with 1263 respondents (5). The buffer in this experiment was considerably larger than those in the previous surveys, consisting of 101 items, which took on the average 16.3 minutes to administer (6). Most of the questions concerned the respondents' use and perceptions of cable television. The others covered the following: the respondents' use and perceptions of the local bus company; their perceptions of housing integration in their neighborhood; their beliefs about the cost of health and medical care and their preferences for various health care plans; and their use and knowledge of transportation alternatives to the automobile (7).

Each of these experiments, then, represents an independent test of the effects of using a buffer under the various conditions created by the content of the three surveys, and the time at which they were conducted. Let us look now at the results.

Results

Level of Political Information

Table 1: Response to Political Knowledge Questions by Survey

1.   "Do you happen to remember anything special that your U.S.
     representative has done for your district or for the people in
     your district while he has been in congress?"

|  | May-June 1983 | Nov.-Dec. 1983 | May-June 1984 |
|---|---|---|---|
| Yes | 12.2% | 12.1% | 13.7% |
| No | 87.8 | 87.8 | 86.4 |
| Total | 100.0% | 99.9% | 100.1% |
| (N=) | (1131) | (1256) | (1255) |

2.   "Is there any legislative bill that has come up in the House of
     Representatives, on which you remember how your congressman has
     voted in the last couple of years?"

|  | May-June 1983 | Nov.-Dec. 1983 | May-June 1984 |
|---|---|---|---|
| Yes | 16.0% | 18.3% | 15.3% |
| No | 84.0 | 81.7 | 84.6 |
| Total | 100.0% | 100.0% | 99.9% |
| (N=) | (1131) | (1251) | (1256) |

3.   "Do you happen to know the name of the Governor of Ohio?"

|  | May-June 1983 | Nov.-Dec. 1983 | May-June 1984 |
|---|---|---|---|
| Yes | 69.0% | 69.2% | 76.8% |
| No, Incorrect Guess | 31.0 | 30.7 | 23.3 |
| Total | 100.0% | 99.9% | 100.1% |
| (N=) | (1124) | (1241) | (1248) |

Table 1 shows the distribution of responses to the political
knowledge items used in the three surveys. As expected from previous
studies, the level of information about politics in the general
public was fairly low: the vast majority (80%-90%) could not answer

either of the two questions about their United States Representative's record in Congress. Furthermore, the percentages in
Table 1 exaggerate the number of respondents who are truly
knowledgeable because many of those who said "yes" when asked the
questions could not remember anything specific when asked further
what their Congressman had actually done for their district or how he
or she had voted on legislation (data not shown here). So the
percentage of people who are truly informed about their Congressman's
record in this sample is probably less than 10%.

The question about the name of the Governor of Ohio indicates
that a little over two-thirds of the respondents could correctly name
the governor in 1983. By May and June of 1984, the figure had risen
to just over three-fourths. So the great majority of respondents
could answer this relatively "easy" political knowledge question,
though it was not quite as easy as had been originally expected. Let
us look now at the effects of answering these hard and easy items on
people's self-perceptions of their interest in government and public
affairs.

Context Effects on Self-Perceptions

Table 2 shows the results for each of the three experiments,
separately, and for all three surveys combined. The data from these
investigations look remarkably similar to each other, so much so that
they can be summarized together. What they tell us is this:

1. People are significantly more likely to say that they follow
what's going on in government and public affairs "most of the
time" if they are asked about it first (as in Form B), that is,
before they are asked any questions about their Congressman's
record or about the name of the governor, incorrect answers to
which might imply that they are not that knowledgeable and
therefore not that attentive to what's going on in government
and public affairs.

2. Asking people a buffer of questions on unrelated topics does
not eliminate or reduce the magnitude of the context effect
created by asking them about their Congressman's record at the
beginning of the interview. We found no significant differences
in the results in any of the three surveys, or when the three
were combined, between Forms A-1 and A-2 or between Forms C-1
and C-2. Nor did we find any consistent relationship between the
length or duration of the buffer for an individual respondent
and his or her response to the question about interest in
government and public affairs (data not shown here).

Table 2: Percent who follow "what's going on in government and public affairs," by form and survey

| Follows Govt. and Public Affairs | Form A-1<br>Hard Items<br>Interest Q.<br>Easy Item | Form A-2<br>Hard Items<br>"Buffer"<br>Interest Q.<br>Easy Item | Form B<br>Interest Q.<br>Hard Items<br>Easy Item | Form C-1<br>Hard Items<br>Easy Item<br>Interest Q. | Form C-2<br>Hard Items<br>"Buffer"<br>Easy Item<br>Interest Q. | Form D<br>Easy Item<br>Interest Q.<br>Hard Items |
|---|---|---|---|---|---|---|
| **I. May/June 1983** | | | | | | |
| Most of the time | 23.9% | 23.9% | 34.3% | 26.8% | 25.7% | 29.0% |
| Some of the time | 29.6 | 34.1 | 33.9 | 28.2 | 32.2 | 33.5 |
| Only now and then | 26.1 | 25.4 | 16.4 | 21.8 | 23.0 | 21.3 |
| Hardly at all | 20.4 | 16.7 | 15.4 | 23.2 | 19.1 | 16.2 |
| Total | 100.0% | 100.1% | 100.0% | 100.0% | 100.0% | 100.0% |
| (N=) | (142) | (138) | (280) | (142) | (152) | (272) |
| **II. Nov./Dec. 1983** | | | | | | |
| Most of the time | 26.4% | 23.6% | 36.1% | 25.0% | 27.9% | 34.3% |
| Some of the time | 31.1 | 29.9 | 37.7 | 31.4 | 29.2 | 31.4 |
| Only now and then | 21.6 | 25.5 | 16.2 | 25.0 | 23.4 | 19.1 |
| Hardly at all | 20.9 | 21.0 | 10.0 | 18.6 | 19.5 | 15.2 |
| Total | 100.0% | 100.0% | 100.0% | 100.0% | 100.0% | 100.0% |
| (N=) | (148) | (157) | (321) | (156) | (154) | (309) |
| **III. May/June 1984** | | | | | | |
| Most of the time | 27.1% | 29.2% | 45.0% | 24.0% | 22.6% | 33.1% |
| Some of the time | 30.3 | 29.2 | 30.9 | 29.2 | 31.0 | 36.8 |
| Only now and then | 21.3 | 26.6 | 15.6 | 22.1 | 29.0 | 13.9 |
| Hardly at all | 21.3 | 14.9 | 8.5 | 24.7 | 17.4 | 16.1 |
| Total | 100.0% | 100.0% | 100.0% | 100.0% | 100.0% | 100.0% |
| (N=) | (155) | (154) | (307) | (154) | (155) | (323) |

Table 2: (Continued)

| Follows Govt. and Public Affairs | O R D E R | Form A-1 | Form A-2 | Form B | Form C-1 | Form C-2 | Form D |
|---|---|---|---|---|---|---|---|
| | | Hard Items / Interest Q. / Easy Item | Hard Items / "Buffer" / Interest Q. / Easy Item | Interest Q. / Hard Items / Easy Item | Hard Items / Easy Item / Interest Q. | Hard Items / "Buffer" / Easy Item / Interest Q. | Easy Item / Interest Q. / Hard Items |
| **IV. Surveys I, II, and III Combined** | | | | | | | |
| Most of the time | | 25.8% | 25.6% | 38.5% | 25.2% | 25.4% | 32.3% |
| Some of the time | | 30.3 | 31.0 | 34.3 | 29.6 | 30.8 | 34.0 |
| Only now and then | | 22.9 | 25.8 | 16.1 | 23.0 | 25.2 | 17.9 |
| Hardly at all | | 20.9 | 17.6 | 11.1 | 22.1 | 18.7 | 15.8 |
| Total | | 99.9% | 100.0% | 100.0% | 100.0% | 100.0% | 100.0% |
| (N=) | | (445) | (449) | (908) | (452) | (461) | (904) |

Chi-square=95.55, $\underline{df}$=15, $\underline{p}$<.0001

Form A-1 vs. A-2:  Chi-square=2.08, $\underline{df}$=3, $\underline{n.s.}$

Form C-1 vs. C-2:  Chi-square=1.89, $\underline{df}$=3, $\underline{n.s.}$

Form A (1 and 2 combined) vs. B:
Chi-square=59.77, $\underline{df}$=3, $\underline{p}$<.0001

Form A (1 and 2) vs. C (1 and 2):
Chi-square=0.36, $\underline{df}$=3, $\underline{n.s.}$

Form A (1 and 2) vs. D:
Chi-square=20.11, $\underline{df}$=3, $\underline{p}$<.001

Form B vs. C (1 and 2):
Chi-square=66.58, $\underline{df}$=3, $\underline{p}$<.0001

Form B vs. D:  Chi-square=13.32,
$\underline{df}$=3, $\underline{p}$<.01

Form C (1 and 2) vs. D:
Chi-square=23.15, $\underline{df}$=3, $\underline{p}$<.0001

3. Giving people an easy question to answer about the name of the governor does not eliminate or moderate the context effect either. In none of the surveys did we find any significant variation in the results between Forms A-1 and C-1, A-2 and C-2, or between the combined forms of A (1 and 2) and the combined forms of C (1 and 2).

4. Quizzing people about the name of the governor at the beginning of the interview, as in Form D, makes them significantly more likely to say that they follow what is going on in government and public affairs "most of the time," as compared to people who are asked the question about the governor last, as in Forms A-1 and A-2, or after the more difficult questions about their Congressman, as in Forms C-1 and C-2. But people receiving Form D are not as likely to say they follow public affairs "most of the time" as those who are asked the question about their interest in public affairs first, as in Form B. So while the question about the governor has a significant effect on people's self-perceptions of their interest in government and public affairs, when asked first, which is equivalent to asking it alone, it does not appear to undo the context effect created by the two difficult questions about their Congressman, as in Forms C-1 and C-2.

The data in Table 2, then, suggest that the context effects produced by the sequence in which the questions are asked in Forms A and C (and perhaps in D as well) probably last as long as the length of the interview and quite possibly beyond that time, depending upon the political experiences of the respondent in the hours, days, and weeks after the interview (see Schwarz & Strack, 1981 for other evidence of such delayed effects on political behavior). If true, this would mean that merely asking people questions about political affairs, or any other subject for that matter, in a certain way, may change their self-perceptions and perhaps their behavior too, in some enduring manner.

Effects of Recency and Relevance

Table 3 shows the percent who said they followed what's going on in government and public affairs "most of the time," controlling for the respondent's answers to the three knowledge questions and for question form. Because the buffer had no significant effect on the results (see Table 2), the data for Forms A-1 and A-2 have been combined, as have those for Forms C-1 and C-2. A close examination of

Table 3: Percent who follow politics "most of the time," by knowledge and question form

| Knows what U.S. rep. has done: | Yes | Yes | Yes | Yes | No | No | No | No |
|---|---|---|---|---|---|---|---|---|
| Knows how U.S. rep. has voted: | Yes | Yes | No | No | Yes | Yes | No | No |
| Knows name of governor: | Yes | No | Yes | No | Yes | No | Yes | No |
| Question Form | | | | | | | | |
| A | 72.7 (33) | 0.0 (3) | 45.7 (46) | 20.0 (15) | 40.0 (90) | 18.2 (11) | 24.8 (464) | 12.3 (228) |
| B | 75.5 (49) | 0.0 (1) | 61.9 (63) | 42.9 (14) | 57.0 (107) | 26.7 (15) | 39.0 (428) | 14.8 (223) |
| C | 63.0 (46) | 0.0 (1) | 44.0 (50) | 12.5 (8) | 59.5 (84) | 30.0 (10) | 23.3 (490) | 5.4 (221) |
| D | 71.7 (53) | 50.0 (2) | 57.4 (61) | 35.7 (14) | 57.6 (85) | 40.0 (10) | 30.6 (438) | 10.1 (237) |

Note: Data for Surveys I, II, and III combined. Percentages are
based on the number of cases shown within the parentheses.

the figures in Table 3 reveals an interesting implication (8): Being able to answer the hard questions about one's Congressman before the question about interest in government and public affairs has no significant effect on respondents' self-perceptions; rather, it is not being able to answer either one or both of the difficult items that has a significant negative effect. If, for example, we combine the data for columns 1 and 2 in Table 3 and compare the responses given to Forms A and B by respondents who were able to answer both of the questions about their Congressman correctly, we find no significant difference in the percentage who say they follow public affairs "most of the time"; in Form A, where the hard items were asked before the interest question, the percentage saying "most of the time" was 66.6%; in Form B, where they were asked after the interest question, the percentage was 74.5% (Chi-square=0.31, df=1, n.s.). In fact, it appears that merely being asked such hard questions beforehand, as in Form B, may lead some respondents to think they do not follow what's going on in government and public affairs "most of the time," even though they can say "yes" to both of the hard knowledge items. But when we combine the data for columns 3-8 in Table 3 and compare the responses given to Forms A and B by respondents who were not able to answer correctly either one or both of the questions about their Congressman, we find a highly significant difference: in Form A the percentage saying "most of the time" was 24%; in Form B, 36.4% (Chi-square=30.67, df=1, p<.0001). Not being able to answer one or both of the hard items before the question about interest in public affairs thus leads many respondents to infer that they do not follow such matters "most of the time."

In contrast, being able or unable to answer the easy question about the name of the governor makes little or no difference in the results (9). The figures for the less knowledgeable respondents (see the last two columns in Table 3) indicate that people who were able to name the governor correctly, but who were unable to answer the questions about their Congressman, were no more likely to think they followed public affairs "most of the time" if they were asked the question about the governor just before the question about interest in government and public affairs (see the second to the last column in Table 3), as in Form C (23.3%), than if they were asked about it immediately afterwards, as in Form A (24.8%). This would suggest that when respondents are asked the question in Form C about how much they follow what's going on in government and public affairs, they do not base their answer largely on the implications of their answer to the immediately preceding question about the name of the governor; instead, they would appear to consider the fact that they were able to answer an easy question about the name of the governor as irrelevant to how much they follow what's going on in government and public affairs, probably because being able to answer such an easy question does not _imply_ that a person is necessarily that attentive to politics. Had they, on the other hand, been able to answer a more difficult question about political affairs (e.g., about their United States Senator's position on increased spending for defense), they might have inferred that they were more attentive to what's going on in government and public affairs. The assumed _relevance_ of the information that comes to mind in answering such questions thus seems to be a more important determinant of the inferences a respondent will make in giving an answer than the sheer _recency_ of the information.

Notice in the final column of Table 3, however, that respondents were less likely to think they follow public affairs "most of the time" if they failed to answer correctly the question about the governor when it was asked just _before_ the question about their interest in public affairs, as in Form C (5.4%), than when it was asked immediately _after_ it, as in Form A (12.3%) (10). Not knowing the name of the governor, in other words, may lead a person to infer that he or she is even less attentive to public affairs than is already implied by the failure to answer the two questions about the Congressman. But the reverse is evidently not true: Being able to answer an easy question about the name of the governor does not mean that the respondent follows public affairs "most of the time" if he or she has failed to answer previous questions about the Congressman's record that imply that he or she is not that attentive to political affairs.

More generally, these findings tell us that question order and context effects in surveys will occur when answers to previous questions in an interview (or instrument) have direct implications for the answer to a question, regardless of whether it is asked with or without an intervening buffer of unrelated items. And the more direct the implications of the answers to previous questions, the greater the context effect will tend to be. Context effects in surveys may thus be a special case of a more general principle of human information processing: Namely, that when people are asked to make judgments of any kind (e.g., answering survey questions), they base them largely on the implications of the most _relevant_ information that "comes to mind." The way to test this hypothesis, of course, is to design further experiments that vary systematically the implications of the information brought to mind by answers to previous questions in the survey interview. In this way we can build a more general conditional inference model of question order and context effects in surveys.

## CONCLUSION

This investigation demonstrates the utility of the information-processing approach in understanding the problem of response effects in surveys. In particular, it shows how the conditional inference model developed by Wyer and Hartwick (1980) can be used to make some theoretical sense of some previously unexplained question order and context effects on people's self-perceptions of their interest in government and public affairs. Furthermore, the model gives us some idea as to how context effects occur in surveys more generally: principally through the implications of one answer to a question for answers to another, regardless of when or where that question was asked in the interview or how long it has been since it was asked. It is not so much the recency of the information that matters, then, as its relevance. And that is certainly useful for us to know if we are to understand and control context effects in surveys.

The results of these experiments also demonstrate how difficult it is to measure people's interest in government and public affairs without changing their self-perceptions in the process of measuring them -- that is, the social science analog of Werner Heisenberg's "principle of uncertainty" (Heisenberg, 1974). Indeed, our experiments suggest, that we may have altered people's self-images about their political knowledge and competence in more than just a transitory way merely by asking them what they knew about their Congressman's record. We have no way of knowing, at this time, how long the effects we created, by manipulating the order of the questions, lasted beyond the interview. But we suspect that they probably persisted for at least some time. This leads us to propose a rather important question for the research agenda, and that is, to ask ourselves: To what extent do we change people's attitudes, perceptions, and opinions in the process of measuring them? Are some people more easily affected than others? And, if so, do these cognitive changes induced by the measurement process lead to behavioral changes subsequent to the interview? Studies of the effects of being interviewed on voting would indicate that such behavioral changes can occur. So there is sufficient evidence to make this a research agenda worth pursuing.


<u>Footnotes</u>

1 The response rate for fully completed interviews with people living in households with telephones in Greater Cincinnati (Hamilton County) was 77.3% (N=1435). The refusal rate was 13.6%. The remainder consisted of partially completed interviews (3.6%), potential interviews that could not be completed because of a language barrier, a hearing problem, illiteracy, senility, or physical illness (4.2%), or because the selected respondent was away on vacation, a business trip, or because they otherwise were not available for an appointment (3.2%).

2 For the exact wording and sequence of the items in the buffer, see the Technical Report for the Spring 1983 Greater Cincinnati Survey, Institute for Policy Research, University of Cincinnati.

3 The response rate for fully completed interviews in this survey was 71.5% (N=1685). The refusal rate was 15.8%. The rest consisted of partially completed interviews (3.2%), potential interviews that could not be completed because of a language barrier, a hearing problem, illiteracy, senility, or physical illness (5.6%), or because the selected respondent was away on vacation, a business trip, or otherwise unavailable for an appointment (3.9%).

4 For the exact wording and sequence of the items in the buffer, see the Technical Report for the Fall 1983 Greater Cincinnati Survey, Institute for Policy Research, University of Cincinnati.

5 The response rate for fully completed interviews in this survey was 71.3% (N=1704). The refusal rate was 14.8%. The rest consisted of partially completed interviews (2.8%), potential interviews that could not be completed because of a language barrier, a hearing problem, illiteracy, senility, or physical illness (5.6%), or because the selected respondent was away on vacation, a business trip, or was otherwise unavailable for an appointment (5.5%).

6 In all of these surveys the number of questions asked of a particular respondent will vary depending upon whether he or she should be asked a given set of questions. Respondents who did not subscribe to cable television, for example, were not asked most of the questions on this topic. The length of the buffer was thus shorter for them than for people who were asked the entire block of questions about cable television. As mentioned below, however, there was no significant association between the length of the buffer and the presence or magnitude of the context effect.

7 For the exact wording and sequence of the items in the buffer, see the Technical Report for the Spring 1984 Greater Cincinnati Survey, Institute for Policy Research, University of Cincinnati.

8 My thanks to Norbert Schwarz for pointing out this implication.

9 A separate analysis (data not shown here) shows that not being able to answer the easy item has no significant effect on the results when the responses given to Forms B and D are compared, combining

columns 2, 4, 6, and 8 in Table 3. Nor does being able to answer the easy question correctly have a positive effect when the responses given to Forms B and D are compared, combining columns 1, 3, 5, and 7 in Table 3. In fact, when respondents are asked the easy item before the interest question, as in Form D, they are significantly less likely to say they follow public affairs "most of the time" (40.3%) than those who are asked about it after the interest question, as in Form B (47%): Chi-square=5.56, $df$=1, $p<.02$. Not being able to answer the easy question, however, does appear to have some effect when we control for a respondent's answers to the two hard items, as demonstrated in the analysis described in the next paragraph.

10 The difference between the percentages for Forms A and C in this comparison is statistically significant (Chi-square for "most of the time" vs. all other responses = 6.48, $df$=1, $p<.05$).

## ACKNOWLEDGMENT

The research reported here was supported by a grant from the National Science Foundation (SES-8218586). I would like to thank my colleagues, Robert Oldendick and Alfred Tuchfarber for their comments on a previous version of this manuscript, which was presented as a project report to the National Science Foundation. I'd also like to thank Norbert Schwarz for his comments and suggestions for revising the manuscript for this volume.

## REFERENCES

Bem, D.J. (1978). Self-perception theory. In L. Berkowitz, (Ed.), Cognitive theories in social psychology. New York: Academic Press.

Bishop, G.F., Oldendick, R.W., & Tuchfarber, A.J., (1982). Political information processing: Question order and context effects. Political Behavior, 4, 177-200.

Bishop, G.F., Oldendick, R.W., & Tuchfarber, A.J., (1984a). Interest in political campaigns: The influence of question order and electoral context. Political Behavior, 6, 159-169.

Bishop, G.F., Oldendick, R.W., & Tuchfarber, A.J., (1984b). What must my interest in politics be if I just told you 'I don't know'? Public Opinion Quarterly, 48, 510-519.

Heisenberg, W. (1974). Across the frontiers. New York: Harper and Row.

Loftus, G.R., & Loftus, E.F. (1976). Human memory: The processing of information. New York: Wiley.

Miller, W.E. (1978). American National Election Study, 1978. Ann Arbor, MI: Inter-University Consortium for Political and Social Research, University of Michigan.

Schuman, H., Kalton, G., & Ludwig, J. (1983). Context and contiguity in survey questionnaires. Public Opinion Quarterly, 47, 112-115.

Schuman, H., & Presser, S. (1981). Questions and answers in attitude surveys. New York: Academic Press.

Schwarz, N., & Strack, F. (1981). Manipulating salience: Causal assessment in natural settings. Personality and Social Psychology Bulletin, 6, 554-558.

Wyer, R.S., Jr., & Hartwick, J. (1980). The role of information retrieval and conditional inference processes in belief formation and change. In L. Berkowitz (Ed.) Advances in experimental social psychology, Vol.13. New York: Academic Press.

Wyer, R.S., Jr., & Srull, T.K. (1981). Category accessibility: Some theoretical and empirical issues concerning the processing of social stimulus information. In E.T. Higgins, C.P. Herman, & M.P. Zanna (Eds.) Social cognition: The Ontario symposium, Vol. 1. Hillsdale, NJ: Lawrence Erlbaum Ass..

# 11 STYLES OF INTERVIEWING AND THE SOCIAL CONTEXT OF THE SURVEY-INTERVIEW

Wil Dijkstra
Free University Amsterdam


Johannes van der Zouwen
Free University Amsterdam

## THE DUAL NATURE OF THE SURVEY-INTERVIEW

Of all data collection procedures in the social sciences, the survey-interview is most frequently used (cf. Brown & Gilmartin, 1969; Wahlke, 1979). Considerable doubt has been expressed, however, concerning the validity and reliability of the information it yields (e.g., Phillips, 1971). The term "response effects" refers to the effects of variables that influence or distort the responses, such as the race of the interviewer, the social desirability of the response alternatives provided, or the way questions are formulated.

Despite numerous pitfalls in survey interviewing, we cannot do without it. This method often is the only way available to obtain the information desired, given the usual cost and time constraints. The survey interview being indispensible, is of paramount importance to gain knowledge about the processes that are involved in the information exchange activities during the interview. Such knowledge will help us: (1) to prevent the distortion of interview data, (2) to correct for distortions that nevertheless may occur.

In our opinion, many distortions originate from the dual nature of the survey-interview: it is a scientific enterprise on the one hand, and a social encounter on the other. As Sudman and Bradburn (1974, pp. 5-6) state: "Indeed, it is this mixture of the special task-oriented character of the relationship and the general charac-teristics of a social encounter, such as problems of presentation of self and social desirability, that is one of the primary areas of interest to those studying response effects."

## STYLE OF INTERVIEWING

Cannell and Kahn (1968) describe the survey-interview as "a conversation with a purpose". Primarily, the survey-interview is intended to yield information that is relevant to some research problem. In addition, the survey-interview very much resembles a usual two-person encounter. Given this social conversational character of the interview, the interviewer must obtain some kind of personal relationship with the respondent. But which kind of relationship should be favored?

There are numerous rules about the do's and don'ts of interviewing, which are intended to minimize response effects. These rules involve, for example, the way questions should be formulated, or the training of interviewers. For example, interviewers are taught not to probe directively, and so on. In general, researchers are in agreement with respect to these rules. However, there is much less agreement as to which kind of personal relationship between interviewer and respondent is preferred in order to warrant undistorted responses.

Some believe that the interviewer should maintain a warm and sympathetically understanding relationship with the respondent. We will call this a socio-emotional interviewing style. Others insist that person-oriented actions of the interviewer should be restricted to a socially acceptable minimum. This will be called a formal style of interviewing.

Moreover, research results on the effects of interviewing style, or related concepts like rapport, on the quality of the responses obtained, are usually contradictory or inconclusive. In this chapter we discuss the effects of exerting one or the other interviewing style on a number of mediating processes or variables, which in turn may influence the quality of the information gathered. These processes concern:
- the (in)adequacy of the respondent's role expectations
- the (in)adequacy of the interviewer's task behavior
- the reinforcement of responses
- the motivation of the respondent
- the respondent's mood

Although a particular style of interviewing may lead to inadequate role expectations by respondents and inadequate task behavior by interviewers, these effects may be prevented by careful instruction and training. However, the distorting effects of the other processes or variables are not so easily prevented. Rather, the researcher should choose a particular style of interviewing, with minimal distortion, on the basis of a model of the interview, taking these variables into account.

## THE RESPONDENT'S ROLE EXPECTATIONS

According to Henson and Cannell (Henson, 1974; Henson, Cannell, & Lawson, 1976, 1979), the respondent who agrees to participate in a survey-interview generally has a vague and rather unclear notion of the task, or of what constitutes adequate role performance. This is directly related to the dual nature of the interview. On the one hand the respondent's actions must be taskoriented. Respondents are expected to give information according to the research goal of the interview, namely to respond adequately and accurately. But, as stated before, the interview also has a social quality because it resembles a social conversation between two persons, which results in person-oriented actions. Respondents may for example try to ingratiate themselves with interviewers by conforming to their apparent opinions or try to make a good impression on the interviewer by giving socially desirable answers or convey to the interviewer private information that is not directly called for by the interview questions.

Because of the dual nature of the interview, respondents' anticipations of their role as a respondent - task-oriented or person-oriented - are quite uncertain. The respondent looks for cues in the interview situation, especially in the interviewer's behavior, in order to reduce the ambiguity of the situation.

In a socio-emotional style of interviewing, respondents may get the impression that they are not expected to be very task oriented, because any answers they give are warmly received. The interviewer's reactions may easily distract respondents from their primary task, that is, giving adequate information. On the other hand, in a formal style of interviewing, the respondents may learn to be more and more task oriented and to concentrate on the task itself and not to engage in irrelevant chit-chat with the interviewer.

To prevent inadequate role expectations, it should be made clear to respondents that their primary task is to provide the interviewer with complete and accurate information. As a case in point, Oksenberg, Vinokur, and Cannell (1979) let respondents sign a printed agreement, stating: "I understand that the information from this interview must be very accurate in order to be useful. This means that

I must do my best to give accurate and complete answers" (p. 80). The respondent should not expect to get help or advice from the interviewer with respect to personal problems.

## THE ADEQUACY OF THE INTERVIEWER'S TASK BEHAVIOR

It is a well-known fact that interviewers themselves are a potential source of bias. They may communicate their own opinions to respondents, who may then conform to these opinions. Further, interviewers may expect their respondents to have particular opinions and hence pose questions in a directive way. In this case, respondents have to choose between a number of response alternatives. Interviewers may also infer the respondent's choice from previous information and make the choice themselves, without asking the respondent.

There is ample evidence that the proportion of inadequate interviewer behavior is surprisingly high. For example, Brenner (1982) found that the majority of interviewer probes were rule-breaching, that is, directive, leading, or unrelated to the task.

The more freedom interviewers are allowed, the greater the risk that they, intentionally or not, inform respondents about their own opinions, or probe directively. A socio-emotional style of interviewing brings along much greater freedom for the interviewer's behavior because reacting in a warm, understanding way and showing personal interest is extremely difficult or impossible to standardize. This freedom, in turn, enhances the risk of inadequate interviewer performance, leading to various kinds of interviewer biases.

To avoid such inadequate behaviors, interviewers should be carefully selected and trained. Furthermore, it is most important to supervise their performance during the fieldwork itself. Cannell, Lawson, and Hausser (1975) have developed useful techniques to evaluate interviewer performance from tape-recorded interviews. These tapes should be evaluated every two or three interviews. Interviewers who appear to be "unteachable" should be excluded from the survey.

## THE REINFORCEMENT VALUE OF EMPATHIC REACTIONS OF THE INTERVIEWER

A socio-emotional style is characterized by the interviewer showing interest and understanding. Such empathic reactions of the interviewer may affect the respondent's subsequent responses by acting as reinforcing stimuli for a particular class of responses. For example, a respondent who tells the interviewer that he or she suffers from severe loneliness, is likely to elicit an empathic reaction from the interviewer. Such a reaction functions as a reward for the respondent, who, in turn, may become likely to bias his or her responses in a more negative direction in order to obtain more such rewards.

In a socio-emotional style of interviewing, where such rewards are given, the respondent may learn which kind of responses are rewarded with empathic reactions by the interviewer. The respondent, for example, may learn that describing others negatively, like "my neighbours are very noisy" is met by the interviewer with sympathy and understanding.

Generally, empathic reactions will occur, contingent on responses that have an evaluative loading, either negatively or positively. In this way, a negative self-presentation by the respondent may lead to an even more negative self-presentation, if the negative aspects of the respondent's answers are reinforced. The same of course, may apply to positive self-presentations, or to answers concerning evaluations about others. Giving such reinforcements can hardly be avoided in a socio-emotional interviewing style (see Figure 1).

Figure 1: The reinforcement effect of style of interviewing on the respondent's evaluative responses

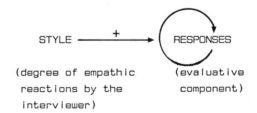

STYLE $\xrightarrow{\quad + \quad}$ RESPONSES

(degree of empathic        (evaluative
reactions by the           component)
interviewer)

## THE MOTIVATION OF THE RESPONDENT

Many researchers think of a socio-emotional style of interviewing as being a prerequisite for motivating the respondent to give
adequate and accurate information, especially if this information
concerns embarrassing or intimate information (e.g., Denzin, 1970). A
sympathetic understanding attitude by the interviewer, or if the interviewer himself reveals personal information, then the respondent's
self-disclosure is enhanced.

Generally, the respondent's motivational level is heightened by
the activity level of the interviewer and the respondent's evaluation
of the interviewer. Apparently, a "socio-emotional" interviewer is
more active and is more positively evaluated by the respondent.
Moreover, showing interest and understanding acts as a reward for the
respondent's efforts in general. It is expected therefore that a
respondent interviewed in a socio-emotional style is better
motivated, compared with a more formal style of interviewing. This,
in turn, will lead to better performance, that is, respondents will
do their best to give responses that are, to the best of their
knowledge, in accordance with their perceptions.

In one of our research projects, for example (Dijkstra, 1983),
we were able to show that respondents interviewed in a socio-emotional style evaluated the interviewers more favourably and gave more
information, performed more accurately and scored lower on a social
desirability scale, than those interviewed in a formal interviewing
style.

Generally, we expect that the better motivated the respondents
are, the more they will do their best to match their responses with
their perceptions (see Figure 2).

Figure 2: The relation between style of interviewing motivation and
response

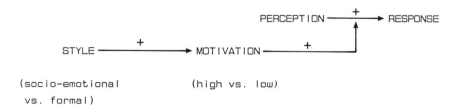

(socio-emotional        (high vs. low)
vs. formal)

## THE RESPONDENT'S MOOD

Existing literature shows that mood influences memory (Bower, 1981), social and cognitive processes (Bower, 1983), as well as the perception, interpretation, and recall of social encounters (Forgas, Bower, & Krantz, 1984). The reason is that positive emotions tend to become associated with positive trait categories, whereas negative emotions are linked with undesirable traits. As a consequence, respondents experiencing a positive mood during the interview may tend to perceive themselves as well as others more positively, whereas respondents in a negative mood evaluate themselves and others more negatively. A warm, sympathetic, and understanding interviewer is more likely to induce a positive mood within the respondent than an interviewer who is acting more formal or business-like. Hence, a socio-emotional interviewing style may lead to more positive evaluations and thus to a more positive reporting.

Further, the reporting process itself affects the respondent's mood. If a respondent is reporting about his or her own personality characteristics that are negatively evaluated, for example about one's own loneliness, or about events like a divorce, it is likely that the respondent's mood is negatively affected. In the same way, the respondent's mood may be positively affected by talking about one's own characteristics that are positively evaluated. Figure 3 shows the different relationships.

Figure 3: The relation between style of interviewing, mood, and evaluative responses

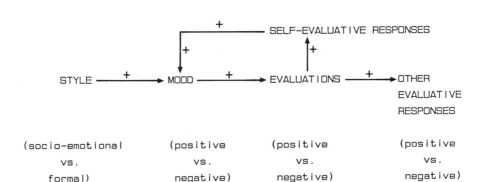

Although this model looks simple, it is quite intriguing. Most remarkable is the positive feedback loop between mood, evaluations, and self-evaluative responses. For example, a negative self-evaluation, leads to a negative self-report. This leads to a negative mood, and this negative mood in turn leads to an even more negative self-evaluation, and so on. Moreover, this whole process is amplified by the respondent's motivation. As we saw earlier, the respondent's motivation affects the correspondence between perception, or in this case self-evaluation, and responses. This effect of motivation bears some resemblance to the effect of alcohol. Drinking alcohol makes a depressive person even more depressed, but makes a cheerful person more cheerful.

## CONCLUSIONS

We started this paper with the question of which relation between interviewer and respondent is most appropriate, or stated otherwise, which style of interviewing should be favored, a socio-emotional one, or a formal one (Section 2).

We argued that the style of interviewing affects the (in)adequacy of the respondent's role expectations (Section 3), the (in)adequacy of the interviewer's task behavior (Section 4), the degree to which previous responses are reinforced (Section 5), the respondent's motivation (Section 6), and the respondent's mood (Section 7). These variables, in turn, affect the quality of the information obtained.

The respondent's role expectations and the interviewer's task behavior are more inadequate in the socio-emotional style. However, these biasing effects may be avoided by carefully instructing the respondents and training the interviewers.

The situation is more complicated however with respect to the other intervening variables. Existing research (Dijkstra & Van der Zouwen, 1982) shows that the occurrence of response effects depends on the interview topic. In short, the probability that response-effects occur is high if:
1) response alternatives differ with respect to their social desirability,
2) the topic leads to anxiety arousal,
3) the topic is not salient.

The effects of mood and reinforcement of previous responses by empathic reactions only affect the responses if characteristics or events are concerned that may be positively or negatively evaluated. This will be the case if response alternatives differ with respect to their social desirability. If the topic is nonevaluative, a socio-emotional style should be preferred, because this style positively affects the respondent's motivation, which in turn yields better performance. This will, in general, be true if response alternatives do not differ with respect to their social desirability.

The situation becomes highly complicated however, if responses concern positive or negative evaluations, and especially self-evaluations. In Figure 4 the relationships between style of inter-viewing, the intervening variables, self-evaluations, and responses are summarized.

Figure 4: Relations between style, intervening variables, self-evaluations and responses

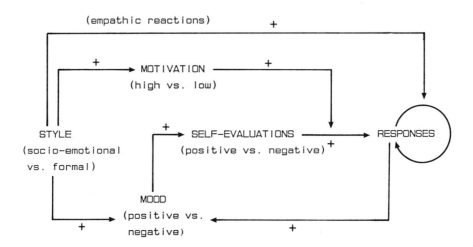

From this figure it can be seen that each style has particular positive as well as negative effects. In a formal style there will be no reinforcement because of empathic reactions, but the respondent's motivation will be low. In a socio-emotional style the reverse is

true. Both styles may affect the respondent's mood, and thus the responses.

If the topic may lead to anxiety arousal, that is, if topic threat is high, for example if the topic concerns death or sexual behavior, the respondent's mood may be negatively affected, which will result in responses that are negatively biased. This effect may be compensated by a socio-emotional interviewing style, which affects the respondent's mood positively. Moreover, this style will positively affect the respondent's motivation. These effects outweigh in our opinion the distorting effect of reinforcing particular responses by empathic reactions.

If topic threat is low and saliency is high, there is much less reason to use a socio-emotional interviewing style. Moreover, the saliency of the topic itself will motivate the respondent. In this case a formal style is to be preferred. However, if the saliency is low, the researcher should weigh the advantage of motivating the respondent against the distorting effect of reinforcing previous responses. In Table 1, these recommendations are summarized.

Table 1: The topic of the interview and the style of interviewing

| SD-DIFFERENCES | TOPIC THREAT | SALIENCY | STYLE |
| --- | --- | --- | --- |
| no | | | socio-emotional |
| yes | high | | socio-emotional |
| yes | low | high | formal |
| yes | low | low | formal/socio-emotional |

Of course these recommendations have a hypothetical character. More research should be done to unravel the intricate relationships between style of interviewing, motivation, mood, interview topic, and so forth, and the quality of the data obtained. However, it will be clear that research results with respect to the effects of interviewing style on the quality of responses are contradictory. First, a number of variables such as motivation or mood may intervene between

style and response. Second, the interview topic may affect these intervening variables. Topic threat, for example may affect the respondent's mood, whereas the saliency of the topic may influence the
respondent's motivation.

## REFERENCES

Bower, G.H. (1981). Mood and memory. _American Psychologist, 36_, 129-148.

Bower, G.H. (1983). _Affect and Cognition._ London: Philosophical Transactions of the Royal Society.

Brenner, M. (1982). Response effects of "role-restricted" characteristics of the interviewer. In W. Dijkstra & J. van der Zouwen (Eds), _Response Behavior in the Survey-interview._ London: Academic Press.

Brown, J.S., & Gilmartin, B.G. (1969). Sociology today: Lacunae, emphases and surfeit. _American Sociologist, 4_, 283-291.

Cannell, C.F., & Kahn, R.L. (1968) Interviewing. In G. Lindzey & E. Aronson (Eds), _The Handbook of Social Psychology_, Vol. II, 2nd edition. Reading, MA.: Addison-Wesley.

Cannell, C.F., Lawson S.A., & Hausser, D.L. (1975). _A Technique for Evaluating Interviewer Performance._ Ann Arbor: The University of Michigan.

Denzin, N.V. (1970). _The Research Act: A Theoretical Introduction to Sociological Methods._ Chicago: Aldine.

Dijkstra, W. (1983). _Beinvloeding van Antwoorden in Survey-interviews_ Unpublished doctoral dissertation, Free University Amsterdam.

Dijkstra, W., & van der Zouwen, J. (Eds) (1982). _Response Behavior in the Survey-Interview._ London/New York: Academic Press.

Forgas, J.P., Bower, G.H., & Krantz, S.E. (in press). The influence of mood on perceptions of social interactions. _Journal of Experimental Social Psychology._

Henson, R.M. (1974). Effects of instructions and verbal modeling in a survey interview setting. _Social Science Research, 3_, 323-342.

Henson, R.M., Cannell, C.F., & Lawson, S. (1976). Effects of interviewer style on quality of reporting in a survey interview. _The Journal of Psychology, 93_, 221-227.

Henson, R.M., Cannell C.F., & Lawson, S. (1979). An experiment in interviewer style and questionnaire form. In C.F. Cannell, L. Oksenberg & J.M. Converse (Eds), _Experiments in Interviewing Techniques._ Ann Arbor: The University of Michigan.

Oksenberg, L., Vinokur A., & Cannell, C.F. (1979). The effects of commitment to being a good respondent on interview performance. In C.F. Cannell, L. Oksenberg & J.M. Converse (Eds), _Experiments in Interviewing Techniques._ Ann Arbor: The University of Michigan.

Phillips, D.L. (1971). _Knowledge from what?._ Chicago: Rand McNally.

Sudman, S., & Bradburn, N.M. (1974). _Response Effects in Surveys._ Chicago: Aldine.

Wahlke, J.C. (1979). Pre-behavioralism in political science. _The American Political Science Review, 73_, 9-30.

# 12 PERSPECTIVES FOR FUTURE DEVELOPMENT

Seymour Sudman
University of Illinois
at Urbana-Champaign

It should be obvious to the reader of the earlier chapters in this volume that the interactions between survey research and social information processing or, more generally, cognitive psychology have just begun. To date, most of the discussions have dealt with the potentials for improvement in survey methods using cognitive psychological insights and, conversely, the potentials for more realistic development and testing of cognitive theories using survey methods. In this final chapter we summarize what we think will be the future developments as well as some priorities for research.

## WHO WILL BE INVOLVED?

It is already clear that the interaction between cognitive psychologists and survey researchers has involved those at the center of their disciplines and not those peripheral to it. As can be seen, the participants at the ZUMA conference who are represented in this volume as well as the earlier Advanced Seminar on Cognitive Aspects of Survey Methodology of the U.S. Committee on National Statistics (Jabine et al., 1984), have extensive records of research in their own areas and are widely cited by others.

To the extent that these researchers become fully convinced of the synergistic effects of working together, they are likely to persuade their colleagues by their new methods and the literature they cite. One would expect in the near future that many, if not most of the researchers in both cognitive research and survey methodology would be aware of each other, although the depth of that awareness might be shallow.

Based on past experience, it is likely that the survey research-ers will be more interested in cognitive psychology results than vice versa. This is simply the result of the fact that survey research is an applied social science interested in practical results, while cognitive psychology is a basic science. One might note that in the physical sciences the engineers borrow more from the physicists and chemists than vice versa. This analogy is, I believe, a good one because it suggests that there are mutual benefits. The physical scientists  need the tools of the engineers to conduct their experiments and they find as well that problems in engineering sometimes lead to important basic science insights.

It is doubtful that survey researchers will persuade many cognitive psychologists to abandon the laboratory methods using small samples of college students and artificial tasks such as memorizing nonsense syllables. What is to be hoped for, and what appears reasonable to expect is that more natural tasks involving real world behavior will be used to test cognitive theories, and student populations will be supplemented, although not replaced, with more general populations, especially when the topic warrants them. Thus, in attempting to measure health behavior, it seems only reasonable to use populations that have a greater likelihood of illness than the typical student, although even here students can be used in early experiments.

It is these two aspects (more natural questions and more natural populations) that distinguish the current survey research methodologists from the cognitive psychologists, rather than a basic difference between surveys and experiments. Survey methodologists use field experiments, and with the current computer technology it is possible  for these experiments to be tightly controlled. Thus, it is really hard to see any significant difference between a CATI (computer assisted telephone interview) study conducted from a central location under tight supervision and using a factorial design to vary interview content with an experiment in a cognitive psychology laboratory.

As a researcher uses more natural questions and populations new sources of variability are introduced. At a minimum, this may simply require larger samples which increase the cost of data collection, but are not impossible if funding sources are available. (The benefits of larger samples are probably obvious, but are discussed in greater detail later.)

Of most concern to the cognitive psychologist will be the absence of perfect validation of the response. Is it possible to know the quality of answers using natural data? This is a problem that has faced survey researchers for decades and methods have been developed for validation that, if not perfect, are usually sufficient to determine which of a series of procedures or hypotheses is most likely to

214

be correct. This leads for many behaviors such as health activities
to the conclusion that more is better. These conclusions are based on
comparisons to outside record sources in some cases and to comparisons of totals to outside estimates of totals when individual
validation is not possible. One must also recognize that for some
kinds of responses, such as attitudes, no outside validation is
possible.

None of the methodological doubts of the cognitive psychologists
will stymie the survey researchers. They will be eager to use cognitive psychology insights as they become available. Here it is likely
that the supply will not meet the demand. To date, much of what the
cognitive psychologists have discovered is still at too abstract a
level to be applied in surveys. It is hoped that in the near future
researchers, either cognitive psychologists or survey researchers,
will think hard about the implications of theories of information
processing and develop applications to survey methodology. Two excellent examples of such applications are the paper by Schwarz and
Hippler and the one by Bishop that are found in this volume. There
are a few others, but we are still very early in the adoption
process.

To date, the dialog has mainly been between the cognitive
psychologists and the survey researchers, but there is a natural
group to bridge the gap between these two disciplines - the social
psychologists. Social psychologists are typically familiar with the
work of the cognitive psychologists but often use survey research or
similar methods. Some of the most notable survey methodologists have
been social psychologists. There is every reason to expect that
interactions between the social and cognitive psychologists and the
social psychologists and survey researchers will continue to expand
in the next few decades.

It should be obvious that there are other links than those
already discussed. Cognitive psychologists will continue to interact
with other groups within psychology and elsewhere. Thus, the work now
being done on artificial intelligence holds substantial promise.
Survey researchers will also be looking to other basic disciplines
such as linguistics for new insights, although to date not much has
transpired in this direction to date.

## WHAT HAVE WE LEARNED?

It has not been a surprise to survey researchers to learn from cognitive psychologists that respondents' memories are faulty and that different question wordings and contexts result in different answers to survey questions. The cognitive psychologists have developed some elegant, but general theories to explain these effects. Thus, Hastie discusses those aspects of information processing theory that he believes to be most useful. For example, he describes "schema" and "schema theory" and "episode schema" as two ways that people have of organizing memory, and then goes on to discuss "spreading activation" principles. At this general level, however, I just don't see any significant contributions to improve survey research in the near future, although Tourangeau does use schema in his design of new experiments.

Bodenhausen and Wyer are more explicit. Among their postulates several do suggest possible methods for improving survey results. Thus, their Postulate 3, which states the importance of memory accessibility implies the importance of transistory moods on responses to more general questions about life satisfaction and possibly other topics. This postulate also explains and amplifies the work of Schuman and Presser (1981) on the effect of context on responses to survey questions. It is likely that there will be many more studies of the effects of different cues in the years ahead.

Another implication of this postulate is that responses may be improved if there is a priming task that increases memory accessibility. This task could be either at the start of the interview, in material presented before the interview or from an earlier interview. Again this would appear to be a method that could be tested in survey research field experiments.

Strack and Martin's model of information processing is even a bit more explicit than the models in the earlier chapters and leads to the experimental study of Schwarz and Hippler that demonstrated the strong effects of anchoring questions, an effect that has also been seen in some of our earlier survey research experiments (Bradburn & Sudman, 1979). Bishop has a fascinating experiment on context effects that demonstrates their existence even when questions are not continuous.

To try to summarize the discussion in this section, it is of limited use to know that different people use different methods of memory storage and retrieval or that even the same person will use different  methods depending on the event of stimulus. What would be more useful would be more specific information--what fraction of people use a given schema and  what determines the schema they use. This requires a variety of real world events and broad population samples.

It is also not useful to know that different events and behaviors are remembered by the same respondent using different schemata unless one can specify, possibly through preliminary questions, what schema was used by the specific respondent for the specific topic under investigation. If  this could be done, it might then be possible to ask questions in the way that would be most likely to activate memory. It seems likely that some efforts in this direction will be conducted in the near future.

The one thing that is fully under control of the researcher is the questionnaire and here progress is possible. The current CATI technology makes possible individualized questionnaires for different respondents that could improve memory retrieval once the process is understood more specifically. The testing and use of alternative cues and anchoring points for closed questions is also already within the scope of survey researchers and only needs to be expanded to additional uses.

## FUTURE PROSPECTS

Predicting the future involves extrapolation of current trends along with some prescriptive suggestions on what would be sensible future trends without knowing if these will indeed occur. It is also impossible to predict what new ideas, techniques, and technology will arise in the future that will make these predictions appear quaintly outdated. Nevertheless, here goes:

1. Among the most useful work in mathematics has been the development of impossibility theorems, which make it clear that certain outcomes are not possible under a given set of postulates, as well as how much relaxation of the postulates is required to make an outcome possible. It is likely that cognitive psychology will be able to demonstrate that certain tasks of memory are simply not possible, such as remembering completely all the details of nonsalient events for a long time period, regardless of all the help that can be provided to a respondent in the form of cues. It is also likely that many specific answers to very specific questions will be recognized

to be estimates. Users of survey data will be more likely to recognize that they are getting estimates that are subject to error and will adjust techniques so as to improve the quality of the estimates. That is, these facts, which are already known to a limited number of cognitive and survey researchers, will become part of the common research tradition.

2. There will be a substantial expansion in the number of cognitive psychologists and survey researchers who obtain protocols from subjects/respondents on how they went about retrieving information that was requested. Cognitive psychologists have been more likely to obtain this information while the retrieval was occurring. Survey researchers who have used such procedures, but only to a limited extent at the end of interviews, will substantially expand their use of this method, both during and at the end of interviews, particularly during pilot tests. The results will be useful not only for the specific study, but also will accumulate over different topics and samples so that there will be a more detailed understanding of differences between people, topics and cues.

3. As researchers obtain a better understanding of how retrieval works there should be a substantial growth in the use of new priming and cueing methods. What form these will take is not known, but it is likely that these procedures will make the current procedures used by survey researchers appear to be primitive.

4. The new knowledge of how different people retrieve information as well as new technologies of data presentation and collection will make it possible to provide individualized cues, anchors or other stimuli to respondents based on their characteristics or responses to early questions. The aim is not to obtain perfect information, which is impossible, but to get the best information from respondents that they are able to provide after being helped.

5. There is every indication that more and more cognitive psychologists will do some of their experiments with natural phenomena and general population samples. These will enable them to improve the external validity of their findings and theories while maintaining control over the methods and stimuli. It is also to be hoped that there will be greater efforts to develop theories that are sufficiently explicit that experimental methods can be designed to test and falsify them if they are not valid. Finally, on pragmatic grounds, there will probably be research funds available for cognitive research on real-world issues.

A famous mathematician who had proved a new theorem was asked, "What good is it?". He replied, "What good is a new baby?". The same may be asked of the interaction between survey research and cognitive psychology. We do not yet know what good this new baby is, but we have high expectations and look forward to watching it grow.

## REFERENCES

Jabine, B., Straf, L., Tanur, M., & Tourangeau, R. (Eds.). (1984). _Cognitive aspects of survey methodology_. Washington, DC: National Academy Press.

Bradburn, M., & Sudman, S. (1979). _Improving interview method and questionnaire design._ San Francisco CA.: Jossey-Bass.

Schuman, H., & Presser, S. (1981). _Questions and answers in attitude surveys. Experiments on question form, wording and context._ New York: Academic Press.

# 13 ABOUT THE AUTHORS

BISHOP, GEORGE F.

George F. Bishop is Associate Professor of Political Science and a Senior Research Associate in the Behavioral Sciences Laboratory at the University of Cincinnati, where he directs the Greater Cincinnati Survey. He is an active participant in the American Association for Public Opinion Research and has published a number of articles on survey research methodology in Public Opinion Quarterly.

BODENHAUSEN, GALEN

Galen Bodenhausen is a doctoral candidate at the University of Illinois, where he received his Master's degree in 1984. He has published several journal articles and chapters in the general area of social information processing. His primary research interests include prejudice and stereotyping, interpersonal and intergroup conflict, and person and event memory.

DIJKSTRA, WIL

Wil Dijkstra worked after receiving his degree in psychology for some years at an Institute for Mentally Retarded Children. He has been affiliated since 1975 with the Department of Research Methodology at the Free University of Amsterdam. He is the author of books and articles on educational psychology and data-gathering methods. His main research interests are interaction processes, experimental designs, and computer programming.

HASTIE, REID

Reid Hastie received his education at Stanford, the University of California, and at Yale, where he was trained to study human memory and cognition. He is now Professor of Psychology at Northwestern University and his primary research interests are in the areas of decision making, social judgment, and social memory.

## HIPPLER, HANS-J.

Hans-J. Hippler reveived degrees in sociology and political science (Dipl.-Soz.; Dr. phil.) from the University of Mannheim. He is currently Project Director at the Center for Surveys, Methods, and Analysis (ZUMA e.V.) in Mannheim, FRG. His main research interests are in the areas of survey methodology, quasi experimental designs, and social judgment.

## MARTIN, LEONARD L.

Leonard L. Martin received his Ph.D. from University of North Carolina at Greensboro in 1983. In 1984 he won the dissertation award from the Society of Experimental Social Psychology. From January to May, 1984, he was a visiting assistant professor at the University of Illinois at Urbana-Champaign. Until August, 1985, he was a NIMH post-doctoral fellow (under Robert S. Wyer) at the University of Illinois at Urbana-Champaign. From September, 1985 to the present he has been assistant professor at the University of Georgia.

## OSTROM, THOMAS M.

Thomas M. Ostrom is Professor of Psychology at Ohio State University. He is also editor of the Journal of Experimental Social Psychology and was visiting Professor (1985) at ZUMA, Mannheim, West Germany. He coedited (with R. Petty and T. Brock) the book "Cognitive Responses in Persuasion", which was published in 1981 and was author of "Sovereignty of Social Cognition" in R. Wyer and T. Srull (Eds.), Handbook of Social Cognition, published in 1984.

## SCHWARZ, NORBERT

Norbert Schwarz is currently "Privatdozent" of Psychology at the University of Heidelberg, West Germany, and is a George A. Miller Visiting Professor at the University of Illinois at Urbana-Champaign, USA. He received degrees in sociology (Dipl.-Soz.; Dr. phil.) from the University of Mannheim and in psychology (Dr. phil. habil.) from the University of Heidelberg. His research interests are in cognitive social psychology, in particular the interplay of affect and cognition in social judgment.

## STRACK, FRITZ

Fritz Strack received his degree (Dr.) from the University of Mannheim where he is a "Hochschulassistent" in social psychology. He has published journal articles and book chapters in the area of social cognition. His central interest is the cognitive and emotional basis of human judgment.

## STRUBE, GERHARD

Gerhard Strube is currently Senior Scientist at the Max-Planck-Institute for Psychological Research in Muenchen. He received degrees (Dipl.Psych., 1974; Dr. phil., 1977; Dr. phil. habil., 1983) from the University of Muenchen. His fields of interest are cognitive psychology and cognitive development, especially memory and language. He has published two main books: "Binet und die Folgen. Die Psychologie des 20. Jahrhunderts," (1977) and "Assoziation" (1984) and various articles in journals and books.

## SUDMAN, SEYMOUR

Seymour Sudman is the Walter Stellner Professor of Marketing in the Department of Business Administration and in the Survey Research Laboratory and Department of Sociology at the University of Illinois at Urbana-Champaign. With his colleaque, Norman Bradburn, he is the author of three major books on questionnaire design, Response effects in surveys, Improving interview method and question design, and Asking Questions.

## TOURANGEAU, ROGER

Roger Tourangeau received his Ph.D. in social psychology in 1979 from Yale University. Since 1981, he has worked at NORC as a survey statistician and methodologist. His current research concerns the processes by which respondents answer survey questions, especially questions about attitudes. In addition, he has conducted several studies of memory problems in surveys.

## VAN DER ZOUWEN, JOHANNES

Johannes van der Zouwen studied sociology and became in 1977 Professor of Research Methodology at the Free University in Amsterdam. He is author/editor of articles and books on sociology of religion, research methods (Response Behavior in the Survey Interview), and sociocybernetics (Sociocybernetics, Dependence and Inequality, Sociocybernetic Paradoxes). His main research interest is interaction processes in interviews.

## WYER, ROBERT S.

Robert S. Wyer received his degree from the University of Colorado in 1962, and taught at the University of Iowa and the University of Illinois at Chicago Circle before moving to his present position as Professor of Psychology at the University of Illinois at Urbana-Champaign. Wyer, a past recipient of the Alexander von Humboldt Special Research Prize, is coeditor of the Handbook of Social Cognition and author of numerous books and journal articles on social information processing.